“There are storytellers. There are painters. There are magicians who marry history with the present. And then there is Yip Yew Chong. He is all three. And more. When I look at his murals, especially when I've stood in the streets and backstreets and watched him paint, he moves everything — my heart, my head, my guts.”

Irene Hoe
Writer, editor and educator

“A young city-state that must continually remake itself to survive and prosper in a world undergoing more-than-usual flux needs social and cultural ballast that stabilizes without allowing sterile nostalgia to hinder adaptation and progress. Yip Yew Chong's delightfully playful yet serious murals thus serve an essential political and strategic as well as aesthetic purpose. They capture what he calls ‘a collective memory’ enriching and enlivening our city-scape, while reminding us from whence we came and who we are and must remain even as we navigate rapid change. An appreciation of his work is long overdue. Congratulations on *Art of Joy*.”

Bilahari Kausikan
Former Permanent Secretary
Ministry of Foreign Affairs

“Mothership first featured Yew Chong in 2017 when he was a part-time artist. My colleague Ashley Tan, who interviewed and written about him over the years, shared that for someone whose works are so sentimental, he is a surprisingly down-to-earth and practical individual.

“*Art of Joy* by Woon Tai Ho is an accessible and introspective look into Yew Chong's life and his second act as an artist. Tai Ho, in his second act as a chronicler of significant and unconventional Singaporeans, managed to bring out the childlike joy of Yew Chong's works into prose, and the book connects and delights.”

Martino Tan
Managing Editor
Mothership.sg

"'A people's artist' sums up perfectly the professional persona behind one of Singapore's most recognised and well-loved muralists. Beyond this description is 'a people's person' — likable, approachable and perhaps, most important for someone as keen an artist as Yip Yew Chong, curiously observant without being obtrusive. To those familiar with the many long-gone scenes Yip captures so vividly, his works are evocative, often poignantly nostalgic. And to those unfamiliar, these same images must surely delight while proffering a sense of time, place and understanding. Kudos to Woon Tai Ho for expressing in words the joy of life that makes Yip Yew Chong the people's artist he is."

Sharon Yeo
Publisher, Friend and Client

"I met Yip earlier this year and came away impressed with his teenager-like zest in mural painting. This book digs deeper into his life story and reveals two other loves. Yip's grandma was a great influence. He remembers her in many of his paintings. Then, his wife. Like him, she was an accountant and did all the sums to convince him to take the dive into making painting a full-time job. As we mark founding father Lee Kuan Yew's 100th birth anniversary, here is a son of Singapore we need to celebrate. Yip Yip Hooray.

PN Balji
Author, Journalist

"Woon Tai Ho's intimate style of writing draws you into the book, much like how Yip Yew Chong has a way of drawing one into his art. The book unveils the captivating journey of Yip Yew Chong from a corporate man to the artist that he is today. An uplifting read, suitable for all ages, you would almost find yourself smiling as you are reading this book! Through Yew Chong's art, we are transported back to our recent past, uniting generations, uniting cultures. We will forever be thankful to the joy Yew Chong and his art have brought to our young family of seven since 2015, and we are excited to continue on his inspiring artistic journey together."

Faith Wong and family
Fans of Yip Yew Chong

"*Art of Joy* helps to document the success of Yip Yew Chong in his switch from the corporate world to the arts and as arguably one of the biggest mural artists, if not the biggest, in Singapore. His works have touched the lives of many Singaporeans and are appreciated across the world. On his murals and especially his 60m painting, you will find many historical nuggets and information, carefully researched and illustrated by Yew Chong, which many Singaporeans can relate to. Definitely more to come from Yew Chong."

John Soh
Art Enthusiast

"Yip Yew Chong's murals are a culmination of our collective memories and histories; I cannot emphasise how important they are for Singapore where the only constant is change."

Darren Soh
Architecture Photographer

"He is Singapore's most well-known muralist. His art connects and unites Singaporeans from all walks of life. *Art of Joy* not only allows us into Yip Yew Chong's nostalgic world, we also get to know the personal stories behind his awe-inspiring works."

Hong Shin
Children Book Author and Illustrator

"A delightful read of the man behind some of Singapore's most popular street art. You'll find the stories behind his street art, especially of the many women who influenced him and turned up in his paintings — his grandmother, aunt, and supportive wife.

"A phrase that crops up frequently is that YC is a 'people's artist'. Part of his popularity, and what comes through in the book too, is his approachability, friendliness, humility — he never says no to a photo. His art is indeed universal — they tell stories and are relatable. You'll find yourself wanting to revisit his street art again, now that you know the stories that influenced him."

Belinda Tan

"I like art that tells stories, and Yew Chong is a delightful storyteller, using our recent and collective history as his story base. *Art of Joy* is a treasure to me, and I am sure to many of his fans, for it goes behind the art into Yew Chong's own story, from his childhood to his marriage, from an accountant to an artist, branching out from murals to canvas, and many other aspects that are both interesting and surprising. An absorbing read."

Aziza Ali
Artist / Author

"What struck me most while reading *Art of Joy* is when Yew Chong explains, 'When I paint, I go back to me when I was a little boy.' No wonder there is so much joy in his work. There is a lot we can learn from the innocence of children. Thank you Yew Chong!"

Colin Low
Art Collector
CEO, Singapore Land Authority

Art of Joy

THE JOURNEY OF YIP YEW CHONG

Other World Scientific Titles by the Author

Soul of Ink: Lim Tze Peng at 100
ISBN: 978-981-123-702-7
ISBN: 978-981-123-773-7 (pbk)

Mo Hun: Bai Sui Lin Zi Ping
[Soul of Ink: Lim Tze Peng at 100]
ISBN: 978-981-124-287-8
ISBN: 978-981-124-288-5 (pbk)

Rainbow After Dusk: Lim Tze Peng Remembers
ISBN: 978-981-12-7454-1
ISBN: 978-981-12-7534-0 (pbk)

George Yeo: Musings
Series One
ISBN: 978-981-125-969-2
ISBN: 978-981-126-128-2 (pbk)

George Yeo: Musings
Series Two
ISBN: 978-981-125-972-2
ISBN: 978-981-126-129-9 (pbk)

George Yeo: Musings
Series Three
ISBN: 978-981-12-5975-3
ISBN: 978-981-12-6130-5 (pbk)

Forthcoming Titles

An Unfinished Canvas: The World of Koh Seow Chuan

I Love SG – The Best is Yet to Be: What You Can Learn from Lim Siong Guan's 50 Years of Public Service

Art of Joy

THE JOURNEY OF YIP YEW CHONG

Woon Tai Ho

World Scientific

NEW JERSEY • LONDON • SINGAPORE • BEIJING • SHANGHAI • HONG KONG • TAIPEI • CHENNAI • TOKYO

Published by

World Scientific Publishing Co. Pte. Ltd.
5 Toh Tuck Link, Singapore 596224
USA office: 27 Warren Street, Suite 401-402, Hackensack, NJ 07601
UK office: 57 Shelton Street, Covent Garden, London WC2H 9HE

British Library Cataloguing-in-Publication Data
A catalogue record for this book is available from the British Library.

ART OF JOY
The Journey of Yip Yew Chong

ISBN 978-981-12-7781-8 (hardcover)
ISBN 978-981-12-7871-6 (paperback)
ISBN 978-981-12-7782-5 (ebook for institutions)
ISBN 978-981-12-7783-2 (ebook for individuals)

For any available supplementary material, please visit
https://www.worldscientific.com/worldscibooks/10.1142/13454#t=suppl

Desk Editors: Nicole Ong/Claire Lum
Design and layout: Jimmy Low, Loo Chuan Ming

Printed in Singapore

Here's to all our second acts.

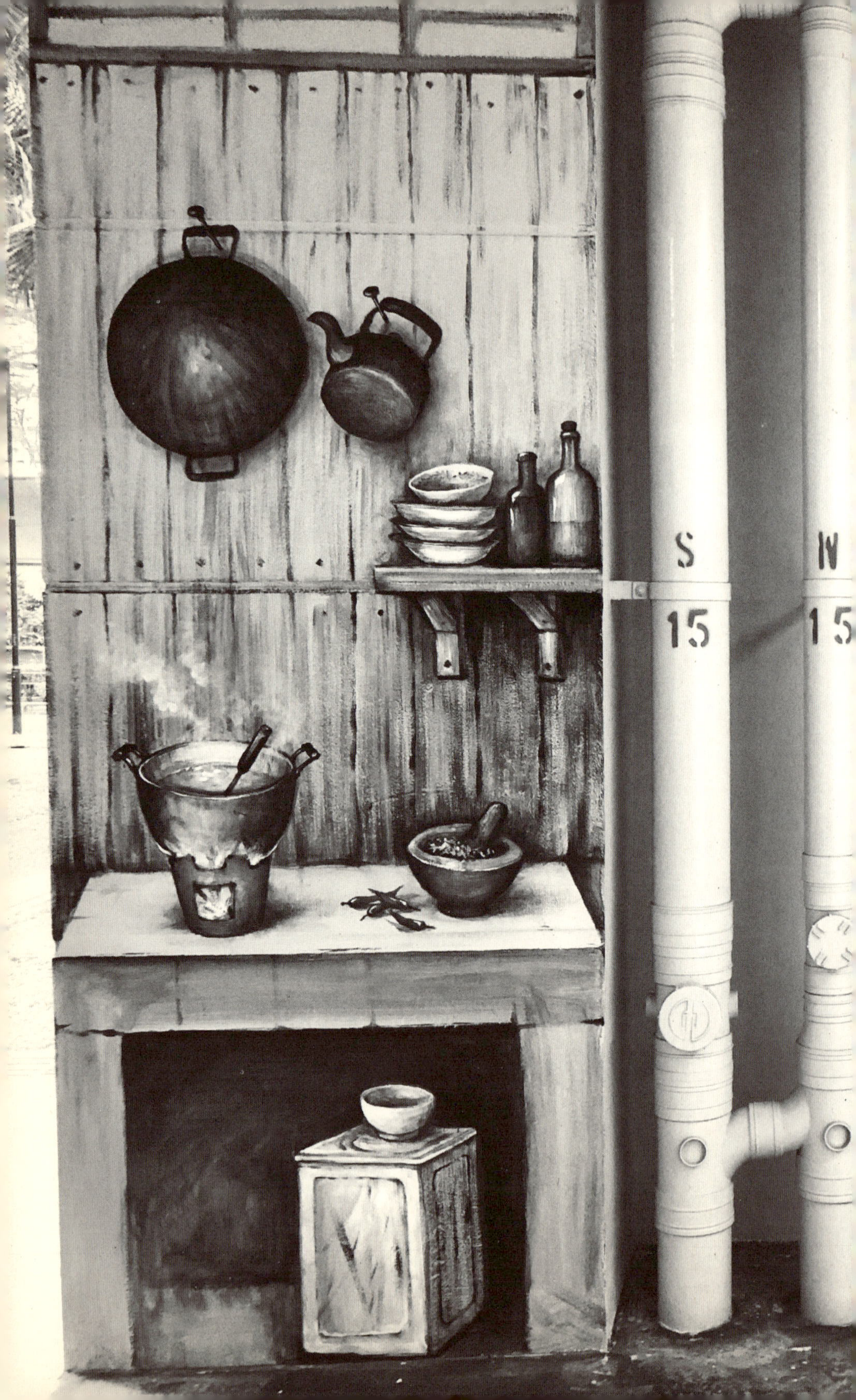
S
15
N
15

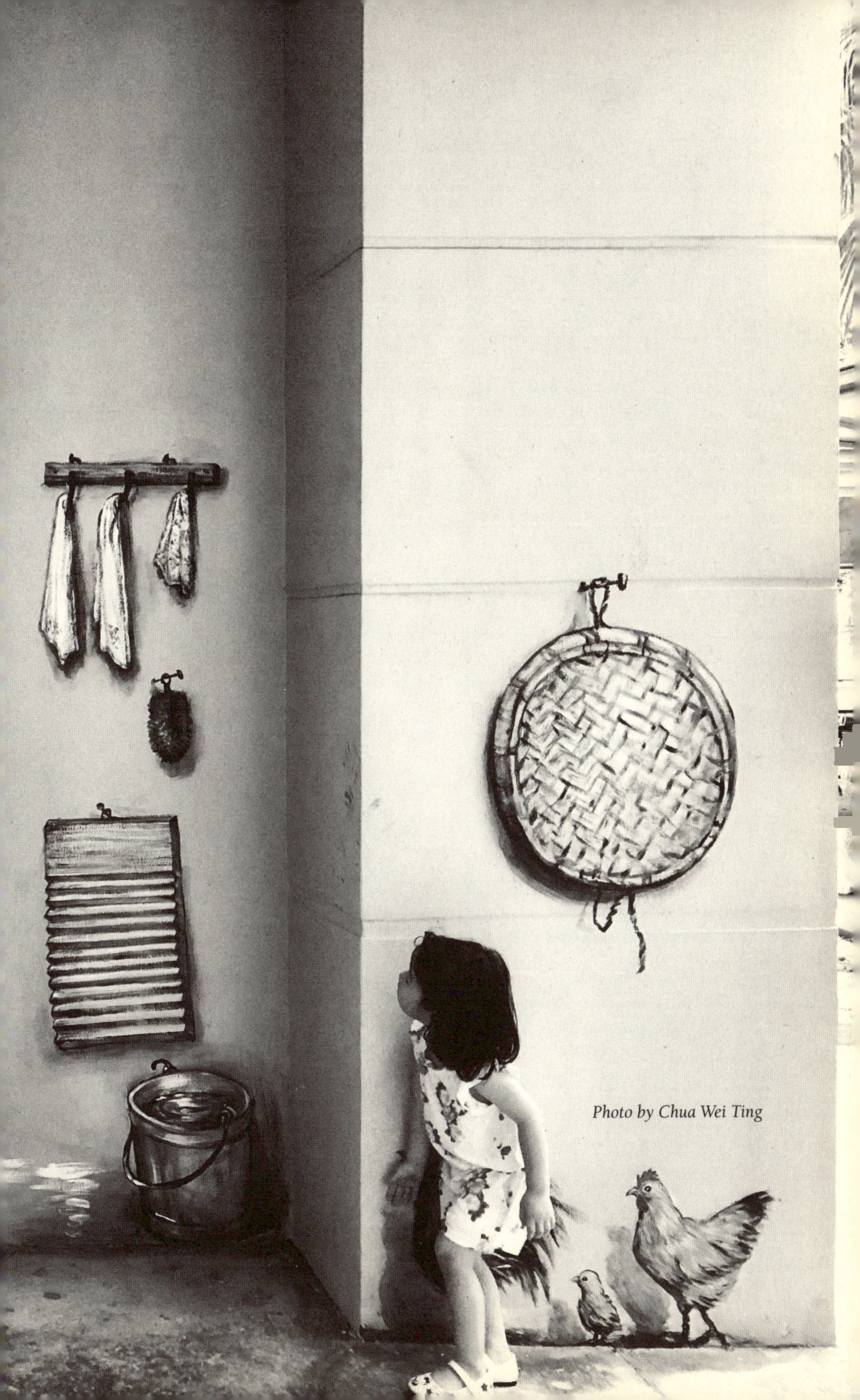

Photo by Chua Wei Ting

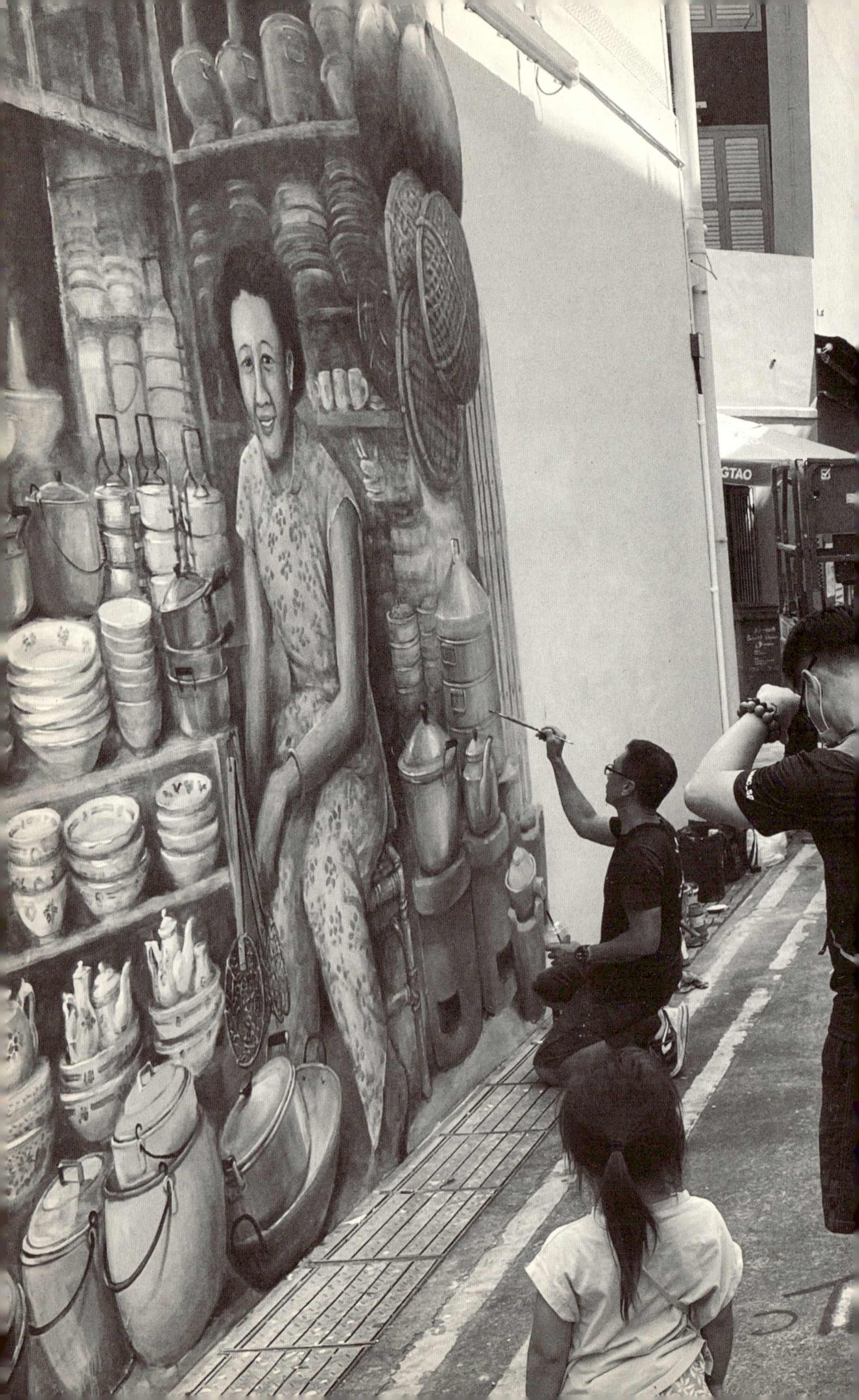

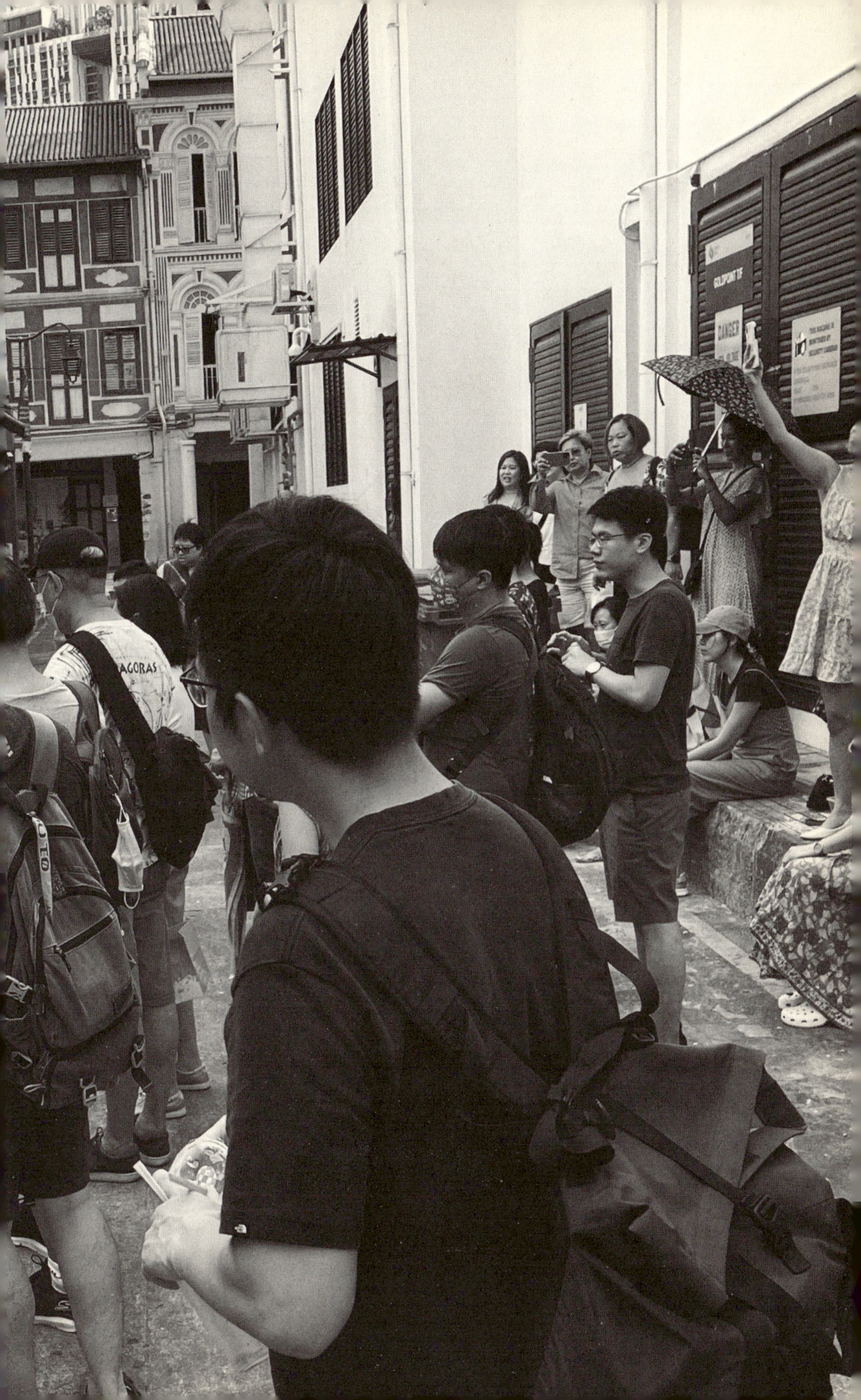
DANGER

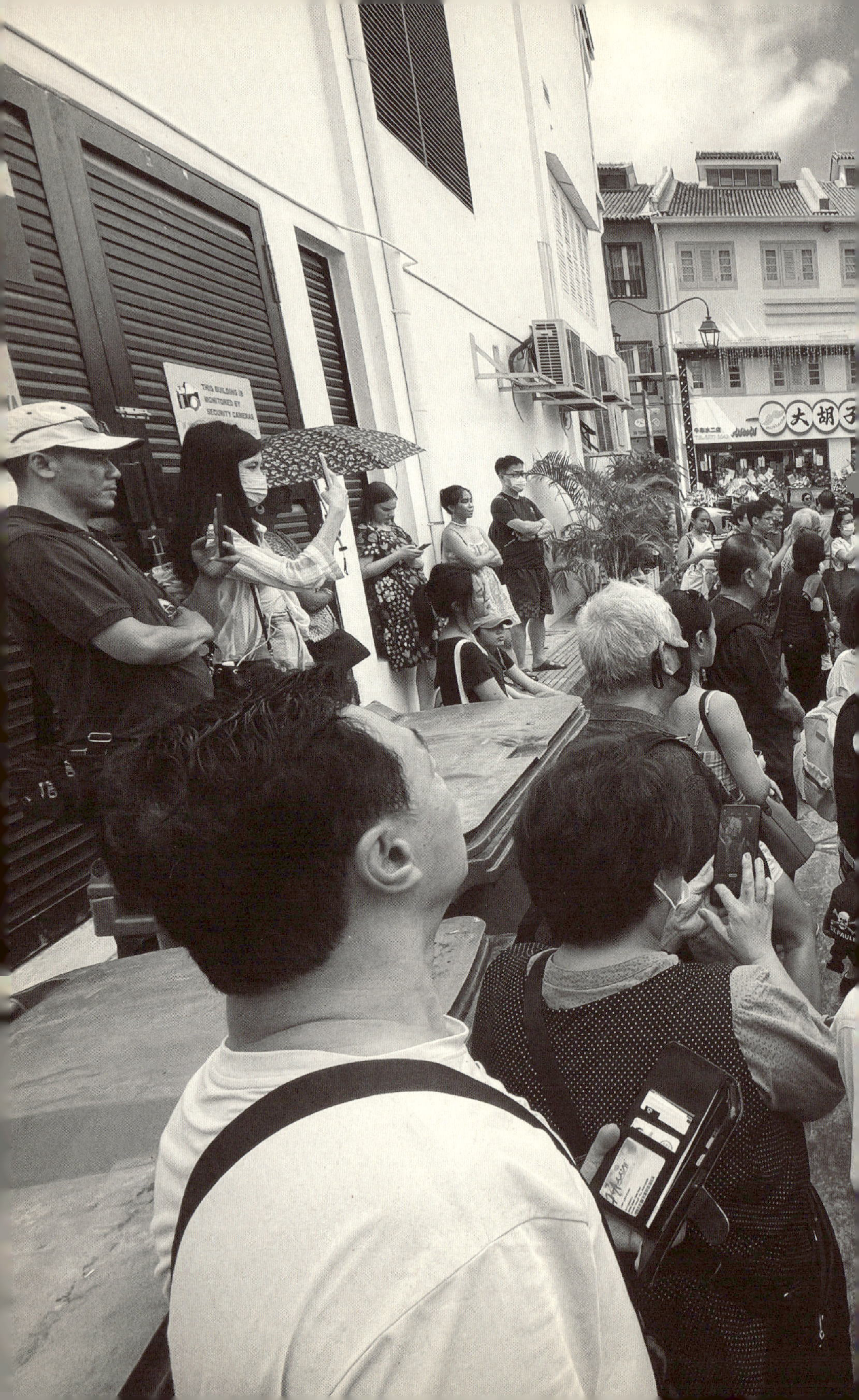
THIS BUILDING IS
MONITORED BY
SECURITY CAMERAS
大胡子

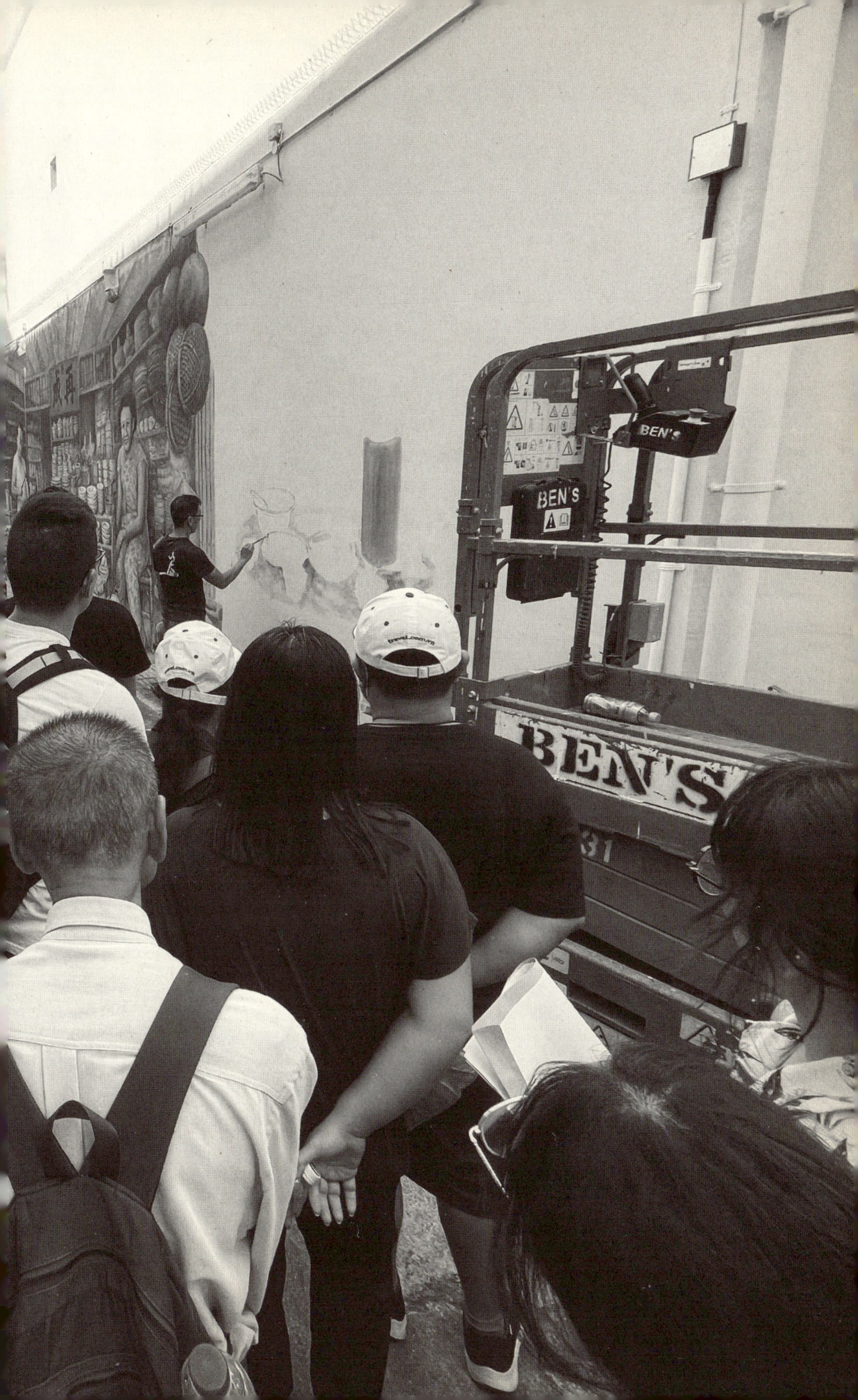
BEN'S
BEN'S
BEN'S

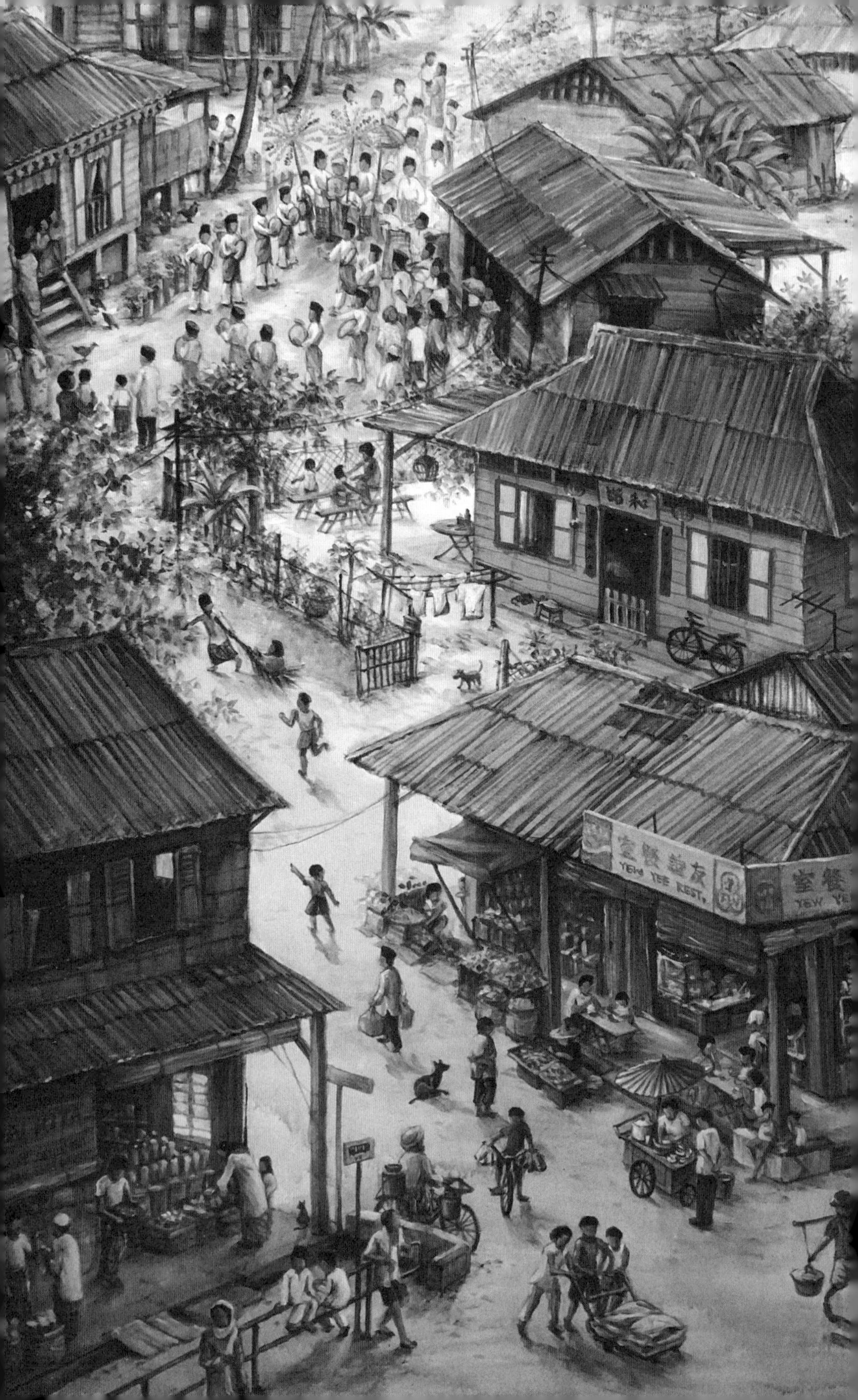
YEW YEE REST.

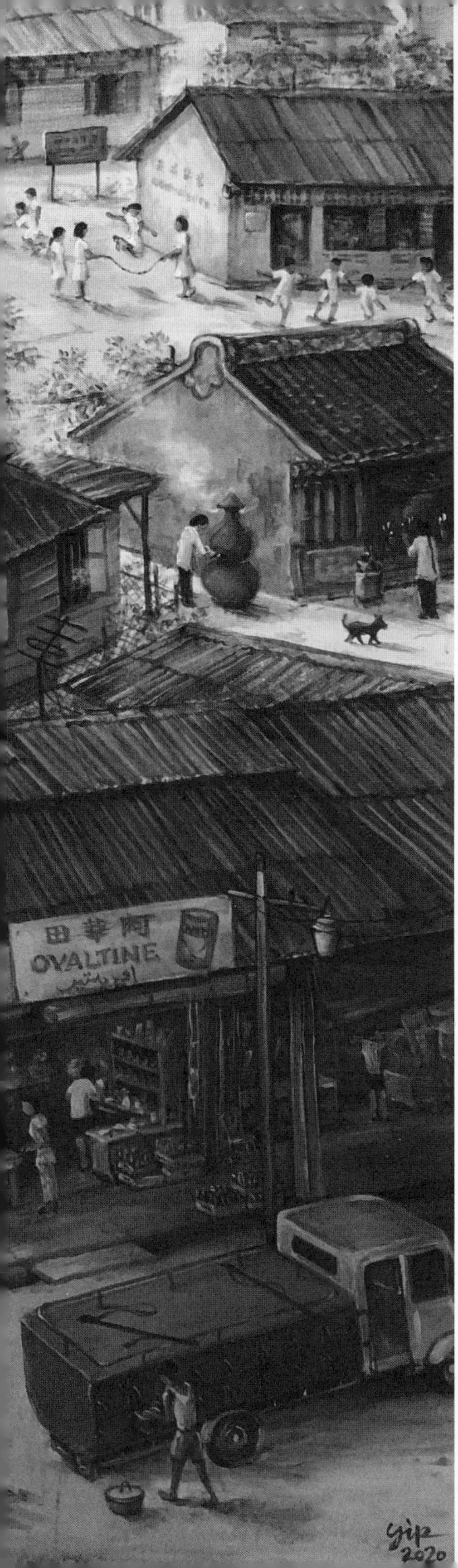

Contents

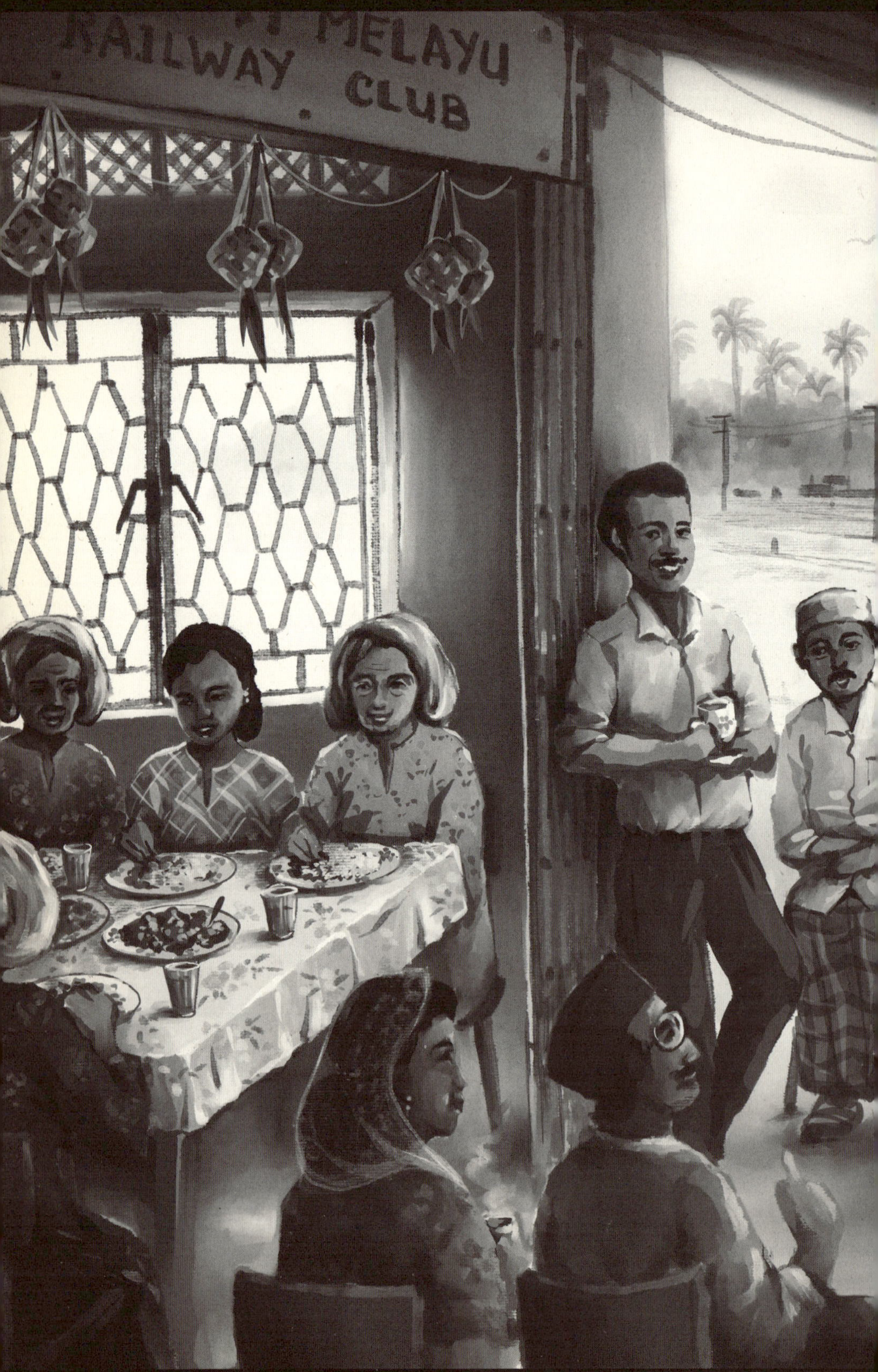
RAILWAY
MELAYU
CLUB

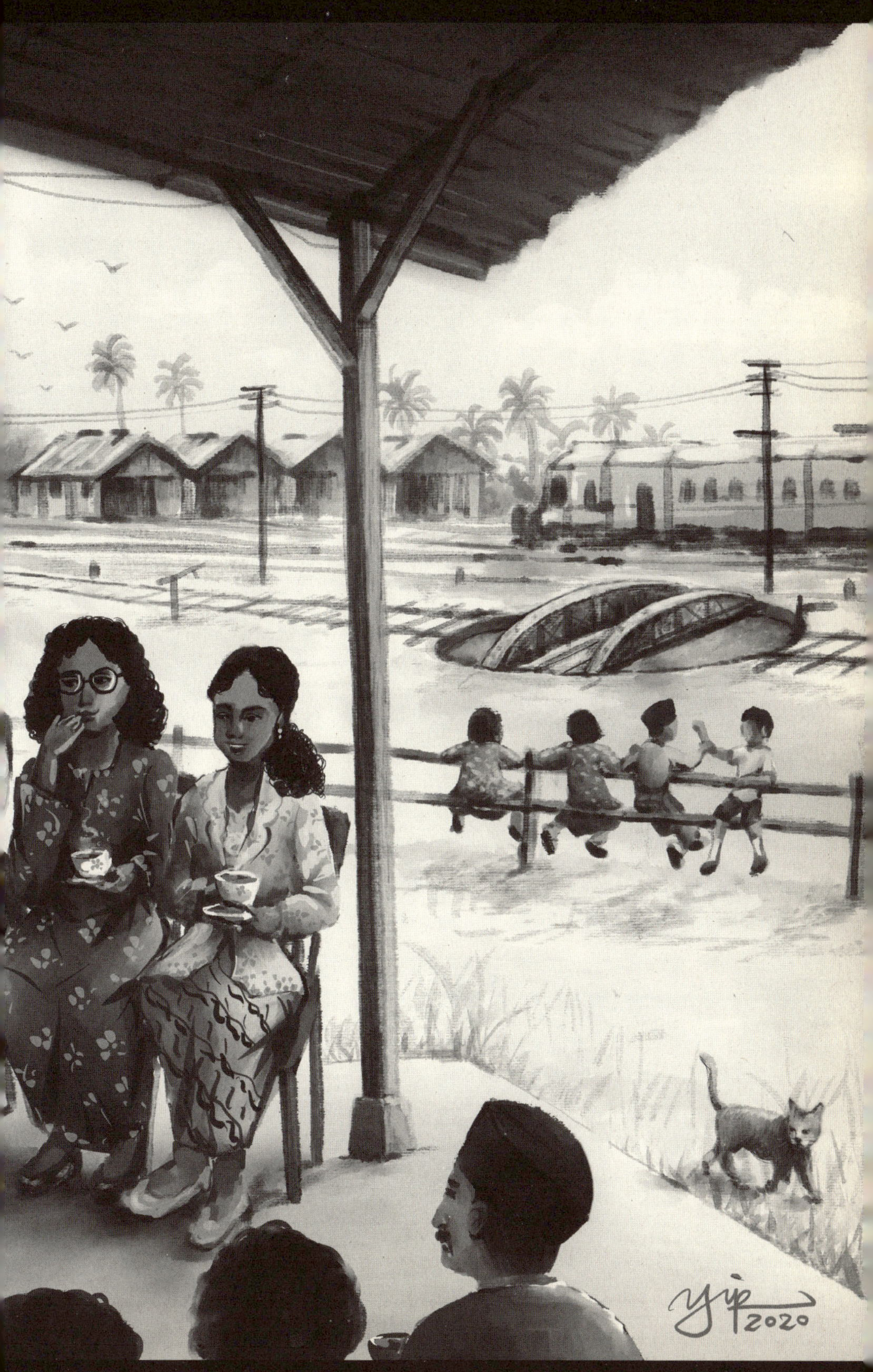
yip
2020

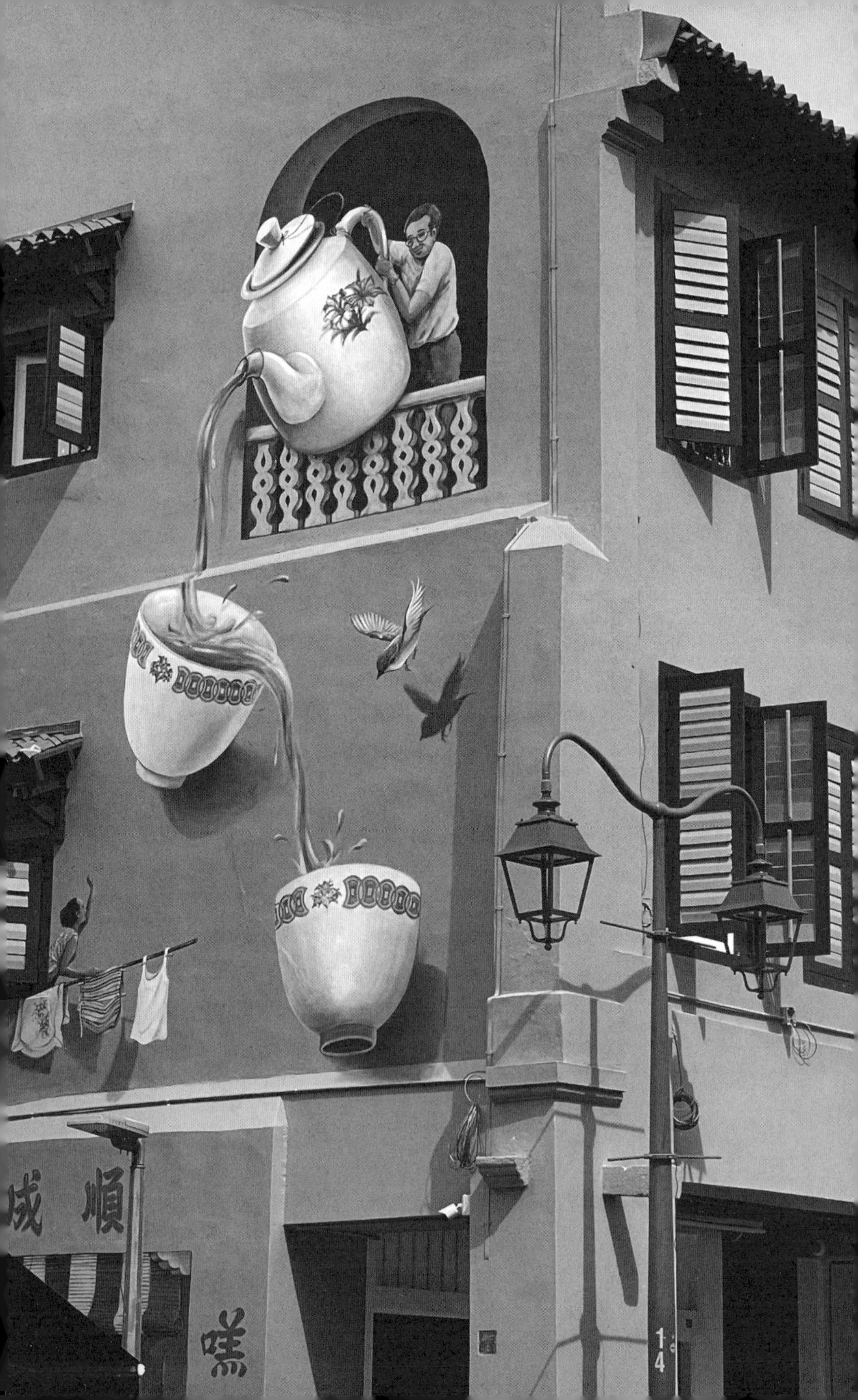
順
14

CHAPTER 1

The Chinatown Native

His landscape is essentially 'human-scape'.

Imagination

A woman screams. Her shrill voice permeates the whole of Temple Street in late morning Chinatown. She cannot believe what she is seeing. The laundry she has put out to dry is now wet, wet with brown tea! "Stop pouring!" she shouts at her neighbour up on the third floor. "Uncle, stop!" With her right hand, she tries hard to pull the pole of clothes into her room as her left hand assumes a life of its own, pointing and cursing at the man.

On the third floor, the uncle holds a larger-than-life teapot, tipping it over. Tea, hot brown tea, streams two floors down. Two giant teacups, barely holding the tea, frolic merrily with the cascade. A large bird, an unlikely witness to the drama, suspends itself mid-air, in total shock.

On the ground, the noise and smell of food provide another kind of spectacle. A man reads his newspapers with one leg up while his friends savour their own freshly brewed tea with dim sum. The aroma of food fills the coffeeshop, and a couple is in deep conversation below an old-fashioned clock. The time is 10 past 10. A lizard crawls out, a lady is deeply engrossed counting money at the cashier counter.

Immediately outside, a hawker smiles as he watches a grandmother feed her grandson the *chee cheong fun* he made, next to them, a cat minds its own business. Within sniffing distance, a provision shop sells dried seafood and soy sauce.

A few steps away, the noise and action slow down. Four older ladies, two seated, one having her hair combed, while the other has her face traditionally 'cleaned', by threads.

Further down, the raw noise, smell and colour return dramatically to the wet market: the vegetable-seller calls out, a fishmonger negotiates with a stubborn housewife, bare-chested men defeather chickens, freshly-cooked, steaming hot ducks hang, dripping in oil. Behind, monitor lizards, frogs, turtles, pythons, look out from cages. A frog escapes, springing into the air.

Yip Yew Chong steps back from the large empty wall on Temple Street, the vivid wet market images still swimming in his mind. It's the last quarter of the year, the weather is getting cool again. He is relieved, it won't be so hot when he starts painting this next mural, his biggest outdoor mural yet. The wet market in Chinatown is long-gone, but he will bring it back onto this blank wall before him, three stories high. He puts a few finishing touches to the single-page sketch in his hand. There isn't much to see on paper, but the brush in his mind is already completing the painting. He can see, smell and hear the scenes in his head: the giant teapot and teacups, the auntie shouting, the coffeeshop, the grandmother and grandson, the cat, the vegetable seller, fishes, reptiles, all the gore of the wet market that Chinatown was known for in 1970s. His mind bubbles with possibilities.

Drama, or happy drama to be precise, is what he is good at. His growing number of admirers all think the stories he tells on the streets are based on his own life experiences. Childhood memories perhaps, but almost all the drama is drawn from one source, his colourful, boundless imagination.

"When I imagine, I am more creative and resourceful," Yew Chong's voice is high when you first hear it. Then you get carried along with its inherent animated excitement. "For me, it helps me form mental images, hear sounds, detect smells and feel emotions beyond my present senses, time and space. It transports me to experience other worlds. And then, I create them."

The tone of his face and arms is a shade darker than most Chinese, a testimony of the many hours of painting outdoors. That, and his lithe physique and full head of dark hair mislead most to think the street artist is only in his 30s, when in fact, he is already in his 50s. As the conversation continues, his calm maturity simmers through.

"I am conscious of how my work affects people," he allows a smile. "As much as my art is drawn from my imagination, it also lives through the imagination of the people who see it. The interaction injects life to both my art and the street."

Theatre, and the ability to see humans as performing characters, is a sharp instinct of his. His landscape is essentially 'human-scape'; each and every single one he paints has been assigned a role. Even when a figure is seemingly still, he contributes to the overall activity. And indeed, his murals are activity-driven; it could be one big activity or many pockets of smaller ones, all in it to tell a human story or a collection of human stories.

"True," Yew Chong adjusts his large black rimmed spectacles. "My works are about people, usually many people. Most of these people you would recognise, a mother, a father, a son, a barber, a hawker, a washer woman… there is no mystery as to who they are and what they do. Unlike abstract art, I aim to make every object or subject recognisable and therefore, relatable. The viewer can relax as he recognises, and from there his imagination gets going as he discovers more."

Most muralists arrive on site with a fairly detailed sketch. For Yew Chong, that sketch is in his head. He arrives at a site armed with emulsion paints, tubes of acrylic and a variety of brushes. There are stages to his mural painting, each stage requiring different tools to actualise the artwork he sees in his mind.

"About 70% of the work is in my head," Yew Chong laughs out. "The rest, the other 30% is my direct experiences on site, the realities of painting… from adjusting my painting schedule because of the weather, to inputs from the crowds who watch me paint. For instance, when it comes to painting 'violence', such as chicken slaughtering, or the killing of the monitor lizard, how much blood do I show? Here I find children extremely helpful. They are honest, so I ask if it is scary for them. When they tell me it isn't, I will allow the gory details to show a little, to make the scene interesting and as real as possible."

While the first stage of his mural painting is done all in his mind, the second stage, however, is done on location, almost alone during the COVID-19 pandemic. "I like to set up the mural with outlines of where things are, like where and what roles the human figures would occupy and play, the things they would hold, where the animals are, and this stage I prefer to do it alone without an audience. There isn't much to see at this stage," his face arranges itself into a toothy grin.

"So, I tell no one."

The third and final stage of this mural painting is a community event. By this stage, the wall would be two-thirds done and he would tell his fans and supporters via social media when and where he would be executing the final stage, so they too can be a part of it.

"The last stage would last for a week or so," his speech is now slightly accelerated. "As the mural is two-thirds done, there are quite a lot of details the audience can see. I try to include two weekends into the final stretch of painting to allow my supporters a chance to see me paint, and be a part of it if they wish to."

His son and daughter, both in university now, used to help out during their school holidays. His mother, too, comes down to cheer him on. She knows from past experience that when it comes to Chinatown paintings, one of the many women he paints could be her.

"Much of what I paint is from a collective memory." Yew Chong speaks of Chinatown with a familiar warmth, it is where he grew up. He moved to Spottiswoode Park when he got married, but his mother still lives there, right in the heart of the buzz. "My memory of Chinatown is still very vivid. My aunt once told me that when my dad was a little boy, he would use chalk to draw on the street floor around Chinatown. He drew mainly opera actors and actresses. People would crowd around him to watch him draw. I believe he loved art, but never had the chance to pursue it. He was a shipyard fitter most of his life. I am thankful I am able to do art… I have painted myself in my murals as well, and of course my mum too. I assigned her different roles, she could be frying cakes in a soot-covered kitchen, or a cashier in a coffee shop. In real life, she did various jobs, including in a rubber factory, sewing clothes, pantry and cleaning, and her last job was making sushi in Yaohan on Thomson Road."

On 27th November 2021, after 24 days of painting, Yip Yew Chong completes *Chinatown Wet Market* at 30 Temple Street. So, after 38 years, the wet market 'reopens'. In a Facebook post on 6th December, he describes how a person would experience the mural:

> *Do look up when you visit the 30 Temple Street mural. The paintings around the three windows give hints to the type of families living inside the house. Close your eyes for a minute, imagine the movements around you. You may smell the wetness of the market, feel the laundry dripping on your head, hear the cat meowing, birds singing, and the lady shouting to the man that his tea is splashing onto her laundry!*

What sets this mural apart from his other local murals, is the running, waterfall effect created by the tea from the giant teapot on the third floor. The artist has thrown actual proportion literally out of the window in favour of packing an eye-catching dramatic punch. And because this is painted at the beginning, at the right corner of the shophouse, it is visible from the traffic junction much further away.

"I have painted about 50 murals in Singapore. This is the first mural that has a giant, whimsical effect visible from afar. It is like a big movie poster starring characters I have created. I knew I had to create something more refreshing than my usual style. The giant teapot and the small human figures around it, the uncle pouring and the auntie shouting all give the mural that larger-than-life surrealist impact. I hope it catches the attention of people at the street junction. I wish I could do more of this in Singapore. The owners of the shophouse who commissioned it are happy. I am glad they went along with it, because this is different from my other murals."

And as with most of his other murals, there is something personal in this one too. "I named the coffee shop (顺成茶室) *Soon Seng Cha Sat*," Yew Chong's face settles into a reflective stare. "Some people have asked if there was such a coffeeshop in Chinatown. Not that I am aware of. *Soon Seng* is actually my late dad's name. My mum said my dad would be very happy if he sees this mural. I think he sees it."

First Home

There is no fridge, no TV, no sofa. But the mural isn't an unhappy one. Far from it. There is playful laughter, and the scene is a peaceful anticipation of one of the biggest festivals for the Chinese, the Lunar New Year.

In the centre of the mural is the dining table with new year goodies. The bulb plants provide the needed green adornment, with the oranges and red packets looking on. In the forefront is an assembly of mouth-watering sweets, from New Year rice cakes, sponge cakes, love letters, to a tray of assorted sweets. In front of a tin are also four bottled drinks with a bottle opener ready. Painted in fresh colours, the goodies are in stark contrast to the muted tone used for the rest of the home. It is as if the artist is saying, "Feast while you can, it only happens once a year!"

But the dining table is only one of four centres of activity; the others are probably more interesting as they are populated by the artist and his family.

"When I finished *Chinatown Wet Market*, I thought it would be the mural I would be most proud of." Yew Chong smiles his mock smile, which means he has something difficult to say. "When I walked back to Smith Street, where I painted *My Chinatown Home* in 2019, I realised nothing would beat this." He looks down, swallowing a lump of emotion that has unexpectedly and stubbornly arisen. "That was the house I grew up in; everyone's there. I didn't paint my father because in my mind he was working. I was a boy, playing with my brother and sister; my mother was young; my grandmother was living with us. We didn't have much, but I remember I was a happy boy. Everyone loves me."

It has been reported widely in newspaper articles and posts on social media that *My Chinatown Home* is his 'most intimate' mural ever painted because it depicts his first home in Sago Lane, where he lived his first 14 years. "Every detail and object in the entire composition was painted based on my fond memories of home — from the common living room, the common long wooden bed where my siblings and I slept on, to the dining area, and then the kitchen. Those were happy years."

Yew Chong's family was the anchor tenant of a shophouse on the second storey, just above the funeral parlour on the ground floor. His family rented it from an Arab landlord and sub-tenanted smaller units to four other co-tenant families.

The mural begins with his grandmother sewing a patchwork blanket. Yew Chong likes to point out the details around her: the

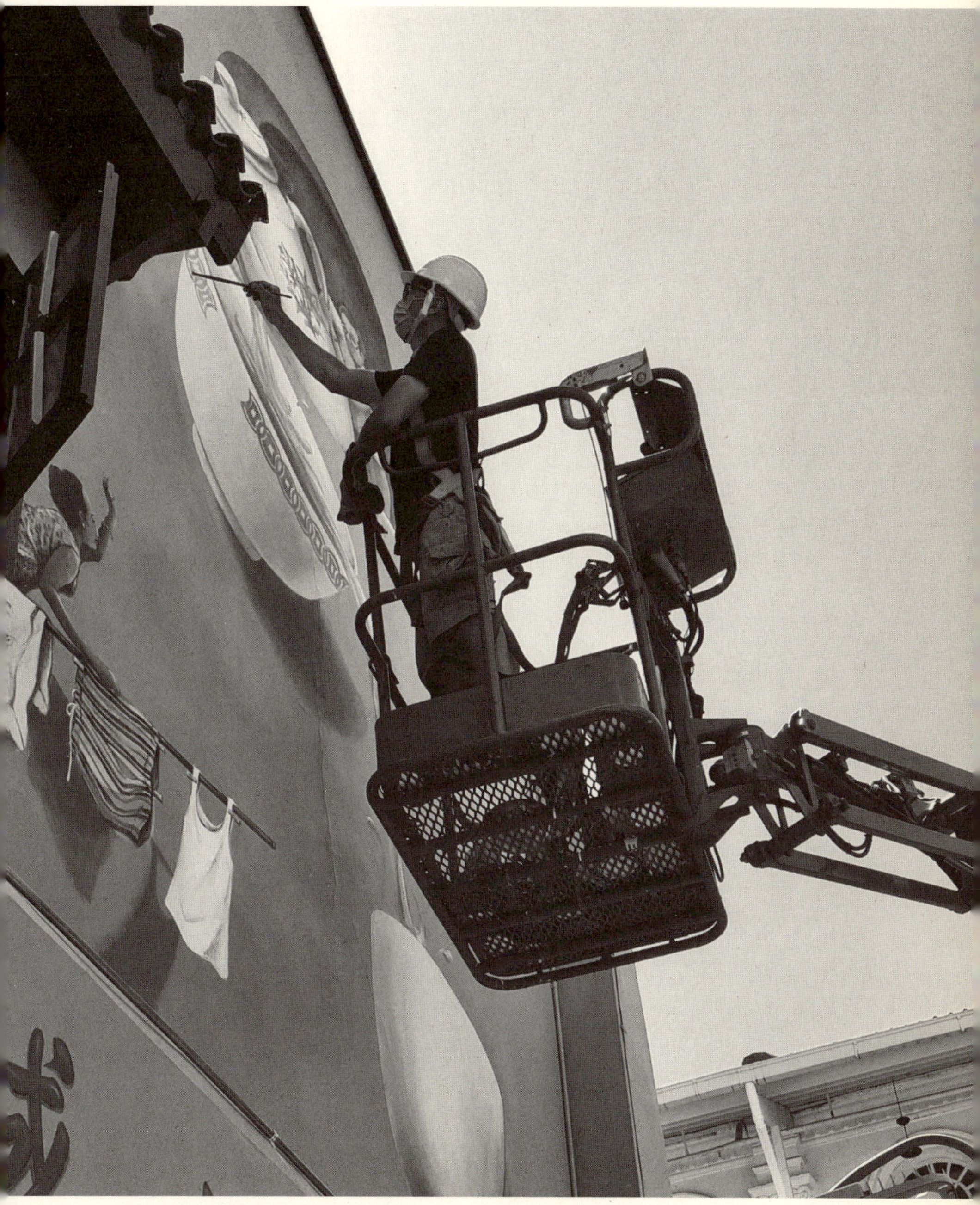

To paint on a boom lift, Yew Chong had to take a boom lift operator course and a work-at-height safety course. (Photo by Victor Yue)

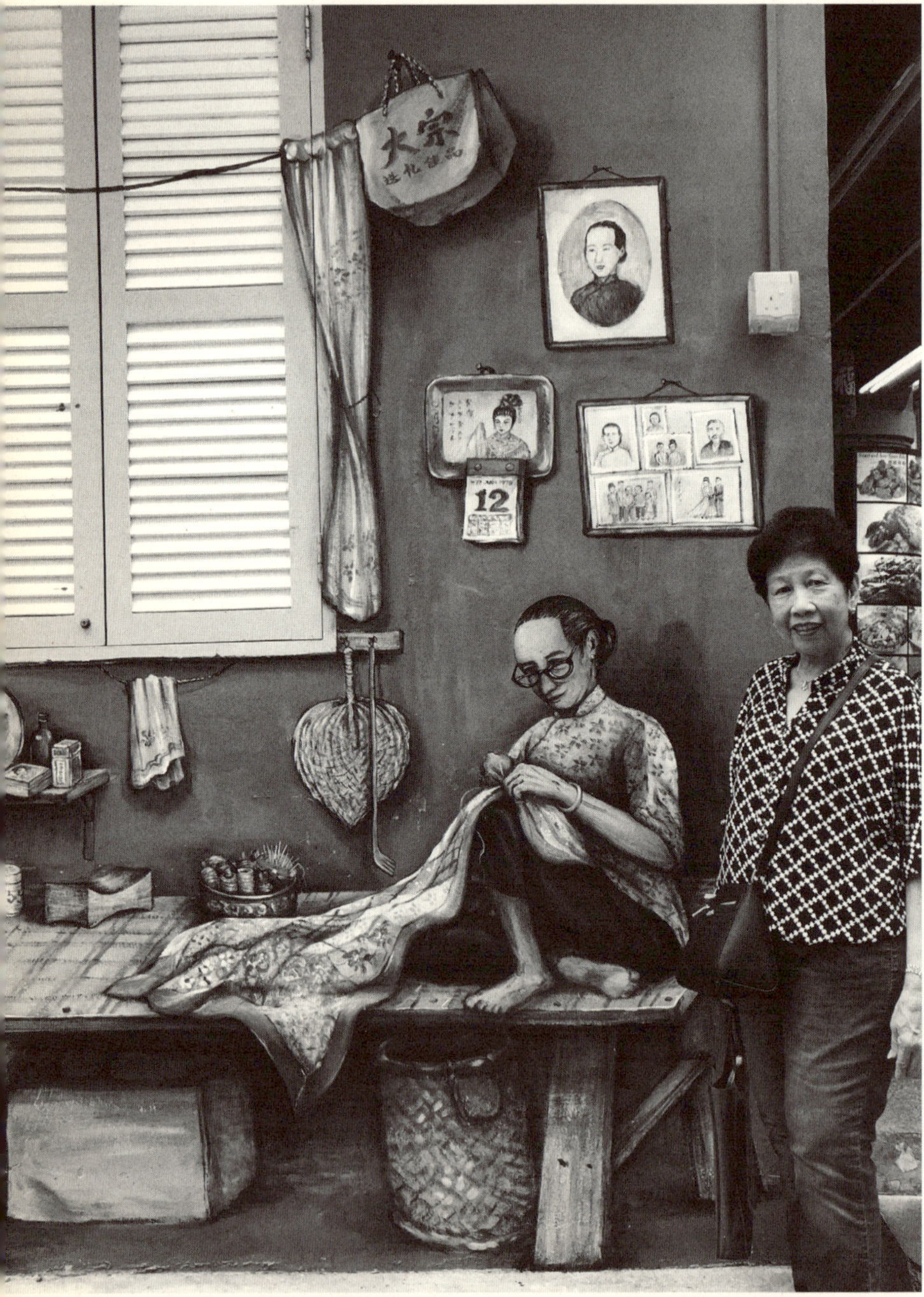

At nine years old, Yew Chong's mother would cook dinner for Yew Chong's grandmother, who rushed from a day shift at the rubber factory to a night shift scrubbing ships offshore.

mosquito coil, the palm leaf fan, and the spittoon. Moving along, the artist and his siblings are playing aeroplane chess on a wooden bed. In the evening, the mattresses would be rolled out and the kids would sleep in a row. After the dining table is the kitchen. Here, the artist's mother is cooking. Below the stove are two chickens given to the family by an uncle who collected waste food from them throughout the year to feed pigs in his farms. The chickens are a token of appreciation. On New Year's Eve, his father would slaughter the chickens for their reunion dinner.

Beside his father and mother, his grandmother has a special place in Yew Chong's heart. To honour her and the memory of his first home, his grandmother takes pride of place in this mural; she is the first person you see.

"I knew I was special to my grandmother." Yew Chong takes a deep breath. He wants to be calm and steady when he talks about her;

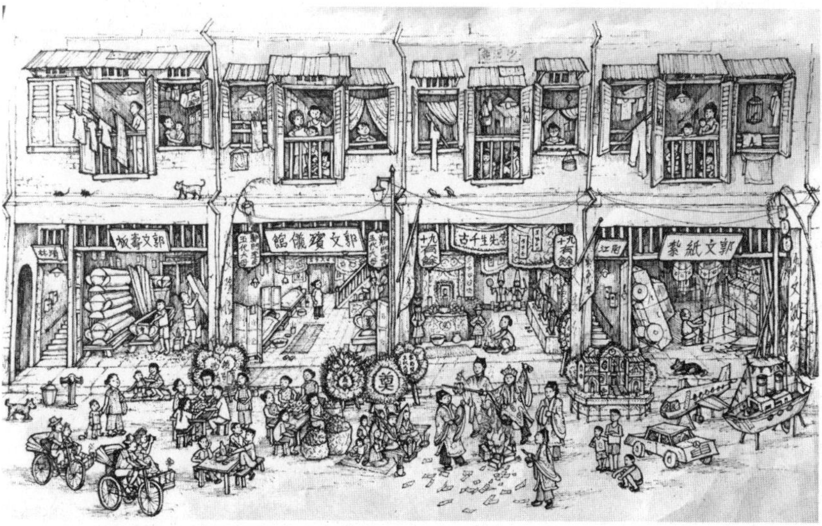

Yew Chong's family lived on the second floor of a shophouse at Sago Lane, also known as the 'street of the dead' due to the funeral parlours there.

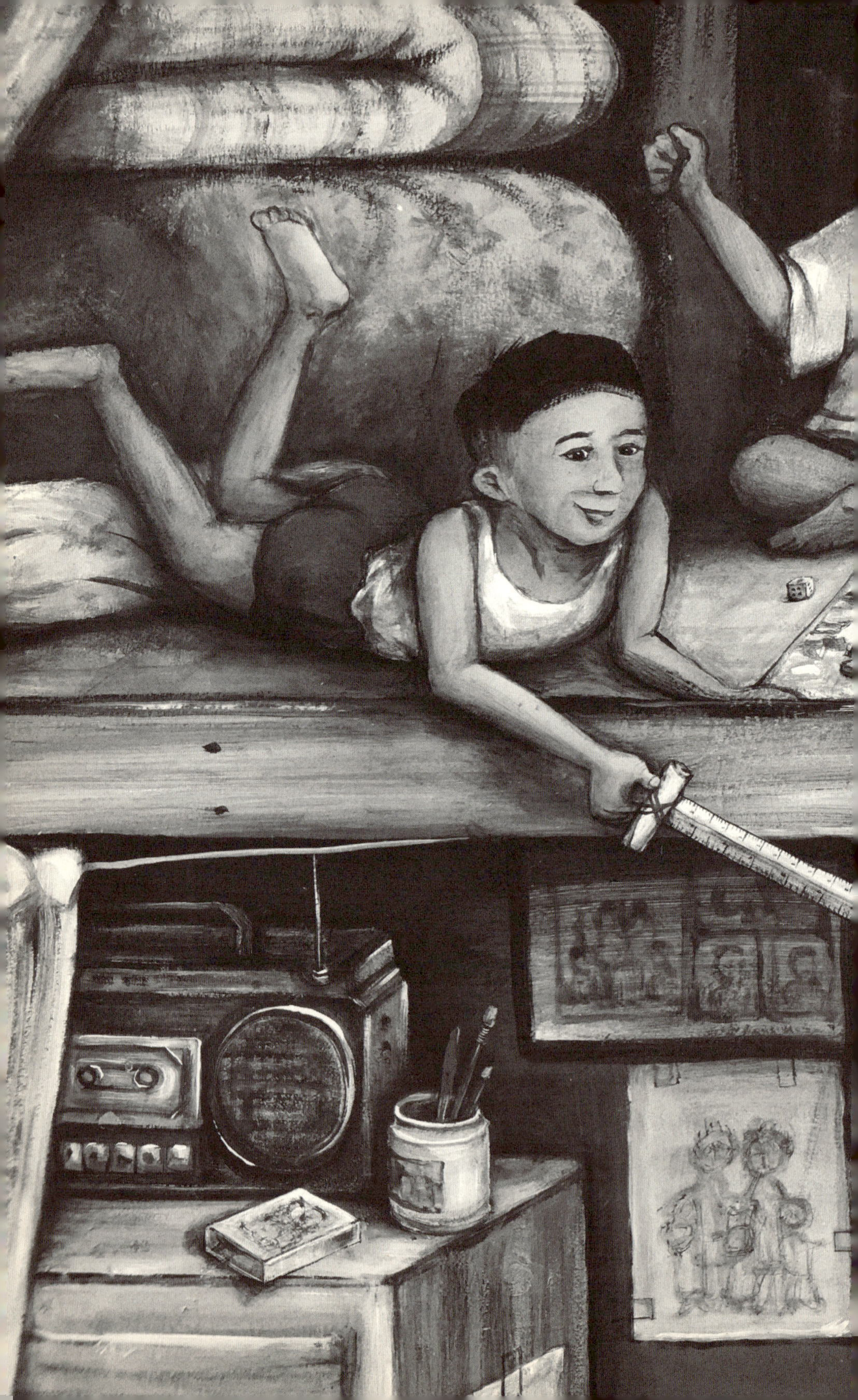

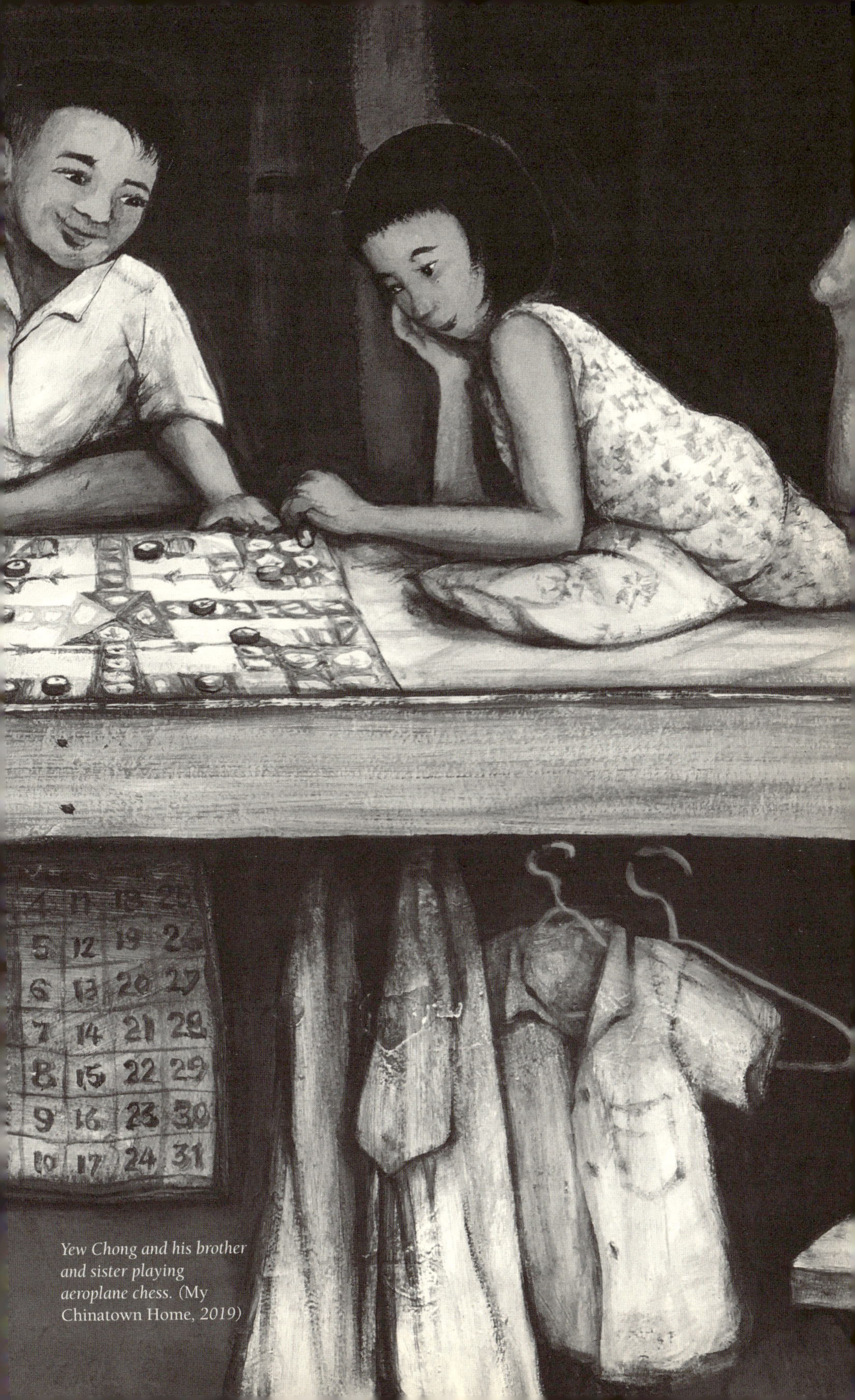

Yew Chong and his brother and sister playing aeroplane chess. (My Chinatown Home, 2019)

he knows he gets emotional when he relives the years with her, how she quietly smiled, her voice, how she called his name. "Like all old people from China, she was partial to sons." He pauses. "Let me tell her story from the beginning. When she was a teenager, she sailed to Singapore from Guangdong, China. It was a leap of faith for a better life. In Singapore, she met my grandpa, who also came from China. She married him as his second wife; his first was in China. In Singapore, Grandma had three children, two sons and a daughter, my mother."

It was not unusual in those days to marry a man who was already married. To be someone's second wife was not anathema. And the women then knew their "place"; in the household, the women did not speak up or go against what the men did or said. In their case, the touchy topic was opium.

"In the early 1950s, the Singapore British government clamped down on opium." Yew Chong's gaze is fixed and faraway. "Grandpa had dealings with opium, so he had to leave Singapore and return to China. He brought with him my two uncles, leaving Grandma and my mother behind in Singapore."

For those years in China, Yew Chong abbreviated them into a sentence or two; he wanted to keep the narrative going. "Shortly after his return to China, Grandpa passed away. Grandma wanted to bring her two sons back to Singapore. She worked hard to earn enough money for it. Two shifts in a rubber factory in the day, and scrubbing ships at night. My mother was nine years old then. She would cook dinner for Grandma so that she (Grandma) could have a quick dinner before rushing to her night shift. She scrubbed the ships anchored offshore till midnight."

His grandmother's story seems to be etched in his head. When it was told to him, he must have noted and took to heart every single detail. "When she had enough savings, she tried to bring both sons back." Yew Chong lets out a sigh. "The family in China only allowed her to bring her elder son back. They kept the second son, knowing that my grandma would continue sending money if one son was still in China. Of course, she sent more than just money — she also sent clothes, a sewing machine, and even a bicycle."

Yew Chong looks down and takes a sip of water. He is preparing himself to talk about his grandma's passing. A brave wide smile. "I was quite close to my grandma. I often teased her in the day, but at night, I massaged her legs and fanned her; it was humid in the shophouse, and there were mosquitoes." He withdraws his smile. "I was serving my National Service in 1988 when my commander called me aside to tell me my grandma had passed away." He removes his spectacles and looks away.

All in, he has painted his grandma nine times, associating her with the sewing kit, mosquito coil, palm leaf fan, old calendar, old clock, patchwork quilt, ancestral altars, food, and more food. "I regret that I couldn't be by her side when she left. In 2014, my mother and first uncle brought me to visit my second uncle, and my grandma's old house in China. I was glad I went. I felt peace; in my grandmother's old house, I felt she was close to me."

While the compositions in his murals may be imaginary, the main human figures are not. They are drawn from his life, past and present… all in, he has painted his grandma nine times. "I like to paint, draw, and create art out of stories, and these stories are not merely stories, they are parts of my experiences in life. That makes it more compelling, more realistic when I tell the stories. When the 'characters' are based on real people, nobody can say it is right or wrong. You can criticise my art — the hand is not right, the head is too big, but you can't say the situation is not right or accurate. For instance, the very first mural I painted, there was a *ma jie*, and she was based on a person I knew, Siong Gu; she lived till 2014. And going back to my grandma, I even included her in *Chinatown Wet Market*. She was the lady feeding the boy by the *chee cheong fun* store. And the boy was me."

Back to *My Chinatown Home*, the abode where Yew Chong grew up in. At any one time, there were about 14 or 15 people in the 'long house', but some tenants like Siong Gu came back only during the weekends, or sometimes only once a month as she was a live-in maid. And when she came back, everyone would know, because she knocked

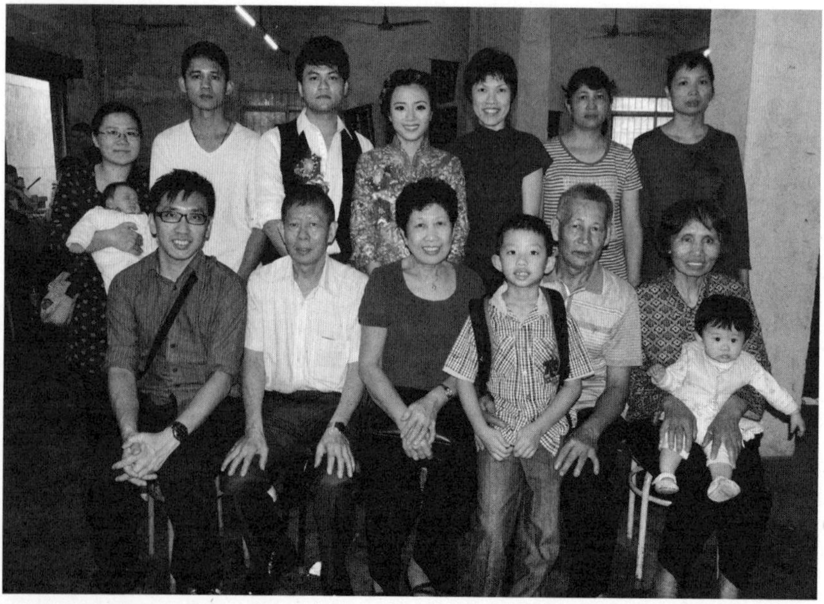

Yew Chong followed his mother and first uncle to visit his second uncle in China in 2014.

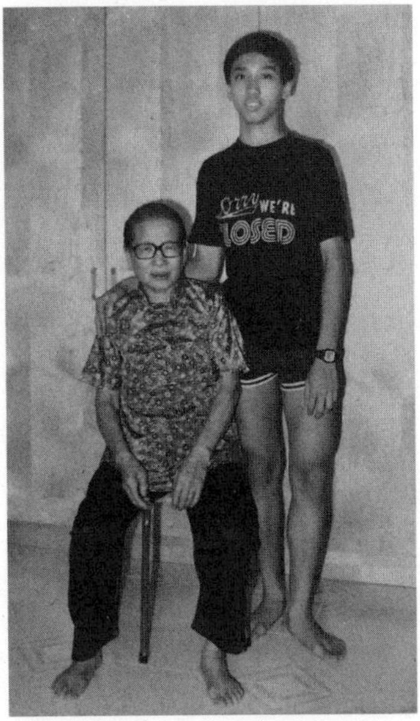

Yew Chong and his maternal grandmother at their new HDB flat above Chinatown Complex, 1983.

on the door hard, partly because she was half-deaf.

There is, however, a hidden story that stays deep in Yew Chong's heart, and it is the story of Dai Soh. One of the tenants of his Chinatown home was an older lady with two sons. He did not paint her in the mural, but only suggested her existence. Behind the dining table is a curtained door and the curtain is half-drawn. That is the door into Dai Soh's world. Yew Chong's murals are positive and happy, especially those depicting his childhood. But Dai Soh's story isn't.

"I told her story in another painting, but not in this mural." Yew Chong's voice is even. "She was one of our tenants, soft-spoken, and she kept to herself. As a boy I was quite fascinated by her, I even wrote a fairly long composition about her when I was in secondary school in Raffles Institution, and my teacher gave me a good grade. Her comment was, a 'moving story'. To a boy, she was very old, probably in her 70s, and she had two sons. One son, who was well-educated, was married to a rich girl, the other had some kind of compulsive condition. He couldn't control himself and would throw his mother's things in the house. She would try to control him, but not always successfully. As if that wasn't sad enough, his other son, who was well-educated and married to a rich girl, was ashamed of his poor background. He never came back to see her. He sent her some money monthly, but didn't visit her."

Yew Chong has a soft spot for older ladies, especially those who are left alone to fend for themselves in old age. "She was a tenant, and our close living conditions were such that we knew what was happening to her. On festive occasions, such as reunion dinners, when the whole family came together, we were always mindful and concerned for her well-being. In one of my canvas paintings, I drew a happy Chinese New Year reunion dinner. But in her room, she too had her own reunion dinner, except it was her waiting for her son to come home. It was a dinner for two, but she was the only one at the dining table."

Even though her existence in the mural is implied, she is 'included' in *My Chinatown Home*. So subliminally, Dai Soh was and still is, in his mind, family.

While his mother and grandma are included, his father is also implied, like Dai Soh. "The one person in my family who did not see any of my murals was my father, who died in 2009. I only started these murals in 2015." Yew Chong remembers; his hand lifts up to support his pensive face. "My mother has said this a few times, if only your father could see these murals, he would have been very happy because he painted on the streets too, the opera performers. He loved to draw and wrote calligraphy for ancestral altars and Chinese New Year couplets. He would buy red paper and golden powder as ink for the calligraphy. As a young boy, I would watch him write. He was an inspiration and inspired that letter writer mural I did."

In 1983, Yew Chong's family had to move out when the entire street was slated for demolition as part of the big Chinatown clean up.

All hawkers, traditional traders, street markets and businesses in shophouses were relocated, many to the mammoth Chinatown Complex. Yew Chong's family moved to the newly-built HDB flat within Chinatown.

"Although the HDB is better, definitely cleaner, but how can anything replace the place I grew up in?" Yew Chong's voice breaks, but he continues. "The old home was rundown, but it was a home. I would bring my friends over to visit me, and I still remember how shocked they were, to see, among other things, firewood, and a toilet without a flush. In the mural, the firewood is right above the chickens. There was a wire-gauzed cabinet hanging from the ceiling. That was how we stored food, we didn't have a fridge. As a kid, I was afraid of geckos, I thought they were little crocodiles! But I added the wall gecko in the mural, together with an old cassette player, the doorbell… I can go on and on."

But he cannot. Chinatown, and what it represents, his childhood, his grandma, his father, Dai Soh … is why the mural is precious, irreplaceable. He adjusts his spectacles again and stops. "When we moved, I was the last person to leave the house, my first home. I told my parents I would like to stay for a few more hours to look around. I took mental pictures of every corner of the place. When I finally left, closed the door behind me for the last time, I had become so emotional I could not see the street outside."

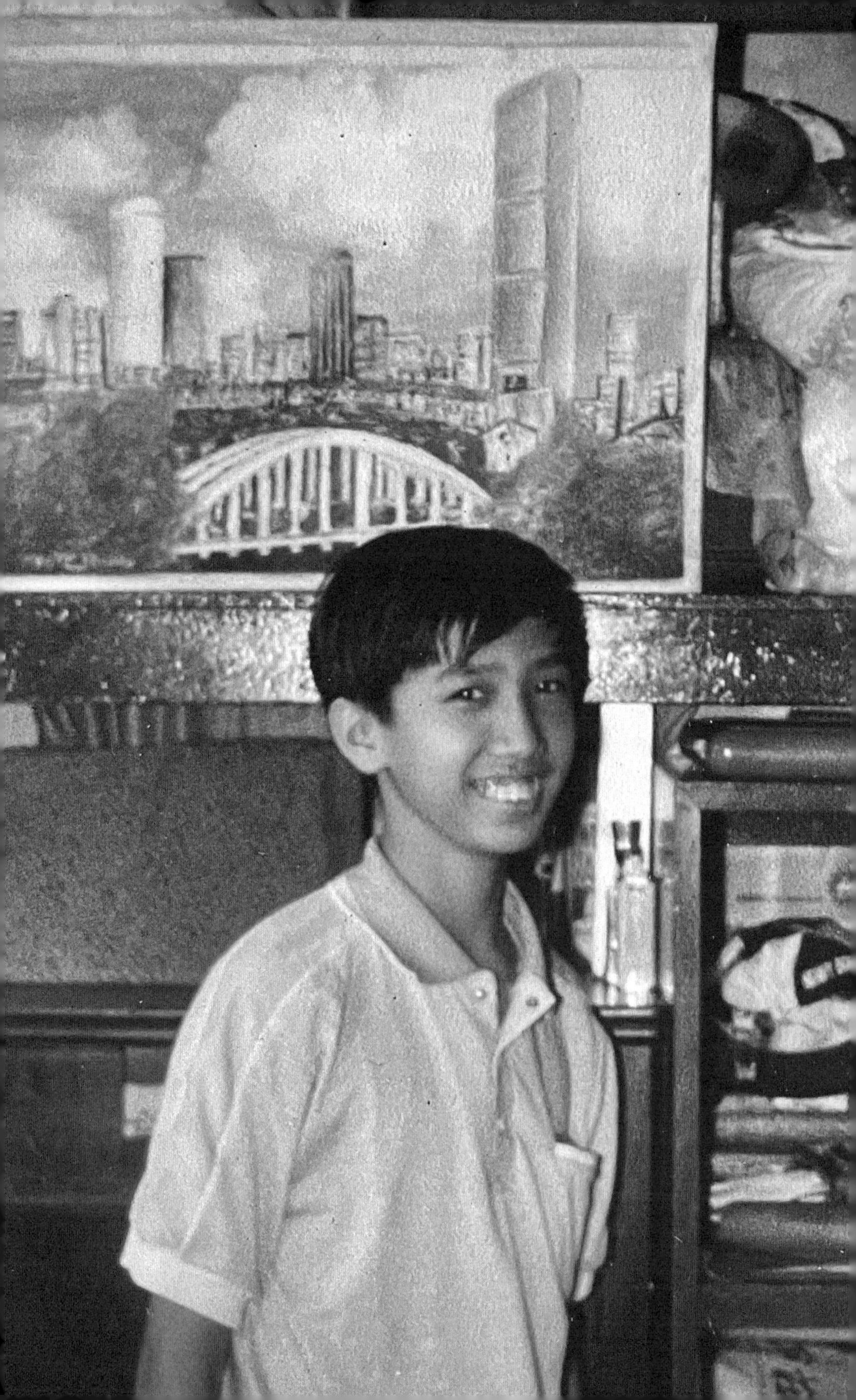

CHAPTER 2

Before the Artist

While luck may have had a say in the way things panned out, a lot has to do with a significant other... girlfriend, wife, mother.

The Boy Who Could Draw

All good artists need patrons, special individuals who do not just look out for the artists, but also encourage and provide opportunities for exposure and growth. In Kindergarten, a buzz surrounded a boy who was skilful with colour pencils and crayons. "When you are that young, you just want to show off." Yew Chong puts both index fingers on his temples, rubbing his forehead, trying to remember. "The adults told me I love to draw for them. But it was really in Primary One that one teacher in particular took notice of me."

The teacher was Miss Leong Oi Lin, who was not only the boy's art teacher but also his Chinese and overall class teacher. "You can draw very well," he remembers her saying. "Even though I was that young, I appreciated how she spent time encouraging me. And looking back, that was important, because I was so impressionable, what I was exposed to, what I was made to do, what I experimented with, stayed with me."

Left: A crayon drawing of the Singapore River, 1981. His parents proudly hung it in the living room.

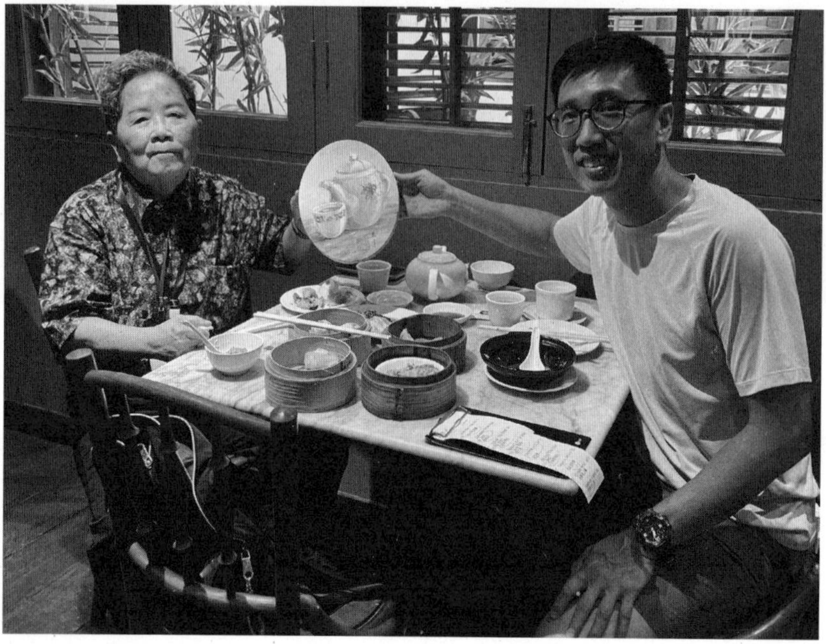

Reunion with Ms Leong in 2021. Ms Leong was Yew Chong's primary school Art Club teacher who availed him with many opportunities to showcase his art.

Crucially, Miss Leong was in charge of the Art Club. Yew Chong recalls fondly how she roped him in and availed him to many opportunities, not just using the pencil, crayon, or the brush, but also moulded his mind doing three-dimensional works, like building models. "I built a model of the school using Styrofoam. I became quite crafty, was involved in all kinds of handicrafts, more so than the other kids."

On his own, he participated in many art competitions, especially those using colours. "I took part in many colouring contests… newspapers where you can tear out the pages, colour them using colour pencils or crayons, then submit them. I won many competitions and in turn I got free subscriptions." His understanding and appreciation of what colours could do started early.

One memory stands out, the drawing of a dollar note. "In Primary Five, I drew a dollar note, the early Bird Series. Looking back, it was silly, but I was really earnest. I drew it life-size, cut it out, and brought it to school to show the teacher." Yew Chong laughs. "I can still see the teacher's face. 'Wow, it's like a real dollar note!' She was astonished. I remember drawing it painstakingly with pencil first, then using colour pencils after to make it look real. I drew both sides of the note. I went on to draw the $5, $10, $20 and $50 notes. I still have these notes in my drawer. They were small, but they were my first 'life-size' paintings."

But what took up most of the boy's free time was his obsession with Chinese TV shows from Hong Kong in the 1970s. "The Hong Kong period dramas. Even in primary school, I knew the actors and actresses well, and would draw them in their iconic costumes and pasted them on the walls of my home in Chinatown. They were like movie posters and billboards. I wish I had kept all those drawings."

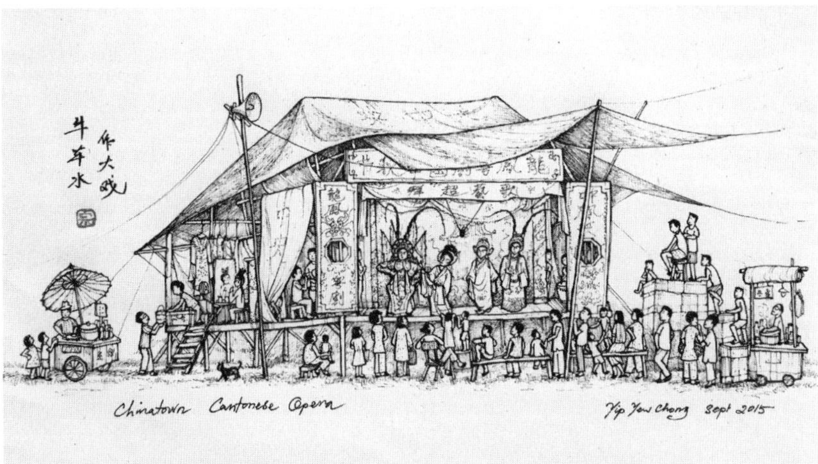

The backdrops and props of Chinese operas influenced Yew Chong's style of art — semi-realistic and 3-D looking.

Looking back at those early years, the recurring experiences that have the most influence on his murals today were the backdrops used in Cantonese opera. “When I followed my aunt to watch Cantonese opera, I was always amazed by the intricate backdrops, 3-D props, flat scenes but painted to give a 3-D look. I was strongly influenced by them, how each scene could literally transport me into ‘another world’. I recall vividly one opera in particular, *The Thirteen Sisters*, a sword-fighting drama. The sceneries were so realistic. I knew I liked the style; I even made miniature cut-outs of opera actors and actresses, where I could change the costumes to match the backdrops. Yes, they all happened in Chinatown, the street operas, and as a boy, I soaked them all into my head.”

His childhood, however, was not lined with one success story after another. One failure was so powerful that it still stays with him and instructs him even today, as an adult. He cannot remember the year; but it was definitely in primary school. “By then, I was winning art competitions and colouring contests. That year, I took part in an SIA Art competition where I was supposed to draw my version of a futuristic Singapore. The theme was about Singapore in the year 2000, about 50 years’ time. Singapore’s MRT was not a reality yet but I drew a tunnel with a train running through it along the Singapore River.” Yew Chong’s face breaks into an ironic smile. “Who knew why I felt the way I did, but I told myself, I must win this. It could have been the winning prize, two return tickets to Los Angeles. My young mind was ahead of myself; I even dreamt about it and found myself asking who I would bring with me. I was that confident.”

He shakes his head and laughs. “I didn’t win.” His Pearl’s Hill

Primary School days rush back. "I was affected by it for a long time, disappointed for several months. I won many competitions, like the McDonald's competition in 1979 when it was introduced to Singapore. My entire class got free McDonald's burgers; they delivered them to my class. I was so proud. But not this, the big prize competition. And you know how it is, when kids are disappointed, it's like their world has come to an end. I had spent so much time on this, trying to create something unique in my application."

Looking back, he now feels it was good that he knew, from a tender age, what disappointment was like. Whenever things don't go his way, the SIA Art competition comes to mind, nudging him to move on. "When I was in the military, I wanted to get into Guards badly. But my Manpower Officer told me to stay in Infantry. Again, I was disappointed for several months. And during those months, I kept reminding myself of the failed competition. It becomes a pointer to remind myself: don't be disappointed. Later, I enjoyed going on my captain course in Infantry. It taught me to be pragmatic, make do with what I have, what I am given. I learn to take life for what it is, rather than look back and make myself go through all the what-ifs. Your given path may or may not be a blessing in disguise, but the truth is, you cannot go back."

Fast forward to present day, he encountered several obstacles in his Chinatown project. "Kelvin Ang from the Urban Redevelopment Authority (URA) understood my frustrations. He advised me to go slow. 'Be patient, better things will come,' he said. Now, looking back, if my proposal had been accepted, I might not have had the experience to execute them the way I do today. If the Singapore Tourism Board (STB), the town council and the property owners accepted my very first proposal to paint the opera mural, way back in late 2015, it might have been sub-optimal. My skills were raw then. I needed a lot more practice to paint that complex scene. So, in that sense, those rejections were blessings in disguise. Later, I was given better walls and my skills were better-honed. Now I have the right murals in the right places and all at the right time. So, it pays for things to not happen all at once; it pays off when things are more spread out."

Disappointments also have the effect of making a person try harder when he is landed with an opportunity. When Yew Chong got into secondary school at Raffles Institution, he was the Chairman of the Art Club. "I was struck by how things that we churned out there were always small-scale. When the principal announced successes at the school assembly, those successes were not from the Art Club. When I was in Secondary Three and Four, especially Four, we tried bigger projects."

He might not have realised it then, but it laid the foundation for many of the big-scale projects he was subsequently involved in as an artist. "We painted a mural that was longer than the swimming pool, which was 50-metres long. The mural was about 70 metres; we also painted a mural on the stage of the assembly hall." Yew Chong's hands interlock behind his head, forming a support as he leans back, reminiscing. "The principal was happy. We also won a silver medal in a Science Art competition. Finally, the principal mentioned us, the Art Club, at the school assembly. I was happy because we were finally recognised. I was proud of it."

25 Years

Not any school kid would draw a dollar note to likeness, let alone a primary school boy. And to do it life-size, cut it out and present it to his teacher in school! He might not have given it too much thought; the hand-drawn note might have portended something significant about how he saw figures, and indeed, money, when he grew up. Today, the hand-drawn Bird Series dollar note is still safe, kept like a real dollar note, in his drawer.

Before Yip Yew Chong became a full-time artist, he was an accountant for 25 years. "In the 1980s, when Singapore was still very much in its development phase, there was a strong emphasis on traditional professions such as law and engineering. I intended to pursue an engineering degree after my mandatory stint in the army. But I met

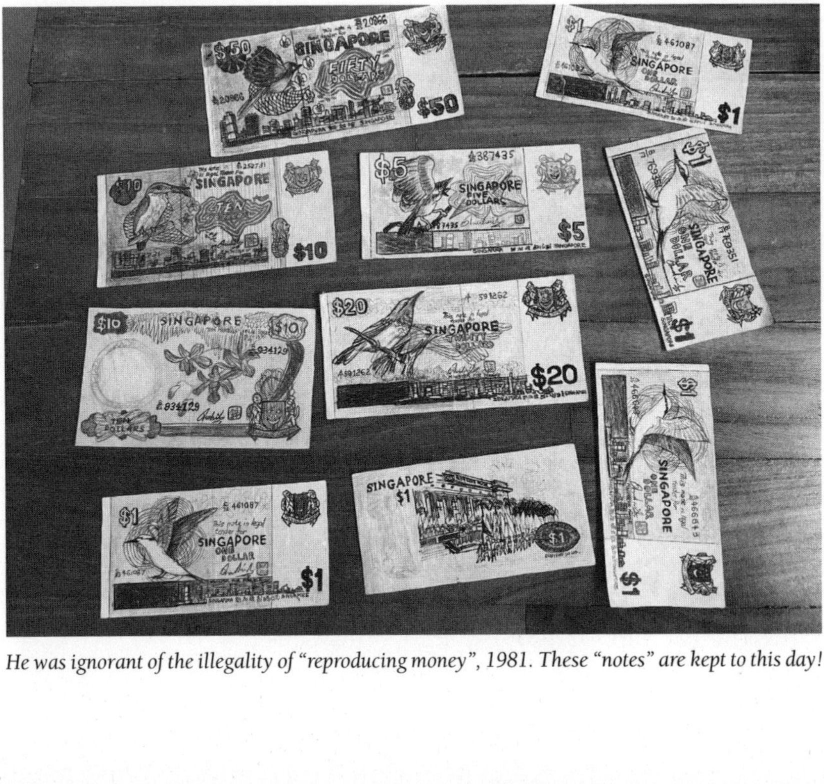

He was ignorant of the illegality of "reproducing money", 1981. These "notes" are kept to this day!

a commander who told me that accountancy was a very versatile skill that would always be in demand in all industries," he recalls with contented calm. "I owe a debt of gratitude to the commander."

Yew Chong studied accountancy at the Nanyang Technological University (NTU) and, true to form, got his first job with a Norwegian shipping company, Thome Ship Management. "I know what most creative people think about accountancy — boring number crunching. But I am proud to say I enjoyed the career. It is different from art, yes. But like art, while I am mindful of the small details, I mustn't lose sight of the overall big picture. For example, if I overly focus on reconciling one cent here and two cents there, or presenting too many details, we might not see the big picture of the financial health of a company. Similarly, when painting a mural, if I spend too much time perfecting one character here or a small shop there, and not paying attention to the overall mural ambience, I won't be able to achieve the intended look and impact a mural must have. In both accounting and art, I learnt to balance the focus on details and big-picture presentation." He pauses, looks up and smiles, "Art and accountancy are very different, but can also be very similar."

He sits up and composes himself, interested in tackling the topic further. "Technical knowledge for both is a given," he says, both hands coming together. "I went to school for accountancy, I didn't for art. After the basic knowledge is acquired, practise, practise and more practise are crucial for both. Finally, deliver consistent results and update your stakeholders with your point of view. All these helped me gain the trust of my boss, my clients and my staff. That trust was hard-earned but so important in my accounting career."

Trust is equally important in art. As an artist who creates public art, there is a certain level of ethics and responsibility involved. "Over the years, I have proven myself to curators and commissioning parties," he says with a look of contentment. "In the beginning, they were cautious and wanted to see my detailed sketches first. Now, they are more trusting. Even if I want to make changes on the spot, I know they would trust me that the changes are for the better. They trust that I will not produce art that is either detrimental to society or to the individual."

As an accountant, what gave Yew Chong satisfaction was applying what he learned in school to the real world. "The experience of working was very different from studying," he says, extending his smile broadly now. "I found fulfilment in knowing that the things I did had a real effect and impact on businesses."

After Thome Ship Management, for his next job at Mas Millennium, Yew Chong was able to apply what he knew onto a global setting. "In this new job, I got to do onsite audits in Taiwan, which was very interesting for a young accountant." From there, he carved out a niche for himself, working with and managing multinational accounting teams. These included Bridge, Thomson Reuters, Visa, and Informa. In 2007, while working in the Netherlands, Yew Chong had the chance to manage a team made up over 20 different nationalities. "It was like a little United Nations (UN). From Western and Eastern European countries, Africa and South America, they all congregated in Amsterdam, led by a Singaporean," he chuckles, obviously enjoying the memory.

There is a word that he likes, but he knows how to use it correctly and in the right context — *pragmatism*. In an international setting, he was able to 'sell' the pragmatic Singapore brand. "I have a very practical approach to problem-solving, there are no 'isms', just pragmaticism. Typically, I stand back and take a look at the big picture, and then identify the practical things that need to be done," Yew Chong says simply, with a shrug.

While being 'practical' may not have been the first word that comes to mind when describing an artist, it is this value that has contributed to the success of Yew Chong the accountant and Yew Chong the artist. "In the accountancy world, I learn to work in collaboration with others. So, I don't insist on sticking doggedly to my own version of things. I consider the comments of others, I accept and modify my work accordingly. Compromise may be a bad word to many creative souls, but is not a bad word to me. It is moderation for the better. Looking back, I realise that if I had gone ahead with my own version for some projects, whether in the corporate or art world, things might not have turned out as well. So, teamwork, collaboration and indeed, compromise were values of the corporate world that I brought to the art world. And these are values that continue to be relevant to me."

Yew Chong likes to point out that in the world of accountancy, there is no black and white. Instead, there are many shades of grey. "It is how you justify, and how you provide evidence to persuade people, such as auditors, to come around to your idea. So, yes, art can be subjective, but so can accountancy."

And it was his love for his accounting career that allowed his love for art to eventually flourish. Yew Chong only planned his secret move to become a full-time artist slightly more than five years ago, while still holding on to a job as Asia's Finance Shared Services Director at Informa. For most of the three years, he would dedicate his weekends to working on his murals. This was done with the full knowledge of his company, who gave their total support, citing his work-life balance as a positive example to others.

It was during this period of juggling the two loves that he decided that it might be time to give art the focus it needed; after all, he had been an accountant for more than two decades. But the bonus was, surprisingly, art also paid well. “I was lucky,” he admits. “I was one of those lucky people in this world who had the luxury of choosing. Having real options was a luxury in life few can talk about.” That art could actually sustain him financially gave him confidence to act.

And so, when his two children entered university in 2018, he took the plunge and became a full-time artist. But this ability to make the switch, he attributes to the rewards that he achieved in his accounting career. “My accounting career gave me financial independence, so I wasn’t taking a big risk.” His hands now rest squarely on the table. “I still have a traditional mindset,” he admits. “I have a family, so that must come first. When that is covered, I am ready.”

Singapore has also changed. “The majority of my works are commissioned by private individuals and organisations; a minority are for the government agencies.” Yew Chong sounds relieved. “A few years ago, you wouldn’t even dream that you could make money from art. One would probably look towards the government or government-related bodies for support and grants. I am glad the private sector has become that much more supportive.”

Even with all the assurances from the art world, he wouldn’t have made the switch had it not been for one person — his wife.

The Good Wife

If one 'follows' Yew Chong around while he paints his murals or when he researches in his studio, it is easy to go away with the idea that he is a loner; an independent creative soul who makes all important decisions inside his head, by himself. As we think of all artists, the creative process begins and ends with them. Yet, there is a much more important stage before the creative process, one that few see.

"There is a mental place I call peace of mind," he begins, the fingers tapping lightly on the table. "It is a peace within myself, arrived at when I know the important things in my life are being cared for, are being sorted out, are resolving and being resolved. So, for me, what's left are my own battles, and these battles are artistic ones only. It's me and

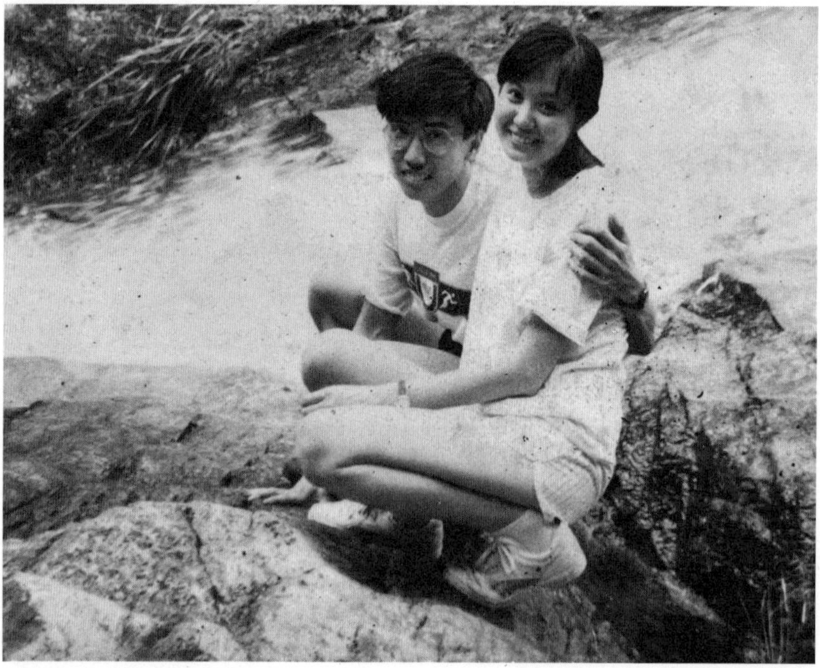

Pui Ying was the only person to show up for the Mt. Ophir training sessions. By the time of the actual climb, they were a couple! At Mt. Ophir, 1991.

myself; it does not get more intimate than this. It is here that I am truly creative. I am free to access the wherewithal within myself to begin the creative process."

The coast is clear to explore and the mind is at peace to create only because the important day-to-day tasks are handled by someone he trusts. "I am lucky." the three words come out like a whisper, afraid that if said too loudly things could change. While luck may have had a say in the way things pan out, a lot has to do with a significant other.

Pui Ying is two years older than Yew Chong; they have been married for 26 years. They have two children, both adults pursuing university education today. Few can say, hand on heart, that it has been 26 years of bliss. She can. In fact, the years got better with the passage of time.

Romance began innocently in school when they were in the same class.

"We knew each other in NTU," he recounts those years with a mix of fun and wonder. "Even though we were in the same class and we, knew of each other, we did not 'meet' in the first year. In the second year, we were also in the same class. I was leading a trekking trip to Mount Ophir in Malaysia and she signed up. When I asked the participants if they needed training, only two girls turned up. Little did I know then that one of the two girls would become my wife. Actually, the other girl sensed something between us and opted out. So, it ended up fatefully with just her… and me." By now, Yew Chong is laughing softly, as 'training' turned out to be an agreeable, early courtship.

During the 'training sessions', young Yew Chong discovered his only trainee was gentle, patient and had the ability to 'really listen'.

"We became close, and I shared poignant episodes of my life with her, especially about my grandmother and how I missed her when she passed away. I cried talking about my grandmother." He looks down, his fingers rubbing on the wooden table. "She consoled me, and I knew we had connected. My guards were down."

Even though Yew Chong's family did not have much, he had a good childhood. His wife, however, had a rough one. The eldest of five children from a single mother, she believed in paying her own way through school, by working. "Her father passed away when she was seven." His tone simmers gently. "Her family could not provide for her, but she knew a university degree was important. After Junior College, she went straight to work and saved. When she accumulated enough, she went back to university. She was one of those who paid everything herself. Her university education was delayed for two years, and when she got in, it was the same year I started after finishing my two-year stint in the army. So, it was fate that we would be together."

He married her when he was 26 years old and she was 28. They became young parents two years later.

"I would describe these 26 years as happy," he says simply. "No arguments, no drama… perhaps a little disagreement on how we took care of our kids, that was that, the usual differences of opinion. It's a good marriage. You need to ask her, but I think she'd say the same, that we have been happy."

When it comes to the children, Yew Chong was easy. "I believe my children should be who they want to be, so my approach to parenting was easy-going. I guided them, but, in the end, they made their decisions on which school to go to, what to study. And also, what they wanted to be when they grow up. My wife was stricter. Here, we did not see eye-to-eye all the time, but in the end, what the children wanted became paramount and it was our children's happiness that guided us."

Pui Ying may be gentle, patient, and a good listener, but these adjectives do not define her. Like Yew Chong, she became an accountant, and worked in the corporate world for 14 years. When Yew Chong was posted to Amsterdam, she gave up her job to be a full-time homemaker and housewife. Unlike many 'professional' women who believe in climbing the corporate ladder first before 'settling down', Pui Ying knew the fate of her family depended on the fate of her husband. With all the skills she had learned and garnered over the years, she focused on improving the financial well-being of the family, knowing that, in turn, would provide the necessary 'support' her husband needed.

"She was an accountant; she is numerically literate." Yew Chong smiles. "She took care of the family finances, literally running the family accounts like she would a corporate entity. Whether it is the stock market or the property market, she researches and invests. Over the years, she has done well for the family."

When she describes herself as a homemaker, the understanding for most is a housewife. In her case, she literally manages the entire household, keeping proper accounts and exploring investment opportunities to augment the family income. "She was so focused on the family income that she even took up part-time work for a while." His eyes are now fixed while he continues. "Most people marvel at how well she manages the family expenses and finances, investing in properties, and buying stocks. But to me, the most difficult part was taking care of the kids. Waking them up, making breakfast, taking them to school, fetching them home, arranging various activities for them on weekends… In my mind, she was, is, a superwoman."

It would come as a surprise, even a shock, to most Singaporeans, that Yew Chong and Pui Ying do not have a helper. "We are simple people, not into the fancy things in life." Yew Chong laughs. "I do the cleaning and she does the washing. We love our home. We have been staying in the same HDB apartment for more than 20 years."

One more thing. She knows what art means to her husband and has been tracking the public response to his works. By the end of 2017 and in early 2018, she knew it was time he became a full-time artist.

"She was the one who told me I could be doing just as well, or better, as an artist financially," he quips, his smile now showing his perfect teeth again. "She saw how difficult it was to squeeze what I needed to do for art over the weekends, or late at night. She kept pestering me to tell my boss, 'Tell him you need to do art full-time; you need to resign.' With her support, I finally made the decision, I took the plunge in 2018."

Classmate, girlfriend, wife, mother, homemaker, financier. When asked what words he would use to describe her, he provides two, "Reliable, capable. I know I can rely on her because I know she is capable." He forgot 'superwoman'.

A Chat with Superwoman

She sits with an aura of quiet confidence; smiles often, like her husband sitting next to her. I am glad they brought *kuey chap* from Chinatown, one of my favourite hawker dishes.

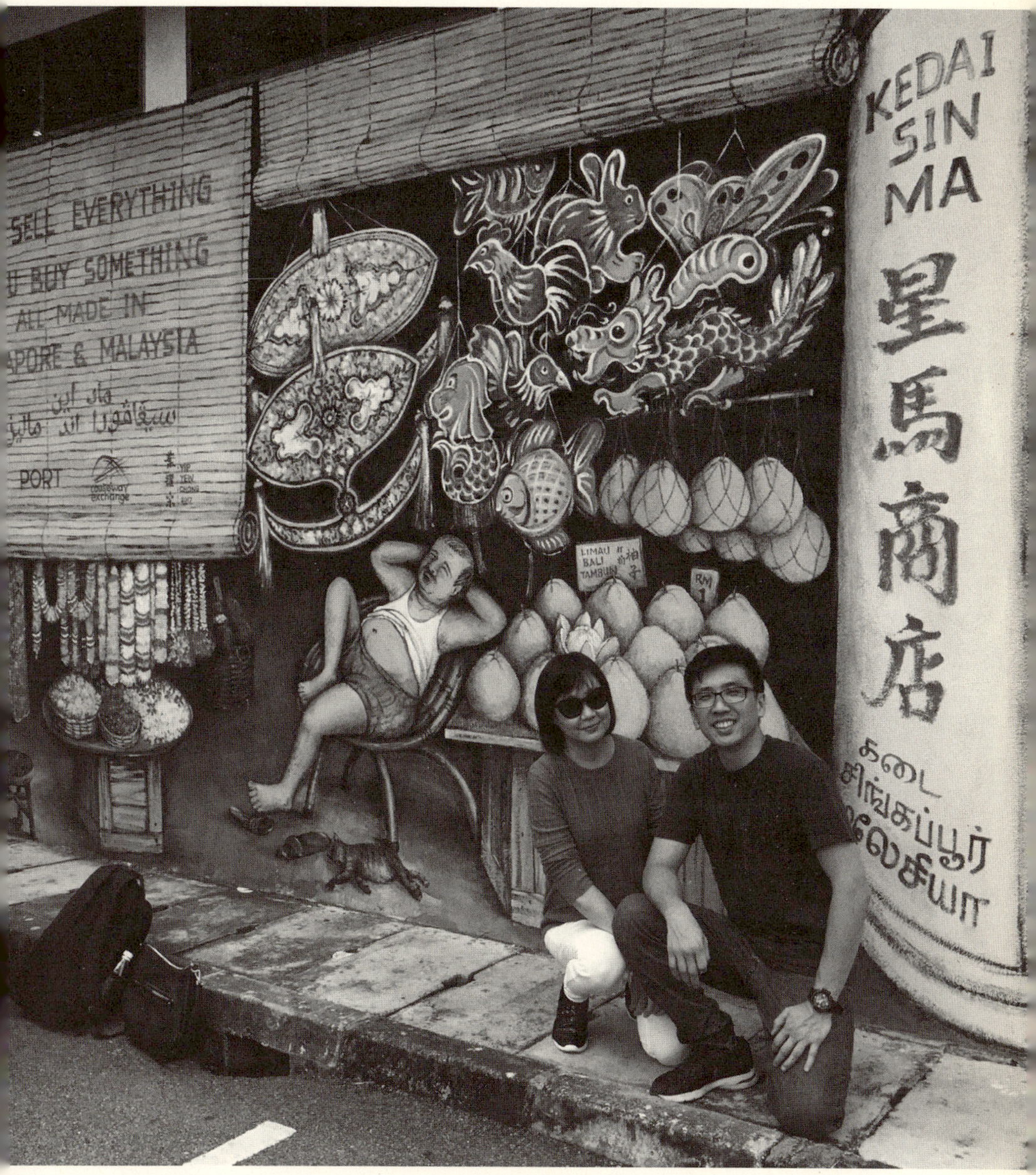

Yew Chong and Pui Ying at the Kedai Sin Ma mural in Ipoh, 2017. It was Yew Chong's first mural painted in Malaysia, organised by the Causeway Exchange.

"The *kuey chap* has soaked up the soup," she laughs. "It's *kuey chap* dry!"

I don't quarrel with *kuey chap*, soup or dry.

She begins by apologising, "I am not much of a communicator." I get the feeling she is more of a doer than a talker, and an observer and thinker. Her eyes scan my apartment like a journalist. When she speaks, she looks straight at me, her eyes smiling.

What does she attribute the success of her husband to?

"I went to school to study accountancy," she begins. "And because I am quite a good student, I did well. Accountancy can be taught. But art, you need to be born with something, talent, or an innate ability. After that, it's hard work, and luck."

Is education important?

"Even though I did well in my A levels, I did not pursue education beyond that. I became a secretary at a law firm. Then, I noticed the lawyers joining the firm were close to my age. I felt it was a pity I didn't give myself a chance to go to university even though I had good results. I decided to go back to school. I applied in 1990."

Did it ever cross her mind that perhaps she didn't need higher education, that her husband would take care of her?

"In my generation, we don't think like that," she asserts lightly. "At that age, I didn't assume I would have a husband to look after me or support me. Because of my background, my mother was not educated, and when my father passed away, she had a hard time. It taught me to be financially independent. Going back to your question about education, it is important, not just for getting a job, but it also nourishes the mind. Looking back at myself, before and after university, the way

I see things, analyse things, it's very different. So, education helps me to be independent, helps me to solve problems in ways I would not have without higher education."

And so, she became independent, she took care of herself. What does marriage mean to an independent woman?

"Honestly, I didn't think too much of it. I met this reasonably nice guy," she looks at her husband. He smiles. "I am not one who puts career above everything. Just a good career is fine, but not climbing up the corporate ladder, being a CEO or something. Just a career that makes me feel I am good and I contribute. Career was never number one in the grand scheme of things. And marriage isn't number one either. If I didn't meet him or a nice guy, I think I would be a happy single. I would focus on career but I won't be an aggressive achiever at work. I went with the flow of my life."

She did meet a nice guy, and marriage came easily. What about the institution of family? How important is it?

"I was 23 when I met him." Her face moves to acknowledge Yew Chong. "I had my first child at 30. I was not old, but I was not young either. Because of my poor background, my difficult childhood, I told myself, when I have children, I will give them my best. My children and my family are very important to me."

Family is important. What would she do for her family?

"In 2007, Yew Chong went to Amsterdam." She looks down, thinking. "Even before that, I brought up the need to quit my job for the family. I was making a good salary. But the two of us were cautious, we waited till his salary reached a certain level before we were comfortable relying on a single source of income. We are prudent accountants," she laughs. "And even after I quit my job, I was looking for ways to augment the family income, whether it was through investments in property or in stocks."

She is effectively the CFO of her family.

"I am not just the CFO, I am also the Home Minister, and the Minister of Education." She covers her mouth, laughing.

Yew Chong chips in, "She is the Prime Minister."

A Prime Minister without help, or, more accurately, without a helper to help out in the house. Why?

"It's surprising. That both of us didn't discuss this, before or after marriage. It's like owning a car; we have never owned one, neither do we want a helper. I was relieved, no quarrel over these. You could say we both have the same values. I have help from my in-laws; both his parents help out. My assumption is, if we have a helper, we need to look after the helper too. And I have heard of stories, like children being closer to the helper than to their parents. And we are both essentially private, to have a stranger staying in the house isn't something we want. But I don't rule out having a helper in the future when his parents are old, or when we ourselves are old."

She has created a comfortable home, and that's probably the most important support she can give her husband.

"It is not just me." She looks at her husband now. "It is also him. He is an extremely easy-going guy and very supportive of the things I do as well. And together, we created a home culture that is an asset to us all."

Back to the question of talent. There are so many talented artists, and not all make it. What are the circumstances that allow an artist to become successful?

"Yes, many talented artists never make it big. I always tell him, be thankful you are given the opportunities, make use of every opportunity. And stay humble, work hard and stay humble. Also, I think his art is easy to understand. He is not trying to be clever or trying to be who he is not. I saw him painting the mural at Spottiswoode Park; many people crowded around, older people, young people and people who have probably never been in a museum before, but their faces say it all — nodding, smiling or just staring. I could tell they were enjoying themselves, enjoying art. So, I tell him, this is the art people want; you connect with them, don't lose it, don't change too much. Improve, but always remember what made them stand there, what made them happy."

Words of wisdom from the good wife.

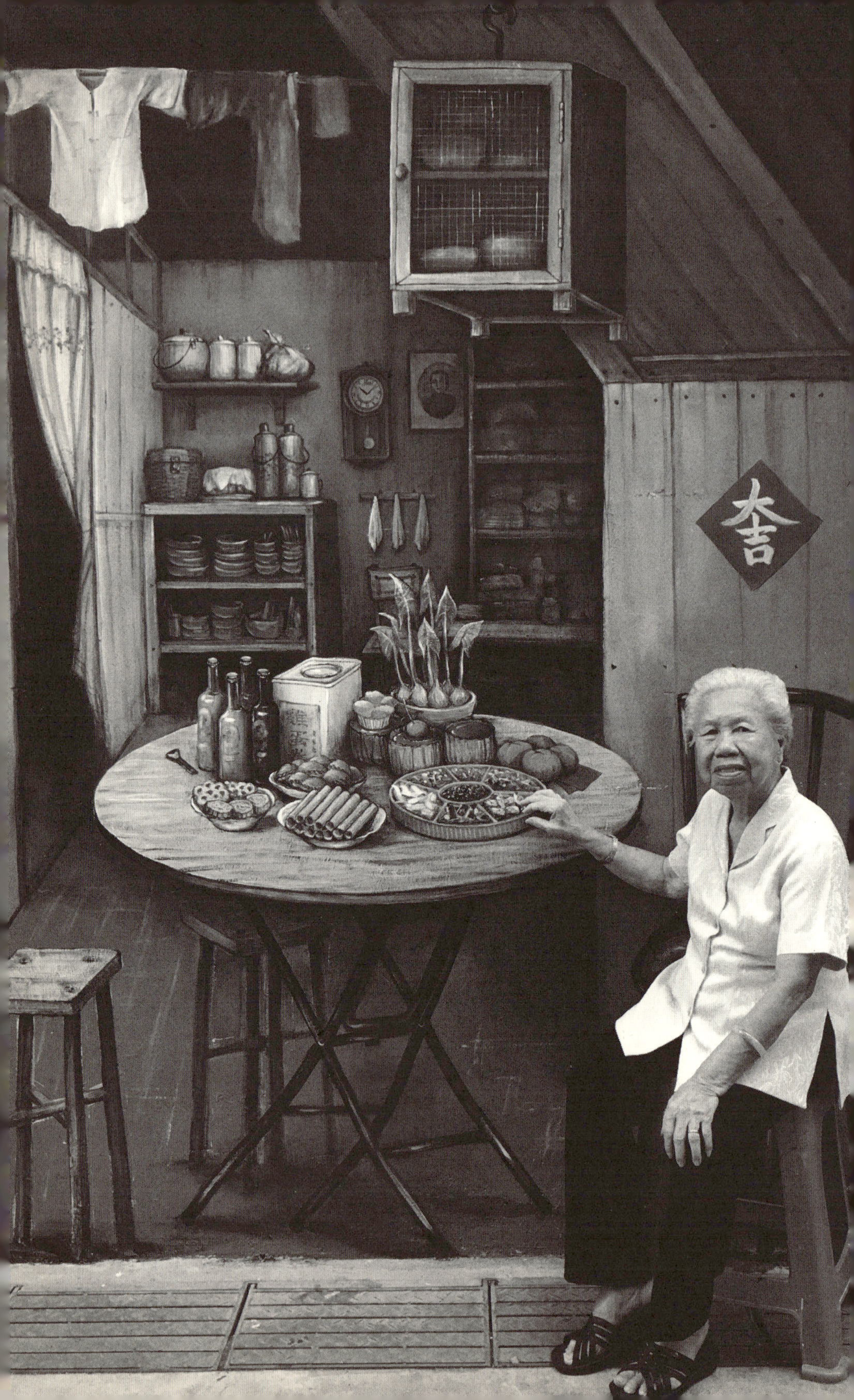
大吉

CHAPTER 3

Chinatown's 'Open-Air Museum'

I am proud of my work in Chinatown, what I call my 'open-air museum'.

Q & A

He has painted more than 80 murals in Singapore and abroad, of which eight of them are in the Singapore Chinatown area. On prominent walls and within walking distance of each other, there is also a consistent style and theme, forming a nice cluster telling a connected storyline. Over the years, the cluster has attracted tourists, heritage interest groups, and students. "This explains why most people know more about my Chinatown murals and less of my other murals scattered elsewhere in Singapore," says Yew Chong as he leans back on an old chair. It's past noon, and we are in a hawker centre in Chinatown for lunch, both having *mee pok*, mine swimming in a thick broth, his is dry with chilli. "I am proud of my works in Chinatown, what I call my 'open-air museum'. People living in Chinatown, outside Chinatown, heritage interest groups, all appreciate the connected stories told in these Chinatown murals." The artist has shared these personal stories on various platforms: social media, TV interviews, and the talks he gives. Less known, however, is how hard it was to get these murals projects off the ground and onto the walls, especially in the first two years.

Today, he has a proven record of popular murals, but not in 2015 or 2016. He literally went from wall to wall, knocking on one door after another, writing and explaining what he had in mind to various approving authorities, and finding the money to fund the murals — it was a long and arduous process. A less focused and determined artist would have given up and stuck to his day job. Not Yip Yew Chong.

I want to know more about the process, from concept to approval to painting, and I want him to relive it walking through the murals with me in Tiong Bahru and Chinatown. The sun is scorching after lunch. Yew Chong is used to the heat and humidity; I am mentally prepared too.

Woon Tai Ho (WTH): Your Chinatown murals are more known than your other murals in Singapore. Apart from the fact that you grew up in Chinatown, what are the back stories to these famed murals?

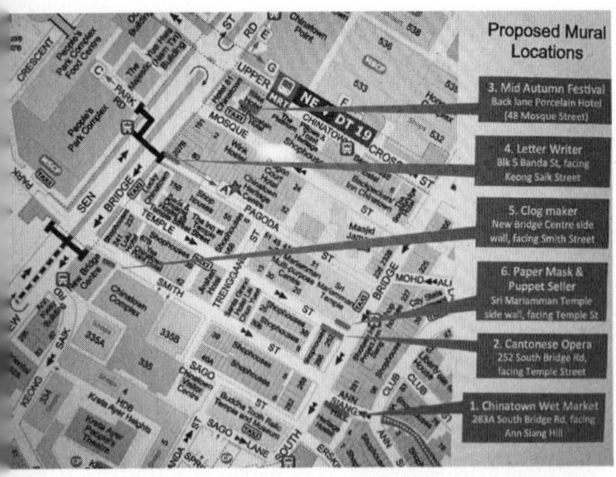

These were the original proposed mural locations. Only one mural, Cantonese Opera, *was painted on the originally intended wall.*

Yip Yew Chong (YC): Way back in late 2015, after I had painted the Everton Road murals which were quite well received by the public, I dreamt of creating more murals elsewhere. I went around looking for new areas. Tiong Bahru was one, Chinatown was another, because I grew up in Chinatown and Tiong Bahru was my childhood playground. Tiong Bahru was my priority because the area had pristine white walls. Chinatown walls were often soiled and greasy due to the high traffic and many eateries. I also eyed the huge white wall at Amoy Street behind the Thian Hock Keng temple (which thankfully I was later commissioned to paint a mural in 2017) and the large grey wall of the Jean Yip salon at New Bridge Road.

In December 2015, I knew I would have little time left for art once I started my new finance job in January 2016. I quickly drew some sketches of murals I wanted to do in Tiong Bahru and Chinatown. For Tiong Bahru, I submitted my proposal to the Seng Poh Road Resident Committee after seeing their 'open call' notice. The notice was pasted beside an existing Tiong Bahru mural by Ernest Goh, his goldfish and rooster photo series. The notice invited anyone to submit proposals for artworks to be installed in the precinct. I drew five scenes relating to Tiong Bahru and submitted them. After a few weeks, I was connected with the committee who showed interest in my proposal. One of the resident committee members, Kelvin Ang, happened to be working in the Urban Redevelopment Authority (URA), in the URA conservation department. Even though I had already started my new job, we continued to pursue the idea. Finally, after all the approvals were obtained from the authorities, I painted three of the five murals in March and April of 2016, done over five weekends. The murals were an immediate hit and received much media publicity, including exposure on TV.

WTH: It started with Tiong Bahru, your childhood playground. Did the success there pave the way for Chinatown?

YC: Not really. Chinatown was not so straightforward. In late 2015, I submitted to the Singapore Tourism Board, STB, a mural proposal — the *Cantonese Opera*, to be painted on the stage of Kreta Ayer Square. I submitted to STB because I knew STB manages Chinatown place-making. The stage had a blank white wall, so I thought it would be interesting to have another 'stage', the opera scene, on a real stage. STB involved the Kreta Ayer Resident Committee in the discussion. Subsequently, they replied that the wall could not be painted on. It needed to be blank to allow for light projection of images on it during events. As there were no alternate suggestions to continue the discussion, I sensed that they were not keen to pursue the idea. Thus, I gave up the idea and moved on to pursue it elsewhere.

I brought the same proposal to two other locations — the large grey wall of the Jean Yip salon building at New Bridge Road, and the Kong Chow Wui Koon perimeter wall. Jean Yip salon declined because they had plans to do renovation. The Kong Chow Wui Koon discussion went a bit further, albeit slowly, but also faded off over time.

WTH: You had your 'Dreams of Chinatown', specific murals you wanted to paint for Chinatown. What was the genesis of that?

YC: After the Tiong Bahru murals, the urge and itch to pursue the Chinatown murals idea came back again. That was in mid-2016. By then, I had known Kelvin Ang well enough to ask him for advice. He told me to do a proper proposal much like the Tiong Bahru mural proposal. He would then share it with STB again. That was how I created a full proposal with 6 murals for Chinatown. I named it 'Dreams of Chinatown'. They were:

1. *Cantonese Opera* (same submission to STB in 2015)
2. *Clog Maker*
3. *Letter Writer*

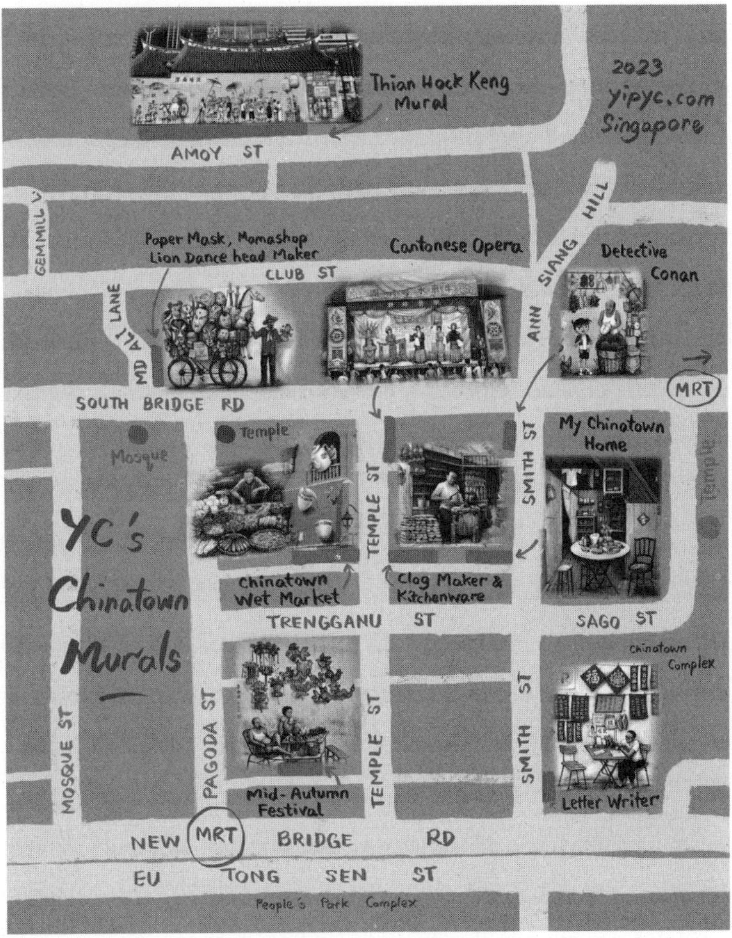

Yew Chong created a mural cluster map for his Chinatown murals, 2023.

4. *Paper Mask Seller*
5. *Mid-Autumn Festival*
6. *Chinatown Wet Market*

I chose these themes for a variety of reasons — my personal connection to them; they were colourful visually; they each had an interesting back story; and they are good representations of the old Chinatown ambience.

To add depth to the proposal, I went around excitedly to identify possible walls for them and drew them on a map:

1. *Cantonese Opera* — Temple Street (exact wall as actually painted)
2. *Clog Maker* — Smith Street New Bridge Centre, the wall where *Letter Writer* was actually painted
3. *Letter Writer* — HDB Block 4 Sago Lane
4. *Paper Mask Seller* — Temple Street, on the perimeter wall of Sri Mariamman Temple
5. *Mid-Autumn Festival* — Mosque Street
6. *Chinatown Wet Market* — Ann Siang Hill or Smith Street's gable wall

WTH: Was STB the approving authority or URA? Who would fund them?

YC: For Chinatown, the property owner must first approve. Thereafter, the next approvers are URA and STB, and other stakeholders like Town Council are consulted. I also have to look for funding separately. URA

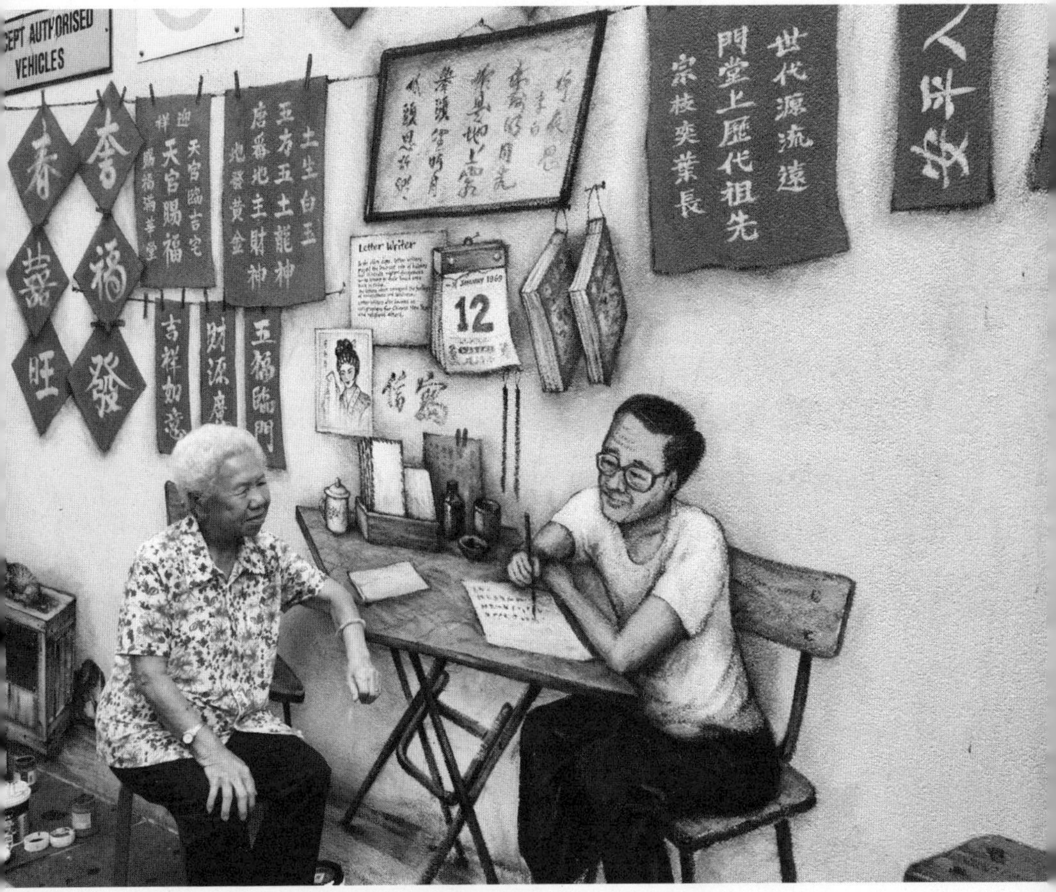

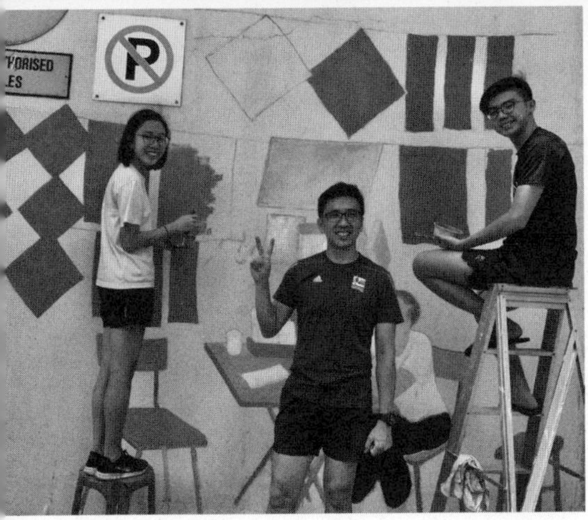

Above: Yew Chong's second aunt posing at the Letter Writer mural as it was still being painted, 2018.

Left: His children helping him paint the mural.

helped share the proposal with STB. They jointly gave me a letter of in-principle blanket approval of the overall project! My next task was to find the walls and funds. In late 2016, I walked the grounds over several weekends and went knocking on the doors of the targeted shophouse walls. It was not easy. At each shophouse, I would first introduce myself as an artist. Then, I would request to be introduced to the shophouse owner to allow me to paint a mural on the shophouse wall. However, the shopkeeper would either say that they were busy, or they couldn't disclose the owners to me, or just asked me to 'go ask the government'. One shopkeeper even shooed me away, saying I was obstructing her business! However, one kind shopkeeper asked me to leave my contact so that she would ask the owner to call me back. Subsequently, I actually received a call from the owner, but unfortunately the owner declined to have his wall painted. I also tried searching through the internet on how to find the owners of other possible houses, but it proved very difficult.

For the targeted walls belonging to the Sri Mariamman Temple and the HDB Block 4, I wrote in directly to the Temple's general enquiry email, as well as to HDB, and even the HDB CEO. There was no reply from anyone. For the HDB wall, I wrote directly to the MP Dr Lily Neo. I was pleasantly surprised when Dr Neo replied me. She said she would like to support the idea. She referred me to the Town Council to pursue the idea. The Town Council assessed my request. They were worried that my mural would distract drivers driving along Keong Saik Road. Thus, they offered me an alternative wall. It was at the carpark gantry entrance off Kreta Ayer Road. I went to look at the site and didn't feel it was suitable. First, it was a secluded area that only cars would drive past as they use the carpark. Secondly, the visual of a letter writer sitting at the entrance of a carpark beside the gantry pole didn't seem right. I decided to decline the offer.

WTH: I remember you sharing these frustrations on social media.

YC: By January 2017, I was feeling frustrated and hinted about it in a Facebook post. Several concerned friends (some whom I had never met personally), contacted me and offered help to connect me to owners. One of them was Belinda Tan. She helped introduce me to her friend Victor Yue. Victor is well known as the "Walking Dictionary of Chinatown". Victor then introduced me to the Chinatown Business

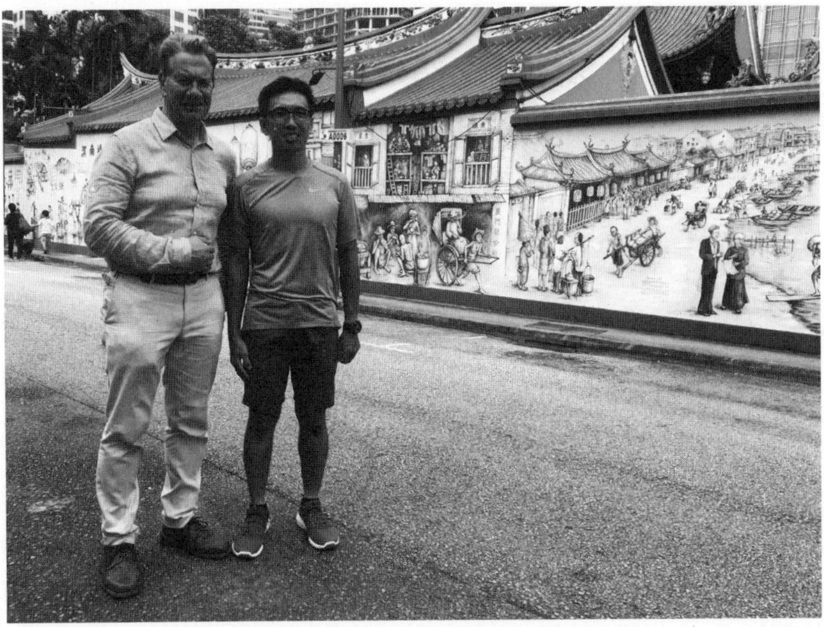

The mural is well-publicised overseas. Various foreign TV stations filmed their documentaries featuring the mural. With Michael Portillo, filming for the BBC Great Asian Railway Journeys, *2019.*

Association and the STB department looking after Chinatown. The Chinatown Business Association looked at my targeted walls. They knew two owners and helped me with connecting to the Temple Street (Opera mural) and Mosque Street (Mid-Autumn Festival mural) property owners.

In September 2017, the Temple Street property owner finally agreed to have the opera scene painted on their wall. However, the Mosque Street property owner declined to have their wall painted. Around that time, Kelvin Ang, who knew of my difficulties looking for owners and walls, was also trying to help me look out for walls in Chinatown owned by government-related agencies.

WTH: I thought you started to get commissioned works around 2017?

YC: No, my first commissioned mural in Singapore was in November 2015. My first overseas commissioned mural was in Hong Kong in December 2016. But my first Chinatown commissioned mural was the Thian Hock Keng mural at Amoy Street, whereas 'Dreams of Chinatown' is a self-initiated project, thus it needs to be funded by either commission or sponsorship or out of pocket.

Backtracking a bit to June 2017, a Temple Street property owner contacted me to explore commissioning a mural of their heritage business — clog-making. However, they said they needed to renovate the property first, which could take several years. It was a godsend because *Clog Maker* was in the project plan, despite it being planned for another wall along Smith Street. I agreed to keep the theme for them. Also, in June 2017, Netflix approached me to do a mural on a wall at Ann Siang Hill. The visual was to have the characters of their show *Orange is the New Black* in a Singapore Chinatown setting. As the mural had the element of 'advertisement', it was displayed for one month and thereafter whitewashed.

WTH: So, in the end, how was 'Dreams of Chinatown' funded?

YC: While I was busy searching for owners and persuading them to let me paint on their walls, I was simultaneously finding ways to get funding for 'Dreams of Chinatown'. I actually wrote in to several individuals, private and public organisations to check if they were willing to fund these murals, co-fund or be the sole sponsor. I realised, very quickly, it was going to be very tough to get money. Most people I approached told me that they liked my works, but they thought a government agency like STB or NAC would be the right parties to fund such public art projects. After having met STB's Chinatown department and having understood their jurisdiction, I explained that it was not within STB's jurisdiction to fund such art projects. STB funds events that attract tourism but not standalone art projects without events. One property owner even thought he should be compensated by the government if he allowed his wall to be painted with public art!

I researched National Art Council's (NAC) grant schemes and learnt that they were rather restrictive. I even spoke to an NAC officer and concluded that for all the requirements to fulfil, and the amount and restrictions of the grant, it was not worthwhile to apply. Thus, I didn't pursue that route. Some friends suggested crowdfunding. I also didn't like the idea. In the end, I decided to fund the murals myself,

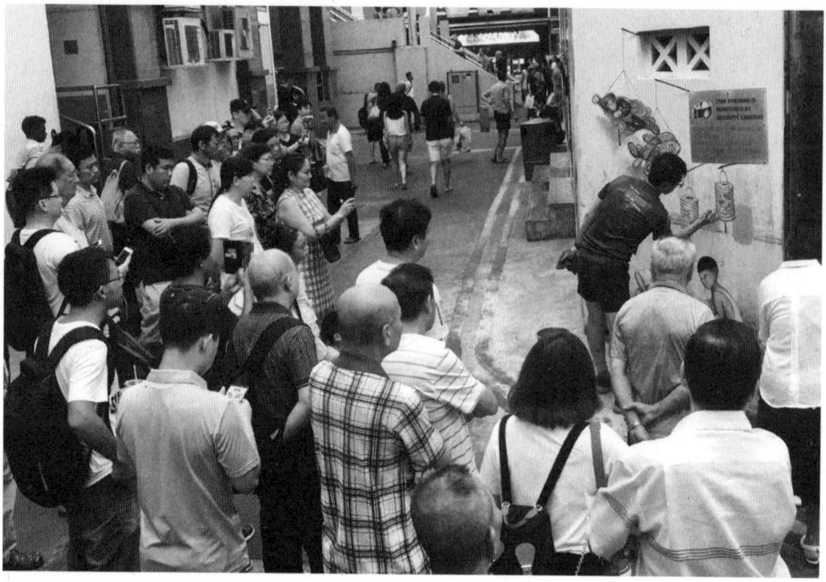

A curious crowd gathered around the mural as it was painted. Mid-Autumn Festival, *2018.*

and see how things would go. Thinking back, this was the same strategy for my early murals in 2015 — I did the first murals at my own expense, when they attracted public recognition, they were like well-invested advertisements. Commissioning requests would come later.

In September 2017, shortly after the house owner of the Opera mural wall gave approval to use his wall, I received good news from Kelvin Ang. He introduced me to HDB and Singapore Power. They were the owners of the New Bridge Centre and Pagoda Street Power station wall respectively. They agreed to let me paint on those walls. Since I had reserved the clog-maker theme for a private owner, I suggested to HDB that *Letter Writer* be painted instead on the Smith Street New Bridge Centre wall. For the Pagoda Street Power Station, I found its gable wall suitable for the Mid-Autumn Festival mural.

By now, I had secured four out of six walls — *Clog Maker*, *Opera*, *Letter Writer*, and *Mid-Autumn Festival*. I was very happy and beginning to feel more optimistic! But aside from *Clog Maker*, which was a potential commission, I had not secured any funding. Anyway, with some walls secured, I decided that I should go ahead and paint a few of the 'dreams' out of pocket. My wife was supportive.

WTH: So, it was out of your own pocket. Of the six 'Dreams', which did you paint first?

YC: Finally, in February 2018, two years since ideation, I painted the *Letter Writer* mural at Smith Street on the wall of New Bridge Centre. My two children helped scrub the grime off the wall and paint the base layer. We finished the painting over two weekends. It was pre-Chinese New Year season, so the red calligraphic couplets of the mural blended especially well with the whole atmosphere. Many passers-by crowded around me to watch me paint. Finally, the first dream of 'Dreams of Chinatown' was done! This 'first' mural proved to be very popular. I think many people hadn't seen my murals elsewhere and hadn't seen a mural of this style in Chinatown, so they might have found it refreshing. Various media outlets helped publicise the *Letter Writer* mural, including Hong Kong's TVB when they filmed it for a variety show.

In June 2018, I left my full-time finance job. With more dedicated time, I painted the Mid-Autumn Festival mural at Pagoda Street, on the wall of the Power Station.

WTH: At what point did your 'investment' start to bear fruit? When did you start to get more commissioned works in Chinatown?

YC: Following the success of *Letter Writer*, I began to receive more enquiries from house owners within Chinatown for commissioned murals. The owner of the Mohammed Ali Lane wall, Heritage Collections, wanted to commission a mural with a Chinatown heritage theme. I offered them the Paper Mask Seller theme. The real mask seller, a Mr Yeo Ban Kok, plied his cart full of his homemade paper masks along South Bridge Road in front of the Sri Mariamman Temple, which is directly opposite Mohammed Ali Lane. The mural theme was therefore very suitable for the wall. Because the wall was rather big, I also added a mama shop, a lion dance head-maker shop and two Samsui women. The mural was completed in October 2018.

In late 2018, I received another request from a house owner to paint a commissioned mural in Chinatown. The proposed wall was directly opposite the targeted wall at Smith Street for the Chinatown Wet Market mural! I was very happy, and offered the Wet Market scene to the house owner. They accepted the idea. However, the wall had two large windows and a door which were never opened. They were dominant in terms of surface area, thus not much space left for painting if I didn't touch them. I decided that I had to paint on them for a wet market scene. A market needs to look busy with goods and people. These large windows and door seemed out of place. Thus, I covered them in my design. I was planning to disguise the door into a chicken coop. We submitted the design to URA. URA rejected it. They said the design must not cover the door and windows because they were features of the house that needed to remain undisguised under conservation standards.

The owner and I went back to our drawing board. I actually felt disappointed because I could not fulfil the last of the six themes in "Dreams of Chinatown". I thought long and hard. What else could I paint without touching the dominant door and windows, yet was something I feel passionate about, while keeping the authentic Chinatown feel? There wasn't much choice really, only a house has a door and windows. A house. My home! My old Chinatown home!

Thus, *My Chinatown Home* was painted in April 2019. It was another blessing in disguise. It became my favourite mural. It also became a favourite for many Singaporeans and tourists, probably the most posed-with, most photographed and videoed mural in Chinatown.

In the same month, April 2019, I went on to paint the Cantonese Opera mural. As it was not a commissioned work, I wanted to make full use of my effort and money for the mural to create other benefits. I partnered with the Community Chest to rally donations that went directly to the charities. The Community Chest invited *The Straits Times* to cover the event to attract donations.

WTH: Wasn't there a Japanese-inspired mural in Chinatown?

YC: Yes. In May 2019, I did another mural in Chinatown — Detective Conan in Chinatown SG. It was an unusual mural for me because I had to paint a Japanese manga character, which I had never done before. This was for the Japanese movie *Detective Conan: The Fist of Blue Sapphire*. STB promoted the movie because it was the first time the popular Japanese movie series was shot outside Japan, and in Singapore. Part of the movie featured Singapore's Chinatown. It was commissioned by STB in collaboration with the Detective Conan creator, the movie distributor, and the property owner. I remembered being quite nervous painting the character because photos of my painting-in-progress were sent to Japan for feedback! I knew I had to get the look right. I was relieved when the movie director, producer and voice actors praised the mural at the launch ceremony.

WTH: How did the pandemic affect you and your work in Chinatown?

YC: When the pandemic hit the world in 2020, like everyone else, I was forced to take a break from painting murals. But behind the scenes, I was busy planning and negotiating. I secured another commissioned mural in Chinatown and re-offered the Chinatown Wet Market theme. It was finally painted in November 2021. I took three weeks, painting daily, I even painted when it rained. The three-storey high mural is my personal tallest in Chinatown and Singapore.

I think the pandemic helped boost the awareness and popularity of the Chinatown murals amongst Singaporean residents. We couldn't travel abroad, so we became local tourists. Suddenly, we realised that we have so many murals in Singapore!

WTH: You have one more dream to paint, the *Clog Maker*.

YC: It's been a long journey since 2015. It seemed like yesterday when I got rejected for the Cantonese Opera mural. It's now 2023. Although

I haven't fulfilled all the Dreams, I feel happy. *Clog Maker* is the last Dream and will be my final mural in Chinatown. I actually feel happy because it has kept me dreaming for the last seven years. Dreaming motivates me to go on and paint better and better. *Clog Maker* was painted in April 2023, turning the "Dreams of Chinatown" into reality.

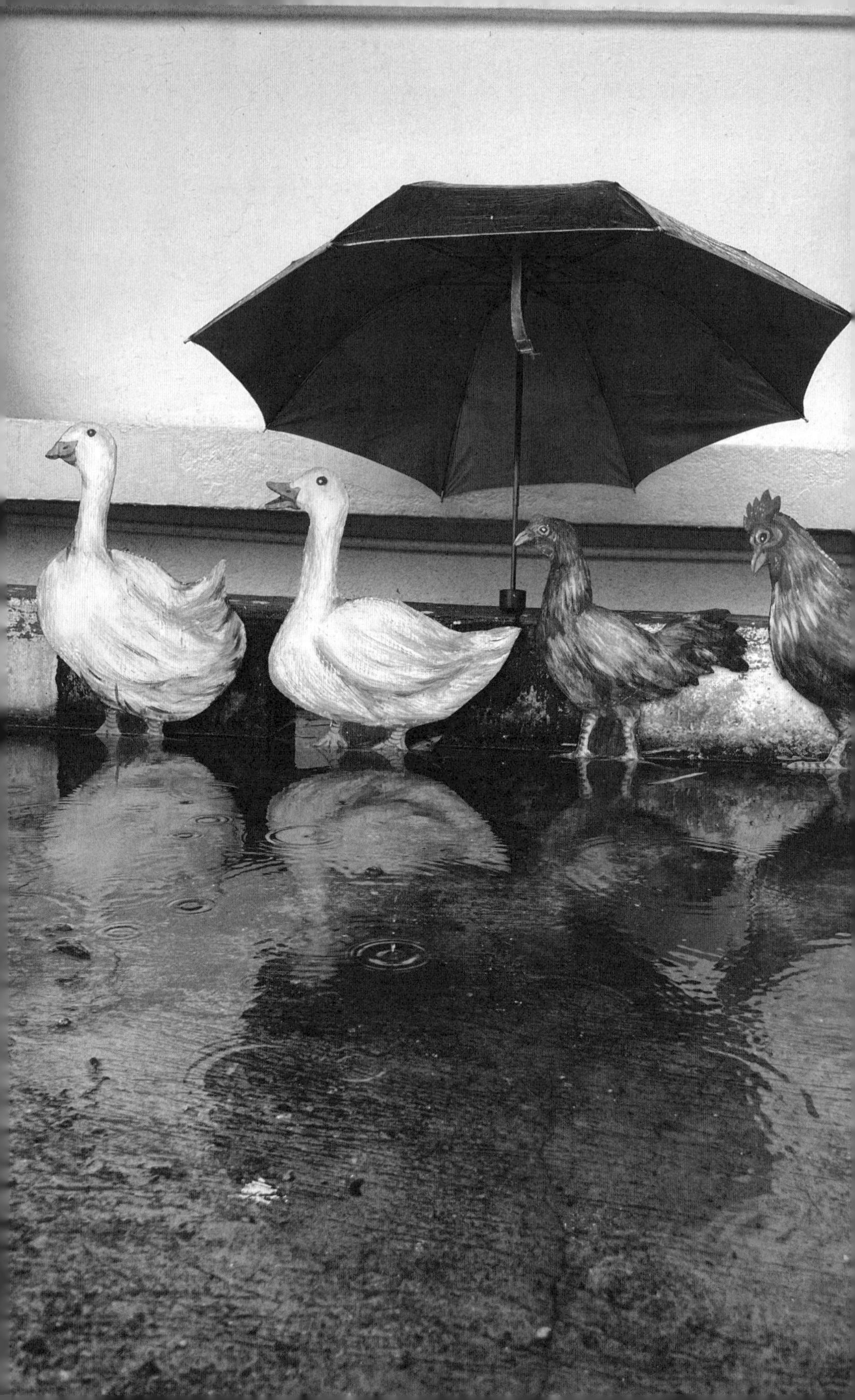

CHAPTER 4

Being Whimsical

When I paint, I go back to me when I was young, when I was a little boy.

Chickens and Ducks

Boxing Day, Sunday. The invitation is simple: *10.45am, photoshoot with kids at the wooden boardwalk below the Art Science Museum. A 5-minute walk from Bayfront MRT.*

The December sun flirts, appears, and disappears, dancing in and out of the clouds. The sky seems confused; it isn't sure if it wants to stay blue or turn grey. Year-end rain is a definite possibility. Everything is up in the air; the elements are in a stage of flux, allowing Yew Chong a free hand.

The boardwalk below the Art Science Museum is a long stretch consisting of wooden stripes, bleached to a light grey by the sun and rain. It soon becomes clear to me why Yew Chong has chosen this for his anamorphic photoshoot. The thin grooves between the wood allow him to 'plant' his mobile art pieces, in this case, life-size chickens and ducks, about 50 of them. Huge clouds have started to form above the Marina Bay skyline, and one quickly sees the dramatic genius that is Yip Yew Chong.

The human eye knows these to be painted cutouts of chickens

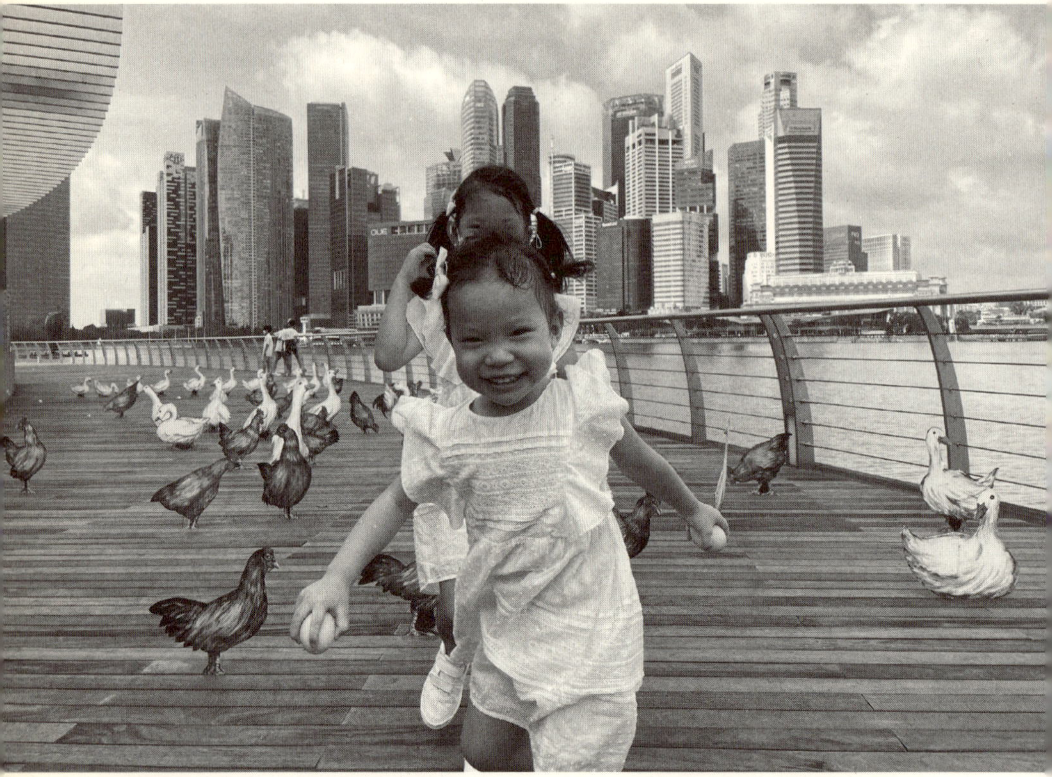

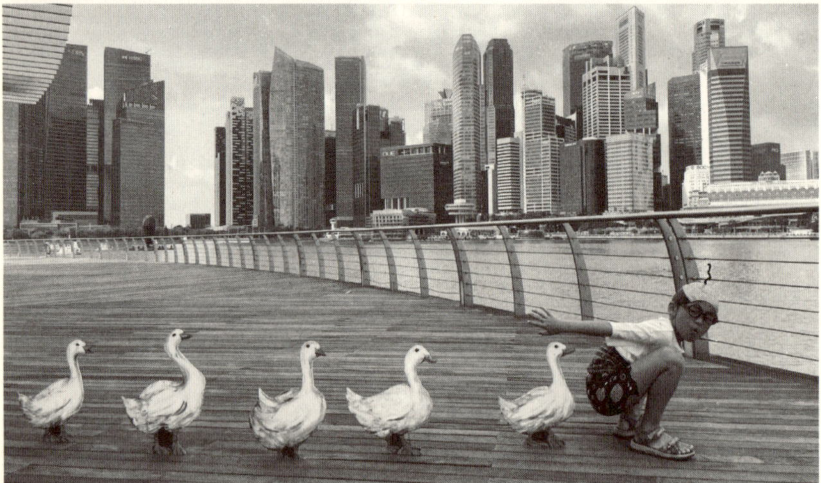

The surreal scene of kids running around the chickens and ducks against a backdrop of the modern Singapore skyline.

and ducks, but because they look so real, their assembly in front of the bay against the Singapore skyline takes one's breath away. It allows the mind to see an unlikely yet entirely probable scenario happening right before the eyes. A "Wow!" moment of farm fowls allowed to run loose right in the middle of Marina Bay with the financial district in the backdrop to provide a striking contrast. As someone would say later to my Facebook post, "Fowl Play, Downtown Singapore Invaded!", only an artist with a keen sense of visual drama can picture and see this in his head.

"I did not get a permit." Yew Chong looks up, holding a painted chicken, adjusting the metal stem as he sticks the chicken into the groove of the boardwalk. "This is a relatively quiet part of the stretch, and it's a one-hour guerrilla art installation, maybe one and a half hour max. I will not leave any chicken or duck behind when I am done." He laughs as he wipes his face, dripping with sweat.

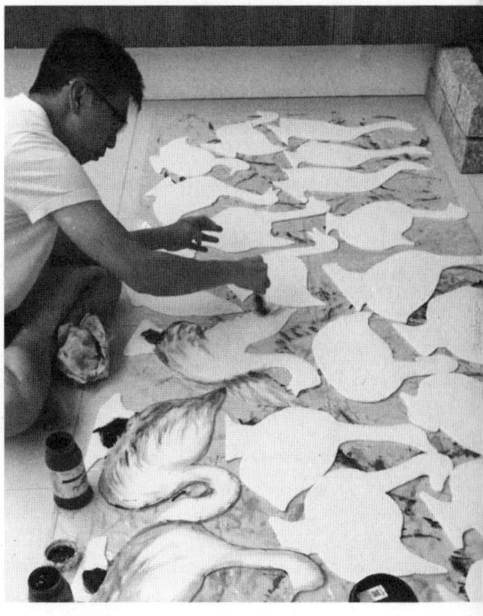

Preparing the Chickens and Ducks *installation at home, 2018.*

An anamorphic image is one produced to create an intentional visual distortion. This morning, the scene before us isn't distorted, but we are teased into seeing an extraordinary made-up 'reality'. And for this to be even more convincing, Yew Chong needs human 'props' too. He has invited some of his fans to bring their kids with them. So, Mikami, a Japanese expat, brings her son; Faith, a long-time fan, her three kids. A professional photographer who has followed the evolution of his works, Kantaya New of Thailand, is invited as well. These followers never miss a chance to participate in Yew Chong's works as it always promises to be a fun day out, with many inventive and playful photo opportunities.

Mikami's son is an attention-seeker and a natural for an anamorphic session. He goes down on all fours and poses on command: chasing the chickens and ducks, catching them, carrying them, arranging the ducks in a row as if they are following him. Faith's kids are overwhelmed by the visual spectacle, initially very careful not to trample on the fowls, only to end up running wild with them. But the person who has the most productive morning is the photographer. Everyone wants special and fun moments with the fowls and readily poses for her. But she has a few surprises up her sleeve too, adding eggs to the chickens, getting a close-up of the boy's shocked face between the beaks of two ducks, arranging the fowls in a flight away from the chasing children… Every shot looks abundantly joyful yet eerily surreal against the Marina Bay backdrop.

The Boxing Day morning session provides Yew Chong with rich visual material to feed his hungry followers on social media. When he puts up the post on Facebook, there is a riot of responses.

"I've always aimed for people to feel happy when they engage with my art," writes Yew Chong, who is also known as YC on social media. "Yesterday, as I watched children immerse in my 'guerrilla' art display for a photo shoot, I was drawn in too, and became a part of my own happy world. I wish everyone happiness and connectedness as you enter the world of YC's Art! These chickens and ducks first appeared in Ang Mo Kio Kebun Baru market in 2018. After crossing many roads, they got tired and decided to take the MRT to Marina Bay… I wonder where they will go next?"

Yew Chong posts 10 pictures, from kids playing, chasing, carrying and walking these fowls, to him posing with his daughter carrying a chicken. There is also a photograph of the fowls in Ang Mo Kio, of them crossing the road and finally of Yew Chong holding a chicken and duck in the MRT train. The last photo alone garnered 350 likes. These photographs are also posted on Instagram with equal fanfare.

A large part of an art installation is about audience involvement and interaction. So, the initial one-hour Marina Bay Sands (MBS) installation is just the first part of this protracted series involving many social media posts, where he chats with his followers, answering their questions, thanking them and basically spending time with them. By treating the fowls as 'real', he is also able to keep his followers 'interested' concerning the fowls' whereabouts and their fate.

"Where will they be this weekend?" asks a Faustina Julianna Lim on Facebook.

Yew Chong replies, "Announcing soon!"

Vivien Zeng exclaims, "Impressive! So vivid and real! Keep it up!!!"

"What a brilliant idea to use local fowl of chicken and ducks!" writes Janet Lim. "Unlike other installations of cows or elephants. So Singaporean!"

"Brings back wonderful memories!" says Lai Ah-Eng. "I used to help my mother rear chickens and ducks. I can call them and they stop in their tracks. Hahaha!"

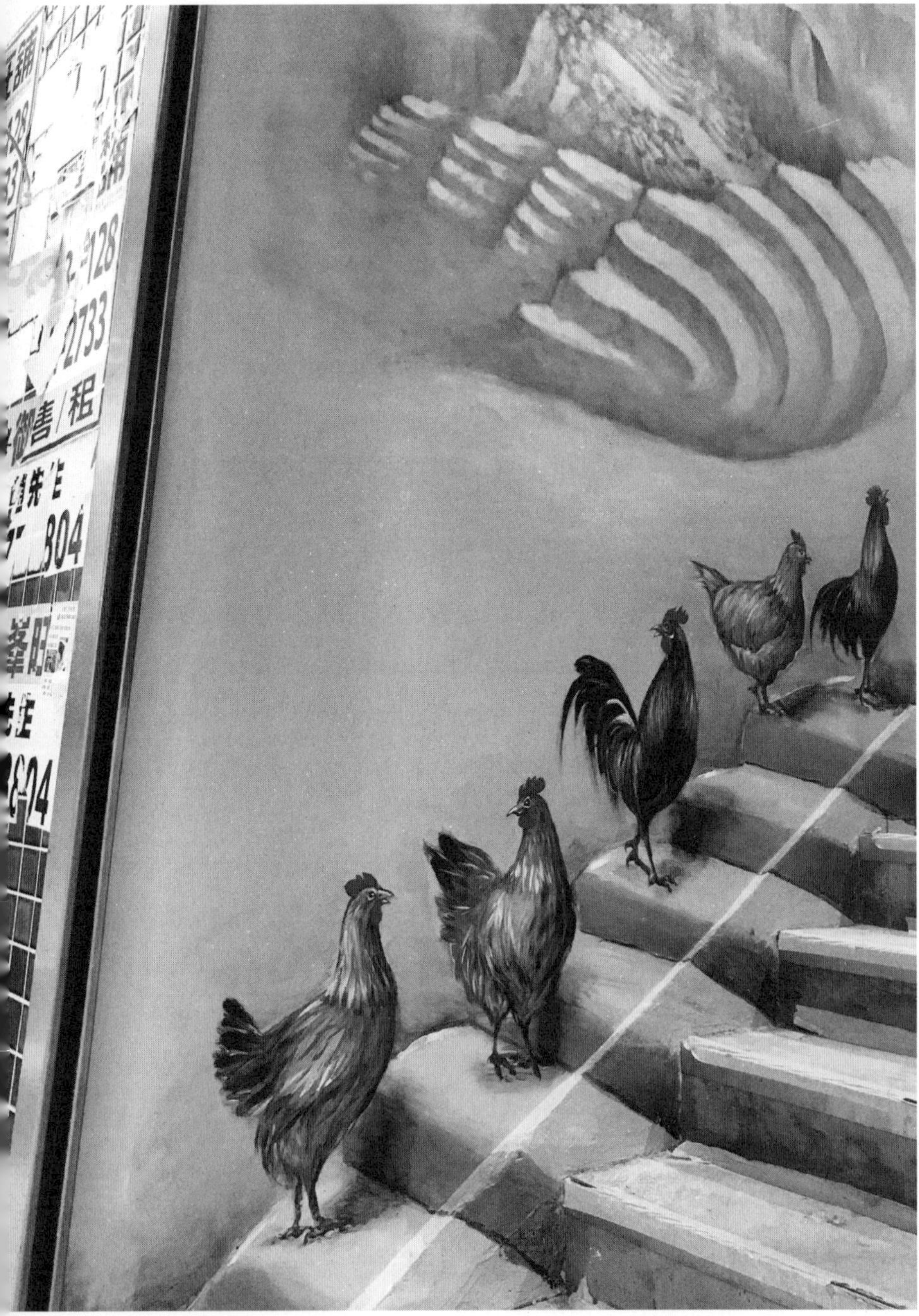

The chickens went to Hong Kong! 2018.

Yew Chong works his fan base by keeping up the fun and suspense. To a question, where is that? He answers, "They told me, 'ku ku ku,' and 'quack quack quack' but I don't understand."

Two days later, he teases with a painting he has just finished, a scene in Hong Kong, where roasted ducks and chickens are hanging by the window in a restaurant, visible from the street:

"Thanks for the warm response and interest to the chicken and duck installation at Marina Bay. Please don't go look for them there. They were there only for an hour last Sunday! I have received various queries about where they will go next, and invitations too! Incidentally, I have just finished painting (on canvas) a scene which shows chickens and ducks, but look where they have gone to [referring to the posted picture of roasted ducks and chicken]! They are fast!! But don't worry, it is just a painting. They will be back alive in Singapore this weekend at two places. This time, I'll keep everyone posted in advance so you can go catch them if you can!"

And then, a day later, in a post where the chickens and ducks are all spread out on his studio floor, them in a bus, and a cat looking on:

"The chickens and ducks are now taking a rest. They will then take a bus to bask at the grass lawns of:

Malay Heritage Centre (Kampong Glam) on Saturday 1st January 2022, 12pm to 5pm

Sun Yat Sen Nanyang Memorial Hall (Tai Gin Road) on Sunday 2nd January 2022, 12pm to 5pm

Everyone is welcome to bask along. Let's hope for sunny days. A 'cat' will be around to *jaga* them, so don't you dare dream of them being your KFC or Crispy Duck."

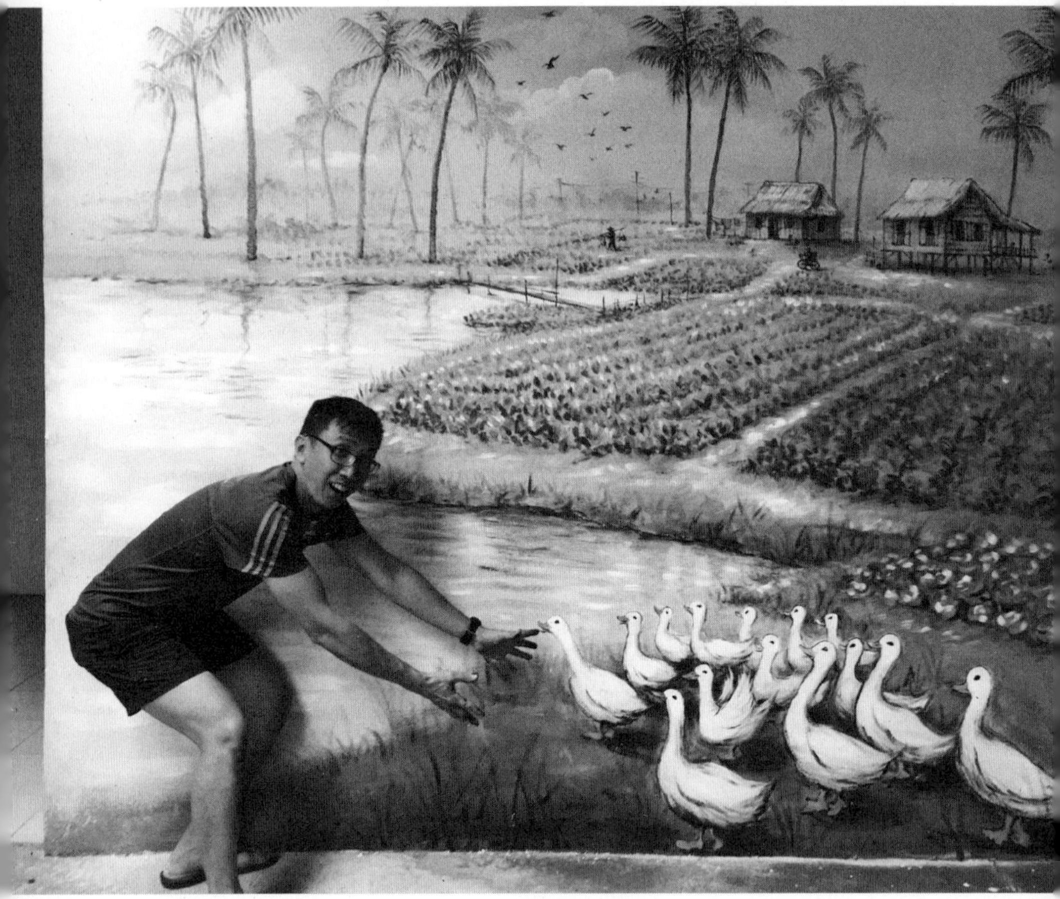

A "duck farm" appeared at a HDB void deck in Woodlands, 2019.

A Maisy Leung is disappointed. "Both dates cannot make it. When and where else can we see them?"

"I will try asking them," he replies.

With thousands of responses on social media, Yew Chong goes through every single comment, engaging them with quick wit and easy grace.

"This is part of the installation process," he says with a shrug of his shoulders. “An installation artist takes the interaction with his audience as part of the artistic process. These days, social media allows for an excellent avenue to interact with the public interested in my work. The actual venue of the mobile installation reaches less than 10% of the audience. I use social media to reach out to the rest, who are keen on my art. This is why good photography of my works is important. It is not just documentation. I see it as a process — install, record, distribute, dismantle, install again. This form of art is interesting because it has many ‘lives’, each different, although the tools I use, chickens and ducks, are essentially the same.”

A communication expert, PN Balji, has been following the artist on social media. A month ago, he brought his grandson to see one of Yew Chong’s murals in Chinatown. “I am not an art person, but I brought my grandson who is eight and loves art.” Balji takes out his mobile phone and shows me images he has taken of the mural. “He had fun posing, just standing, sitting and interacting with the human figures. In the end, I enjoyed it as much as he did.”

He flips to the Facebook pages of the artist. “He is followed by so many people on Facebook and Instagram.” Balji smiles as he shakes his head in disbelief. “More so than some politicians and famous public figures. He is a whiz when it comes to harnessing the power of media, especially social media. The posts are always light-hearted, whimsical, and clever. These days, famous people take care of their own marketing, and he is a good example. He knows his audience, and he takes them seriously. The best kind of marketeer. He has a good brand.”

What is his brand?

“Whimsical.” Balji’s one-word description of the artist.

Through a Boy's Eyes

Who does an artist paint for? Most artists, when they paint, have an 'audience' in their heads. It could be one person, a few people, or even a group of people. I know an artist who 'seeks the approval' of his peers when he paints. Another artist listens only to the 'inner voice', a voice whose standard he lives by. Yet another paints for his teacher; if his teacher doesn't like the work, he throws it away and paints all over again. When I present the question to Yew Chong, he becomes quiet momentarily. He knows it is a simple question, and the intuitive answer is himself. But he pauses.

"My murals typically have many characters." I can see him thinking, casting his mind over the many characters he has introduced to Singapore. "When I paint a person, I am thinking about that person. Who each person is would not be obvious to the public, but each and every one of them is real to me, very real! I know who they are, and when I am painting each one, I am living through my experiences with each of them. In a way, getting their permission, seeking their approval to portray them in the way that I am going to. So, my references are many."

Beside the characters, there is someone else. "But who gives the final approval of the entire army of characters? Is there someone watching over you when you paint, who says yes or no?"

"Myself," he says simply.

"Yourself. Okay."

"But not myself now," he clarifies. "When I paint, I go back to me when I was young, when I was a little boy. So, when you look at my murals, they are all from a child's point of view. It is my world, when

I was a happy child. And I almost always add a calendar showing my date of birth."

Through the prism of a child. Yes, that explains a lot. If a child hasn't tasted abundance, his world of little would actually be a world of plenty; when a child is showered with love, he will see his meagre environment with loving faces and happy animals. He does not replicate old or torn clothes because to him, they are new and bright. Nothing is torn, broken, or old. The ambience of his murals is joyful even when they depict a Chinatown on the eve of evacuation, spaces where there were too many people in small cramped places, and when the food was just enough, or barely so.

"I was a happy child." He remembers with a grin. "And today, when I paint, my mind needs to be happy. My mind is always happy when I paint. Even when unhappy things happen, I erase them from my mind when I paint. Which is why painting is therapeutic for me. I feel like I am in a different world, a happy and optimistic world where I am just creating. When I create, I go back to the days when I was a child."

And he explains, being a child doesn't mean being close to a toy, a person, or a favourite food. It is being brought back to a time. "Like most people, when they think of the time when they were kids, things were simpler, not complicated. And happier. People say my art is the art of nostalgia. If nostalgia means going back to a simpler and happier time, then yes, my art is the art of nostalgia. Even though life wasn't as good as it is now, there was this simple contentment. I know it sounds cliche, but it is true. Most of our childhood days were more innocent days. So, you can say that my paintings, my murals, are what I see through the eyes of a younger self. Of course, there were bad times, but our minds don't focus on those times; we don't cling on to bad times. We remember the good times, at least most of us anyway."

The good times… through the eyes of a boy. What constitutes bliss, what constitutes joy to a boy? What does the boy see that makes him happy?

"It's never about one object or thing. It is the scene, the whole ambience, a composition of things and people." Just talking about it brings a smile to his face. "Even the posture, of a man putting his leg on a chair, a woman cooking, a grandma carrying a child, a table setting of food, a boy lighting up a string of firecrackers, lighting a candle to burn the lantern, catching a lizard, catching a cockroach. They come together to create a mental scene in my head… it was, is, my happy world."

The boy sees a confluence of images, what device does the artist use to help the boy convey his sense of bliss? Contemporary artist Yue Minjun of China, for instance, paints bald-headed images of himself with frozen, full-teeth wide-mouth smiles to hide his sense of alienation. Claude Monet produced around 250 paintings based on water lilies that were growing on the pond at his home in Giverny. As he was growing blind in old age, these water lilies attest to his gritted determination. The works typically have no horizon, nor any sense of scale, just reflections of the sky and the lilies themselves. They have since become some of the best paintings of flowers ever seen, conveying despondence and hope.

"My device, things that people can relate to," he begins. "Family, food, a way of life. It is important that I paint things or scenes that people can recognise."

So, he has come to the nub of his art, the ability to recognise. "Why is that important?"

"It makes it real, and you can have an affiliation with it," he says simply. "When I share something recognisable, something people know, I establish connection. That's important, and for me, that is why art is powerful. In the last hour, we have used many terms to describe it, nostalgia, familiarity, connectedness… they all point to it, painting something that people can relate to. I talked about the scene earlier, the ambience. Am I able to capture a mood that the person standing in front of my mural can feel? If I can, I have achieved my reason to paint."

Ironic that his device is through the lens of a boy, whose emotional state of happiness allows him to access a world pre-modern, pre-urban, and importantly pre-adult. Recognisable. Yes, we all retain the memory of our childhood, our history. So, when we look at Yew Chong's murals, we are also accessing our own childhood, drawing into the levers of familiarity to connect with our own nostalgia.

"When you see something and recognise it instantly without explanation, that is connectedness," he continues. "And for most of my mural, my art, that connectedness makes you happy. That's my device, if you like."

He has touched on it earlier, but this bears repeating. The most powerful visual lever he uses to connect is his frequent use of family, immediate, extended, and also 'adopted'. The institution of family is perhaps the strongest visual foundation of Yew Chong's murals. When a child looks out at the world, that is his most immediate touch point, what he sees first, people he knows intimately, and what he relies on emotionally.

"When I include myself in a mural, I appear as a boy." His face is calm with a hint of amusement. "I could be playing with my brother and sisters, accompanying my grandma to the market, watching Cantonese opera with my aunt. Without even being conscious of it, I bring in a familial context into my work, because to the child, it is a safe place, a protected place, and yes, a happy place. For me, that's the womb of comfort, the core of love. Simple and unconditional love."

And because we all have family or the memory of family, the scene, the ambience, the composition of people and what they do are also the most recognisable, and we feel connected to his art.

Yee Gu (Second Aunt)

Bukit Merah is a mature HDB estate; at the hawker centre, there are groups of seniors having breakfast with their sons and daughters. A few elderly men, who are obviously done with their breakfast, linger on, nursing cups of tea or coffee. They do not look like they are in a hurry to go anywhere or do anything. Two men, probably in their 80s, nod at me as I sit down at a table next to them. The nine o'clock morning air is humid; I am pleased to see ceiling fans rotating above me.

Yew Chong sees me and waves. "I'll go get her; she stays just a block away."

Madam Yip Soon Yong is Yew Chong's second aunt, his father's second eldest sister, or *Yee Gu* in Cantonese. Because she chose not to marry, she stayed with her brother in Chinatown and took care of his family while both parents worked. For the first 14 years of Yew Chong's life, she was like a mother to him. Today, Yee Gu is 95 years old.

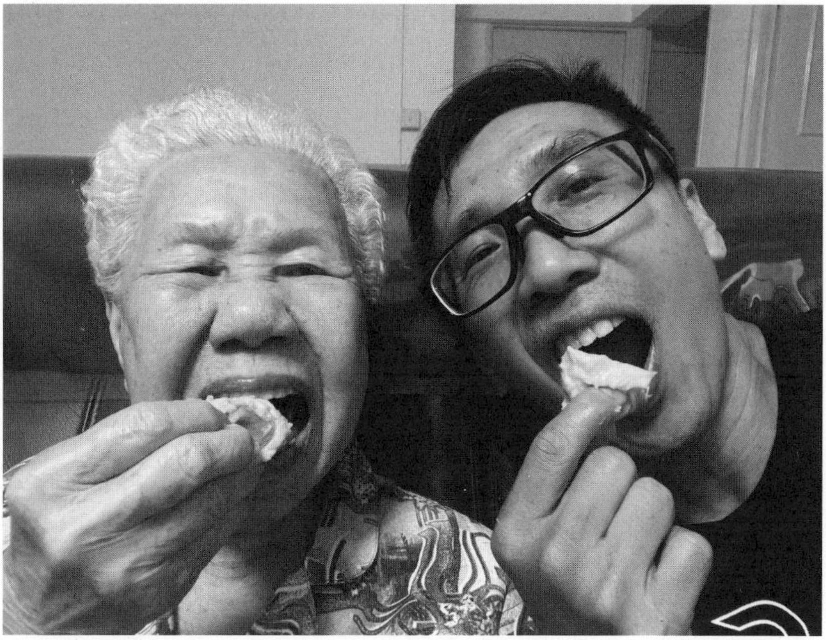

She loves durians.

The woman who appears does not look 95. With the gait of a 50- or 60-year-old, she is slight but not small. A full head of white and immaculately-coiffed hair, her face is taut and lifted, courtesy of a perpetual wide smile. But the real surprise is her gregarious spirit. She does not recognise anyone, she declares, but almost everyone at the hawker centre seems to know her.

"I apologise." She looks a man right in the eye. "I don't recognise you because I am old. But I am very grateful that you are a friend of Ah Chong."

The man, decades younger, holds both her hands. "You look very well. Stay well, stay healthy."

Ah Chong is her term of endearment for Yew Chong. Her small

eyes are kind and they smile at me; her mouth follows with a wide grin. "Thank you for being a friend of Ah Chong," her voice loud and low. "He is a good boy, *gwaai*." she looks towards Yew Chong who is returning to the table with a tray of dim sum, a glass of barley water, and two cups of coffee.

"To her, I will always be a boy." Yew Chong puts the glass of barley by her side.

With her small left hand, she lifts the plate of *siew mai* and pushes it to my side of the table. "Eat," she offers with another smile. "Ah Chong did not go to school to learn drawing." She slows her otherwise rapid-fire Cantonese. "But his public drawings are very nice; a lot of people have gone to see them, and really like them." Her eyes look at Yew Chong now. "I have been to all of them; when he paints, I go watch him paint. The ones in Chinatown are really not bad." Not bad is the polite Cantonese way of saying good or very good. " For those murals outside of Chinatown, my relatives or friends brought me there because I am not familiar with those locations."

With a straw, she sips her barley water. "He started drawing when he was just a boy, and at home he drew many things, what he saw in Chinatown, what he saw on TV. His father was the one who started drawing outside, on the road. A lot of people saw what his father did, liked what he drew. He did not go to school for art too; he was clever at drawing, just like Ah Chong. I think Ah Chong takes after his father."

Yee Gu does not read; she is not educated. "I tried night classes, but fell ill. In the day, I had to work. We were too poor; I had to help my parents; I started working very young." The kind eyes are now tinged with a little sadness, her face is pensive. "Before the war, I sold many things, fish, vegetables, melon seeds, bananas. My mother bought them from the central market and I sold them on the street. Then, the war came. I worked for the Japanese soldiers, cleaned their premises, disposed their waste in order to make 90 cents a day. During the Japanese occupation, there was no rice unless you worked for them. And I did, to get 21 *kati* of rice."

She pauses and looks at the table. "You must finish the dim sum, I had my breakfast early, bread and coffee. So, I can't eat anything until later, lunch time. Please." She flashes her toothy wide smile again as encouragement.

"My parents were working in a rubber factory," she continues her story without prompting. "My sister and I took over when my parents couldn't anymore, supervising the workforce. I was there for 29 years, until they closed down the factory, and we were all retrenched. So, as you can see, I have done many things."

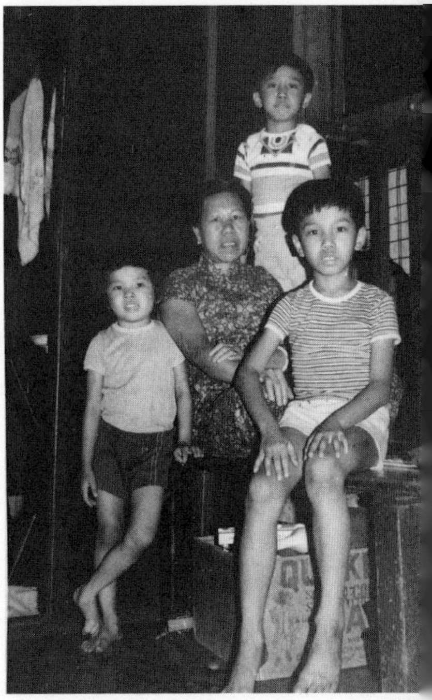

Yee Gu, Yew Chong and siblings at their Chinatown home, circa 1970s.

She stops and looks at the two of us. It is clear she is done talking about her odd jobs. From the way she looks at Yew Chong, I know she wants to focus on him. "Ah Chong was an obedient boy. *Gwaai*." *Gwaai* in Cantonese combines a filial element with "good".

"In Chinatown, I slept beside her when I was a boy until I was 14 years old." Yew Chong looks at her, his eyes simmering with warmth and care. "It was a wooden bed with a thin mattress, so I knew the time she went to sleep and the time she woke up. From the wooden bed, we used to watch TV together."

By the time Yew Chong was 14, they had to move out of the old Chinatown shophouse; the whole area was being redeveloped; Yew Chong's family, his grandmother and Yee Gu all moved to a nearby HDB flat within Chinatown. A few years later, Yee Gu moved to an old flat in Kim Tian Road. The old flat was part of an en-bloc sale for redevelopment, and she moved again to her present residence at Bukit Merah. She has been in Bukit Merah for 20 years now.

I am fascinated by her steely, unwavering decision to stay single. Yew Chong nods. "She was popular when she was a young woman." Yew Chong looks at her; he smiles teasingly. "Quite a few guys proposed, but she rejected them. She wanted to be independent. She would tell them she was taken. She was the sort that would run around doing all sorts of things herself. She did not want to be tied down."

Then, quite suddenly, Yee Gu looks at me in the eye. "I took care of my brothers, especially Ah Chong's father. When Ah Chong's father and mother worked, I took over. I went marketing; I cooked their meals, cleaned, and washed. Took care of the children. And because I was single, I needed company to go places, including watching the street opera or go down to the city centre. I would bring Ah Chong. He was such a good boy."

The good boy, who is now in his early 50s with a family of his own, holds in his heart dearly everything Yee Gu had done for him. And because she has chosen to be single, lived through the war, suffered under the Japanese, family and relatives have rallied around her. In

2013, when Yee Gu was 86 years old, she yearned to revisit her relatives in China. Yew Chong accompanied her and they made the trip together. For many of the murals, especially those in Chinatown, she was the 'model' and became quite the celebrity when the media chased stories of the artist and his sources of inspiration.

Because she often appeared in Yew Chong's social media posts and media publications, many of Yew Chong's followers can recognise her. What made her better known was a series of interviews Yew Chong did, called *Story of my Aunt*, uploaded on YouTube and highlighted on social media, five heartfelt episodes with Yee Gu against a stark black background telling her life story. Five to six minutes each, she told of her childhood and youth (that she was fostered, then returned to her real mother), how she survived the Japanese occupation, what she did to eke out a living, and the trials she went through for a better life. Because she was not educated, her primary means of communication has always been verbal. And over the years, her ability to relate acquired a raw visual quality, her way of telling it as-it-was. The series was action-packed, thrilling, sometimes comical, but always moving. There was no need for embellishment, her life played out like a good movie script, except everything happened, a part of Singapore's history, but it was also her story. From the colonial times to the war, from independence to nationhood, told from the vivid memory of a woman who saw and lived it all.

It is 10.30am, and we are the only ones left in the hawker centre. Even the elderly gentlemen at the next table have left. I ask if she is tired and wants to go back and to rest. She shakes her head.

"I have one last question." I rest my head on both my raised palms.

"Life has been so eventful, hard, and some of it unbelievable to the younger generation. Yet, you look unbelievably young and you look happy. What is your secret? Turning back the clock, what is it that you remember best? What are your memories of Chinatown?"

She offers that Yee Gu smile again. "I eat what I like, go where I want. Before the pandemic, two years ago, I would take the bus, or take the MRT train alone. I have been independent all my life, and as long as I can walk and do things on my own, I shall continue to be independent. I am lucky. I have relatives I can live with and a *kwai* boy like Ah Chong who visits me often to check on me, keeping me company. If I am troubled by something, I let it affect me for a while. Then, I move on. I live moment to moment, a day at a time. People ask me the secret of staying young, staying healthy, well, it is to know how to be happy."

I look at her. "What are your memories of Chinatown?"

"Even though life was tough in Chinatown, I have happy memories. It was my world, my little universe. I can buy anything and everything in Chinatown, I just needed to walk down to the street where I could get anything I wanted. I didn't have to take a bus or a taxi anywhere, everything I could get by foot. Provision shops, department stores everywhere. Now, these are all gone. But I remember those days with fondness. Small things like keeping cats so that they could catch and even eat mice; everyone watching TV together, eating dinner at the same time, telling each other what happened in the day." She pauses, sipping her barley water. "There were always neighbours around to keep an eye. And we knew all our neighbours well. We took care of one other, not just within the family; we helped each other out."

She pauses again; this time she leans towards Yew Chong. "I love him because in the murals he painted, those in Chinatown, my life is on the murals, not one or two, but almost all of them. You see, in those days, we do not have access to cameras. Our lives, if they were photographed, were official or big events like weddings. The day-to-day life, things we do in the living room, kitchen, bedrooms, our neighbourhood, they were not recorded. The murals are our records, and they are painted so well, in colour."

I see now why people of her generation look at the murals with such delight and gratitude. They were not just a celebration of their lives; they were, more importantly, a record, down to very small details like the calendar, the mosquito coil, and kitchen utensils. Many no longer exist anymore. Hard life, simple life, but the good life, all remembered, thanks to an artist's childhood.

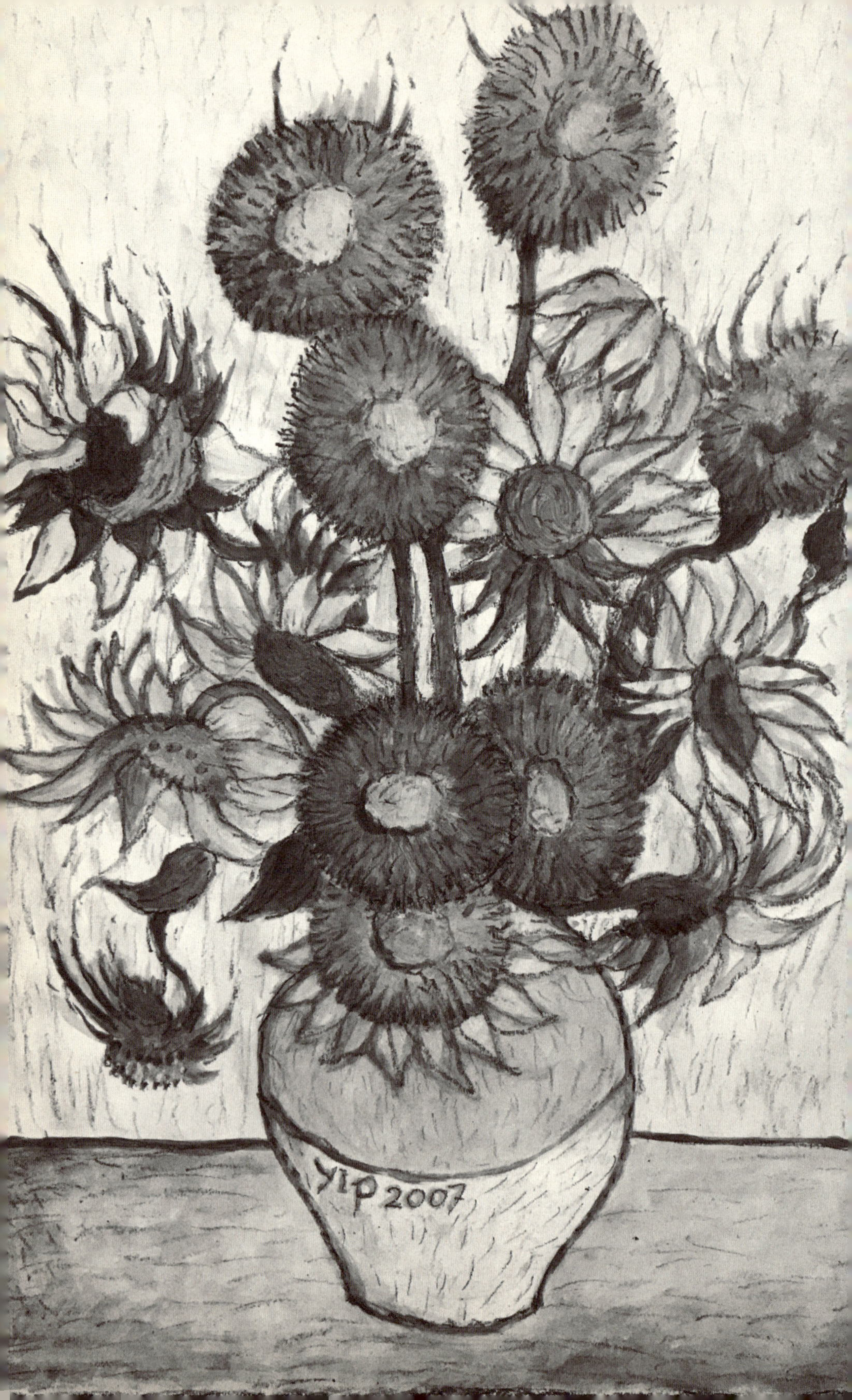
YIP 2007

CHAPTER 5

Nothing Lasts Forever

I can measure my success by the reception of my murals.

Turning 53 and Thoughts of Van Gogh

The story of Vincent van Gogh is well known; the Dutch post-impressionist, who posthumously became one of the most famous and influential figures in western art history, died penniless. He sold just one painting while he was alive. In a decade, he created about 2,100 artworks, most of which date from the last two years of his short life. He struggled with severe depression and poverty, eventually leading to his suicide at age 37. The one painting he sold, *The Red Vineyard*, was for 400 francs in Belgium seven months before his death.

Anyone who knows Yew Chong's murals knows he includes an old-fashioned calendar in almost all his murals, displaying his birthday, 12th January. The calendar is one page per day, with astrological information on each page. He turns 53 in 2022, but is too busy to meet or celebrate. He agrees to have breakfast the following day.

The Chinatown Complex Market and Food Centre combines the wet market and hawker stalls effectively in one complex, and Yew Chong walks through it as if he is in his own backyard; he knows the place like the back of his hand. "Let me bring you to this *yong tau foo* stall." He walks with the celerity of a teenager. "I gave them a drawing of their stall and they have pasted it up to show all their customers." We stand in line, with three teenage customers ahead of us. "By 10 o'clock, the line will snake all the way to the other end of this building."

We order our *yong tau foo* with soup. This is a dish from Hakka cuisine consisting primarily of tofu filled with ground meat mixture or fish paste. Yew Chong has also added vegetables and fishcake.

"I did nothing on my birthday." He laughs.

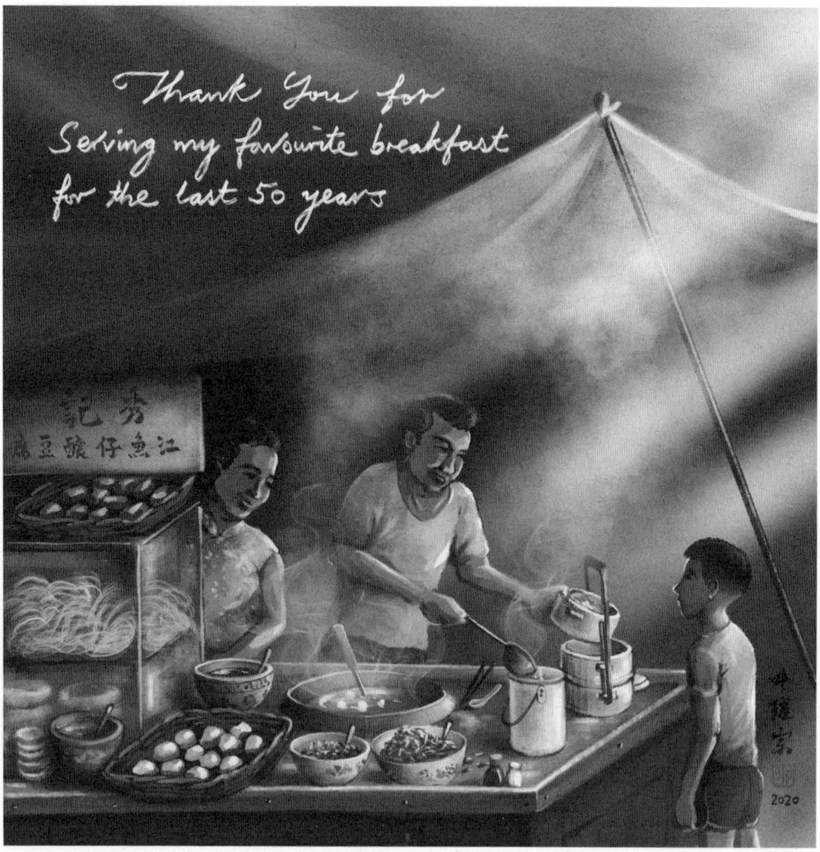

Yew Chong gifted a print of this digital painting to his favourite hawker, who displayed it at their stall, 2021.

"Tell me about the nothing you did not do." I suspect he is one of those who regards his birthday as just another day.

"I normally don't celebrate birthdays." His mind focuses more on the *yong tau foo* than his birthday. "I try to keep it as ordinary as possible. So, yesterday, what did I do? In the morning, I had grocery deliveries, so I needed to stay in the house. At 2pm, the air-con repairman came, and after that I cleaned the house. I left for the studio after that; I wanted to paint, but ended up doing some admin work. So, nothing earth-shaking. At 6pm, I attended a volunteer group that mentors ex-inmates to meet up with my mentees who are interested to paint murals."

"These are ex-prisoners who are already artists or learning to be artists?"

"Learning to be artists," he says matter-of-factly. "I met three of them. They are painting murals for the first time, commissioned to do murals at a halfway house. One of them has been studying at an art school for three years. So, they are serious about being artists. They make me think of going back to school, to an art school myself. It would take three years of my life." Going back to school to get a formal art education has always been at the back of his mind. But the required three years is not practical for him. "Perhaps it's better for me to create, produce more art now; when I want to study more about art, I can do it later. A lot of what I do is intuitive, I don't have names or terms for the way I paint. I think an academic stint will give me some formal grounding. It is for self-fulfilment, nothing else."

One day after his birthday, he is telling me of his birthday wish, or wishes, what he wants to be, when he 'grows up'. Many of his supporters would not want him to grow up if it means changing what he does, and I am one of them.

"Your supporters, so many of them, follow you because of your own unique style." I try not to put my point across too strongly. "Most good artists, famous artists, are self-taught like you. They did not go through a formal curriculum to conform their art to theories and norms. So, they were not told what's right, what's wrong. The art they produce is organically theirs, a result of their own backgrounds and circumstances. Nothing formulaic. I think that's the best way to come up with one's own style, one's own signature style, like how you have come up with yours."

"But the purists dislike that," he adds without elaboration. I understand he has heard comments from 'purists' who thought his art did not conform to any 'rules'. They told him his compositions were not accurate to actual historical landscapes, his style bordered on being childish, and his references were random. Well, if the purists had their way, we wouldn't have Picasso, Van Gogh, or Wu Guanzhong.

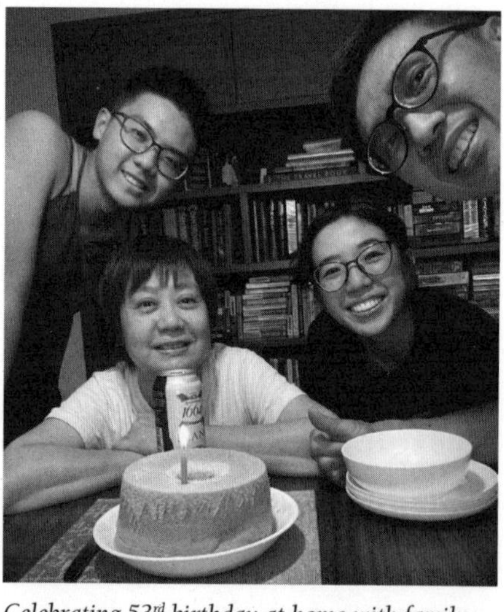

Celebrating 53rd birthday at home with family.

"I think you should ignore purists; they are theorists, nothing more. Let's get back to your birthday. Did your family come together for a meal?" I don't want to talk about purists on his birthday.

"I got back late, around 11 o'clock." Yew Chong allows a belated birthday smile. "They know I like chiffon cake, and they had ordered one. My son came back from the hostel so all four of us got together around the cake." He flips open his mobile phone and flashes a photograph, a 'wefie' taken by the artist with his wife, son and daughter around a candled chiffon cake. My heart lifts; such a comforting and happy assembly of a family.

"A good picture, ah, your son." I have met his wife and daughter; this is the first time I get to see his son, a lean man who seems taller than his father.

"You'd notice I don't post pictures of either my wife or my son on social media." Yew Chong retrieves his mobile. "They are both private; my wife in particular is shy and does not like to socialise so much."

Looking at his face, I see pride and contentment dancing in his eyes. He likes to brush everything off as 'everyday' and does not like to talk about 'celebrating' a birthday, but the photograph of the family together seems like an 'occasion', a happy memory he would keep. Even though it was late, they waited for him. "They sang, wished you happy birthday and you blew the candle." I lean forward. "What was your birthday wish?"

"I don't pay any real significance to birthdays," he asserts again. "Even on my 50th birthday, I was painting." Again, he takes out his phone. "I painted this with my friend Trase, on the road." Another anamorphic work, two big balls painted on the road, and the two artists look as if they are sitting on them. Dramatic and striking.

"When I was with the ex-inmates on my birthday, I heard another mentor explaining the painting style of Van Gogh." He brings the conversation back to his birthday. "And it got me thinking of a post I did just before my birthday on Van Gogh. His life makes me think of what I am doing with mine, and I am happy that my life has unfolded the way it has; I am on track. I don't want to be like Van Gogh, who led a miserable life even though he is now one of the most influential names in the art world."

In 2007, he had the opportunity to work and live in Amsterdam when he was working in finance. During his stay there, the one and only drawing he did was a rare rendition of Van Gogh's famous sunflowers using crayon and gouache on cardboard paper.

"I drew to decorate the bedroom, my way of welcoming my family when they came over to visit." His face lights up like a lantern; Amsterdam must have been a good posting. "I wanted to decorate the room with a Dutch theme. I also made some Dutch canal houses using cardboard boxes which thrilled the kids."

Yew Chong explains that it was only after a year in Amsterdam that he finally visited the Van Gogh museum to see the master's original paintings. "Only one of the five versions of the 'sunflowers in a vase' paintings resides in the Netherlands, the rest are in New York and Tokyo."

I sense there is something else on his mind he wants to say about Van Gogh. "Apart from not wanting to die penniless, any other thoughts about Van Gogh?"

"It was after his death, the lesser heard story of Vincent van Gogh, was Jo, his sister-in-law." Again, his eyes dance. "Jo was widowed shortly after Vincent's death and she inherited all of her brother-in-law's paintings and drawings. She saw value in the artworks. With ingenuity and a strategic mind, she raised their profile and value, not initially through a gallery, but by first setting up a boarding house in a strategic place, and expanding on a network that appreciated the artworks. She also carefully curated and released the artworks over the years, with stories accompanying them for better appreciation and understanding."

I notice how intense his gaze has become. It is an important takeaway from Jo. "What's the moral of the story?"

"Yes, there is one big takeaway." He laughs softly. "From Jo's story… art, as with many things in today's world, is not just about how good the art itself is, but also how we market and tell their stories. Of course, we also need a lot of luck!"

"You don't want to be penniless and miserable; good art needs good marketing. Lessons from the Dutchman. At 53, where are you veering towards?" I ask. "Where do you go from here?"

"I don't know." He flashes that birthday smile one more time. "When I joined the army, I went in without any expectations. It turned out to be very good; I enjoyed it. Same with being an accountant. I did not plan to go this or that way, and just went with the flow. Again, it turned out very well. When I travelled, I try not to plan everything, I do not get into the details. And when I am on the road, I sometimes go off-course, and I enjoy that much more. I don't want to know too much about the future; I don't want to over plan. I just have a general direction; I want to be happy; I want to be positive. I really have no specific detailed plan for the future. For my art, I only know I want to develop my art, diversify, yet keep it rooted to where I come from, which is mural painting. I don't want to drop murals totally in the future in favour of doing something new, but I also recognise that I can't stick to it forever. The one area which I have gone into seriously is canvas painting, and I keep an interest in digital art."

I remind him of his installations. “You have been able to bring what you do with huge murals to massive installations. So far, your installations have a scale and scope few can rival.”

He nods. “Oh yes, I forgot about installations. But massive? I think you included the real skyline!” He laughs.

Nothing Lasts Forever

In a Facebook post, Yew Chong laments:

> *The Tiong Bahru murals are coming to six years old. I am glad that over these six years, the Tiong Bahru murals have assimilated well with both the people and environment there, inspiring further creations. However, nature ultimately has its call. The outdoor murals are especially faded.*

“Most outdoor murals last for five to six years.” Yew Chong is realistic; this is what he tells those who commission him to do murals. “The sun and the rain are relentless in Singapore. And nothing is sadder than a beautifully-rendered mural which has seen better days. I am glad the Resident Committee has decided to keep the murals in Tiong Bahru for a longer period.”

In the same Facebook post, he announces:

> *I will be doing some restoration of the murals. Weather permitting, you can come watch me restore them tomorrow, Sunday 16 January 2022, between 11am and 5pm. I’ll be starting with the ‘Pasar’ mural at Eng Watt Street.*

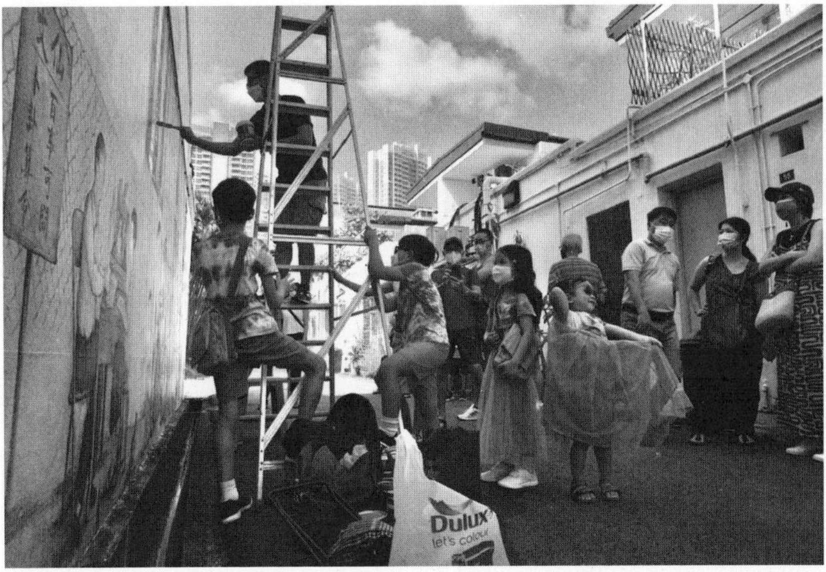

Children helped stabilise the ladder during the Pasar *restoration, 2022.*

Tiong Bahru, Sunday.

Whether you are looking to invest in property or want to find out more about Singapore's history, whether you are a foodie or a shopaholic, Tiong Bahru is the place to be. Although it is the oldest housing estate in Singapore, when you visit, you will immediately notice an intriguing mix of the old and new. While many older residents have lived in the shophouses and flats for decades, the younger generation flocks in for the food, shops, and culture. The neighbourhood is easily one of the hippest places in Singapore today.

I decide to have breakfast in Tiong Bahru. At 10 in the morning, the iconic Ah Chiang's Traditional Porridge on Tiong Bahru Road is almost full. There is inside dining and outdoors where the tables are interestingly close to the road. I sit at a small square table inside and order chicken porridge and *teh c kosong*. I notice the customers are mostly young couples dressed in Sunday casuals. The service staff are middle-aged women who are friendly and accommodating.

Eng Watt Street, next to Tiong Bahru Community Centre, is less than five minutes by foot from *Ah Chiang's*. The mural, *The Pasar Tiong Bahru*, literally jumps out at the left end of the community centre. It is not only faded, but it also harks back to an earlier phase of Yew Chong's works. Painted in 2016, it does not have the proportions of his later murals. An Indian man sells food on a bicycle, the food seems disproportionally large. An Indian lady carrying a basket looks on. She seems overdressed for the market scene. At the extreme left end, a woman consults with a fortune teller. The faces, hands, and feet of this mural are not as refined as his later murals.

"When I look at this mural, I cringe." Yew Chong's eyes sweep across the wall. His face is a mix of amusement and dread. "My skills as an artist were not honed yet, so this looks awkward and somewhat amateurish compared to the ones I did from 2018 onwards. The heads are large, and the figures are not as fluid as I would like them to be. But this morning I am only restoring, touching up; I am not altering anything. It needs to stay as a record of my development as an artist."

There is a marked difference between this mural and the murals now. But it still stops you and makes you stare at it. The multiracial sense of community, the ability to use tradition to fascinate, attention to cultural details, and most importantly, the mood the mural commands, are all there. I can see how back in 2016 when this was completed, it was ahead of its time and would have taken the Tiong Bahru community's breath away.

Slowly but surely, the people start to arrive, and a crowd forms, just before 11 o'clock. I recognise the Wong family and their four kids from the MBS installation. Two loud motorbikes roar in, a middle-aged woman with a rather large basket looks around, spots Yew Chong, and walks up to him. When she puts the basket on the floor, I can see refreshments for the artist.

"Are you starting soon?" Marcus, one of the sons of the Wong family, asks. "May I help you?" It's quite clear to the boy the artist is a rock star.

More people arrive, young couples, older couples, men on bicycles with camera, women with umbrellas; the scene fills up as the artist starts to stir and mix his paints. The kids get excited and start running around. The 11 o'clock carnival is about to start.

"I need a ladder; I will restore from the top down; it's easier that way if the paint drips." Yew Chong looks at the growing crowd; he expects a crowd, but probably not so many people so early. "I have asked someone to bring the ladder." He looks towards the community centre.

A woman taps on his shoulder. "May I take a picture with you?" The artist obliges.

I look around and notice something unusual. Even as the entire Eng Watt Street fills up, this is not a usual crowd. The street is strangely quiet, even with so many people. All eyes are on the art and the artist; no one wants to 'disturb' the artist who will be restoring his art momentarily. Quite unreal.

The ladder arrives to applause, and the artist unfolds it and places it just before the small drain along the wall. "It's not stable." He lets out a sigh. "The ground is not even; it can be dangerous." He tries to stabilise the base of the ladder as he brings his paint up with him on the ladder. A kid holds one side of the ladder, another on the other side. Two more kids join in to hold the ladder as the artist starts painting the top of the mural. It is a heart-stopping moment, his fans, mere kids, making sure their idol is safe while he paints. Again, applause, this time for the kids. The artist looks down. "Wow, thank you."

"Don't make it too real," one of the kids shouts out. "Some people may walk into the painting." Laughter.

By now, Eng Watt Street resembles a Sunday morning picnic, except everyone has a mask on, and lots of mobile phones are capturing the artist and the mural. When the artist gets down from the ladder to get a new can of paint, admirers have formed a line to take pictures with him.

"I need to restore fast," he says as he breaks out laughing, happy that his fans have turned up in such overwhelming numbers. "By afternoon, the sun will move, and I am afraid all of you will be standing in the hot sun."

When the artist is done at the top, he starts to paint over the faces, arms, and legs of the figures in the mural. "The faces have faded and the skin tone almost washed out. These are important to bring life back to the mural." The restoration of the mural has been strategic; not every part of it is restored. The parts that get treated are the highlights, faces, limbs, clothes, and the food.

"Yew Chong." Faith Wong, a mother of the four kids, walks up to the artist as he squats to get fresh paint. "Have you had your lunch? Can we get lunch for you?"

"I had brunch," he shouts out. "Thank you." He turns to face the

Wong family. “Some students want to interview me; after that, I’ll be available.” He smiles. They nod. Now, I wonder what he would be available for.

Faith turns and sees my curious face. “We have prepared a cake for him; we want to celebrate his birthday, belatedly.” She cannot hide her excitement. “It means the world to the kids to celebrate his birthday.” Charles, her husband, takes out a tray of 12 cupcakes with two candles, one at each end of the tray, with the words ‘Happy Birthday’ sticking out in the middle.

“We started following Yew Chong painting his murals as early as 2015,” Charles says with a laugh in his voice. “Then, it was just the two of them, the other two weren’t even born. Now, when we take out the photos, we can actually see how the kids have grown up with his murals, year by year. From babies to toddlers to grown kids. It has been amazing. They really love his art and the second boy Matthew wants to be an artist like Yew Chong.”

Just then, Matthew pushes through. “Mummy, Uncle Yew Chong is ready.” All the kids, including many who have just arrived, more than 10 of them, gather by the cake as they sing ‘Happy Birthday’. The adults join in, clapping and singing.

The clouds wink and cooperate by making it a cloudy rather than sunny afternoon. By late afternoon, almost 5pm, the mural is restored. The faces have been mostly redrawn, fresh skin tone added to the limbs. The clothes sparkle with brighter tones and the food looks freshly cooked. It has taken longer than expected because of the crowd, the photo-taking, and the birthday celebration. Yew Chong would need to restore his other Tiong Bahru murals another time.

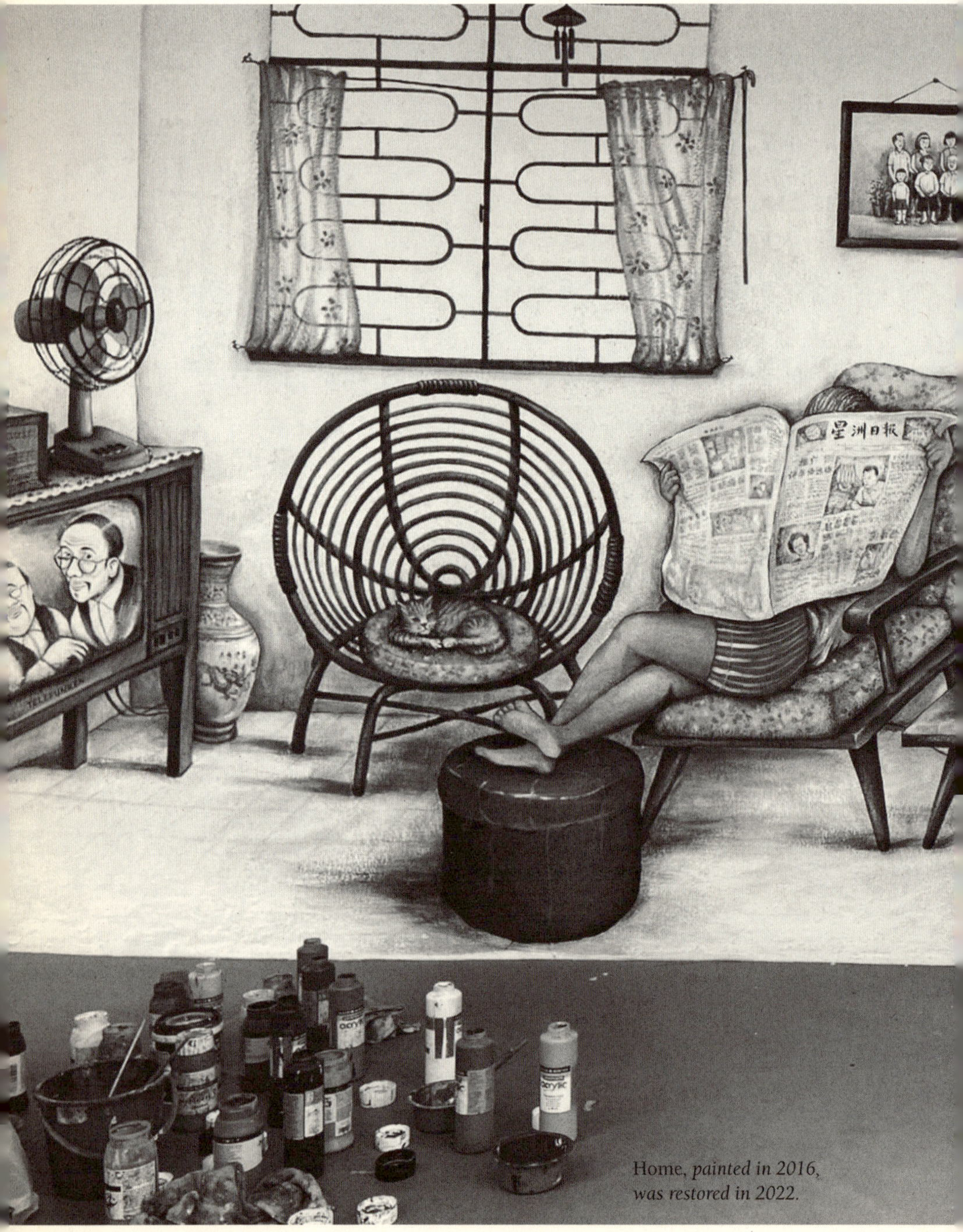

Home, *painted in 2016, was restored in 2022.*

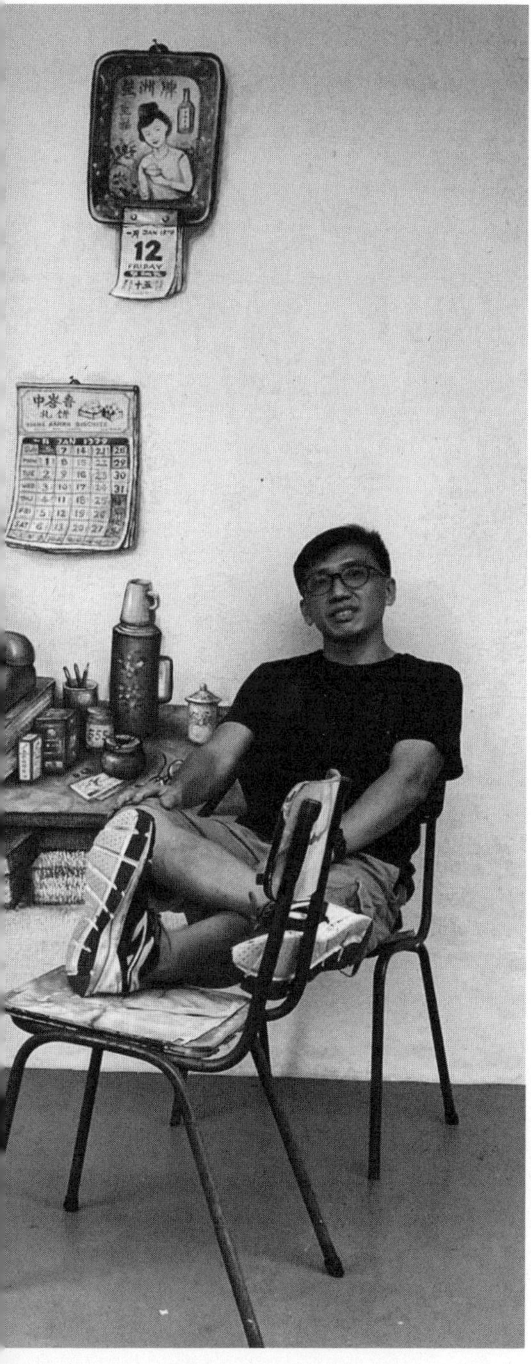

He knows, and he needs to remind himself, that if he makes an announcement in social media, about painting, restoring or even just appearing at the sites of his murals, there will be a crowd. And he needs to make time for them.

"Some people call me a people's artist." He looks down. "It's an honour to be called that. A large part of an artist's success is because of the support he gets from the public. As a mural artist, I can't measure my success by sales, unlike more traditional forms of art. I can measure my success by the reception of my murals. And this is through word-of-mouth, how they follow me on social media and the turnout for my art when I work on them. Their turnout, their physical support, they are so important."

The life of a street artist.

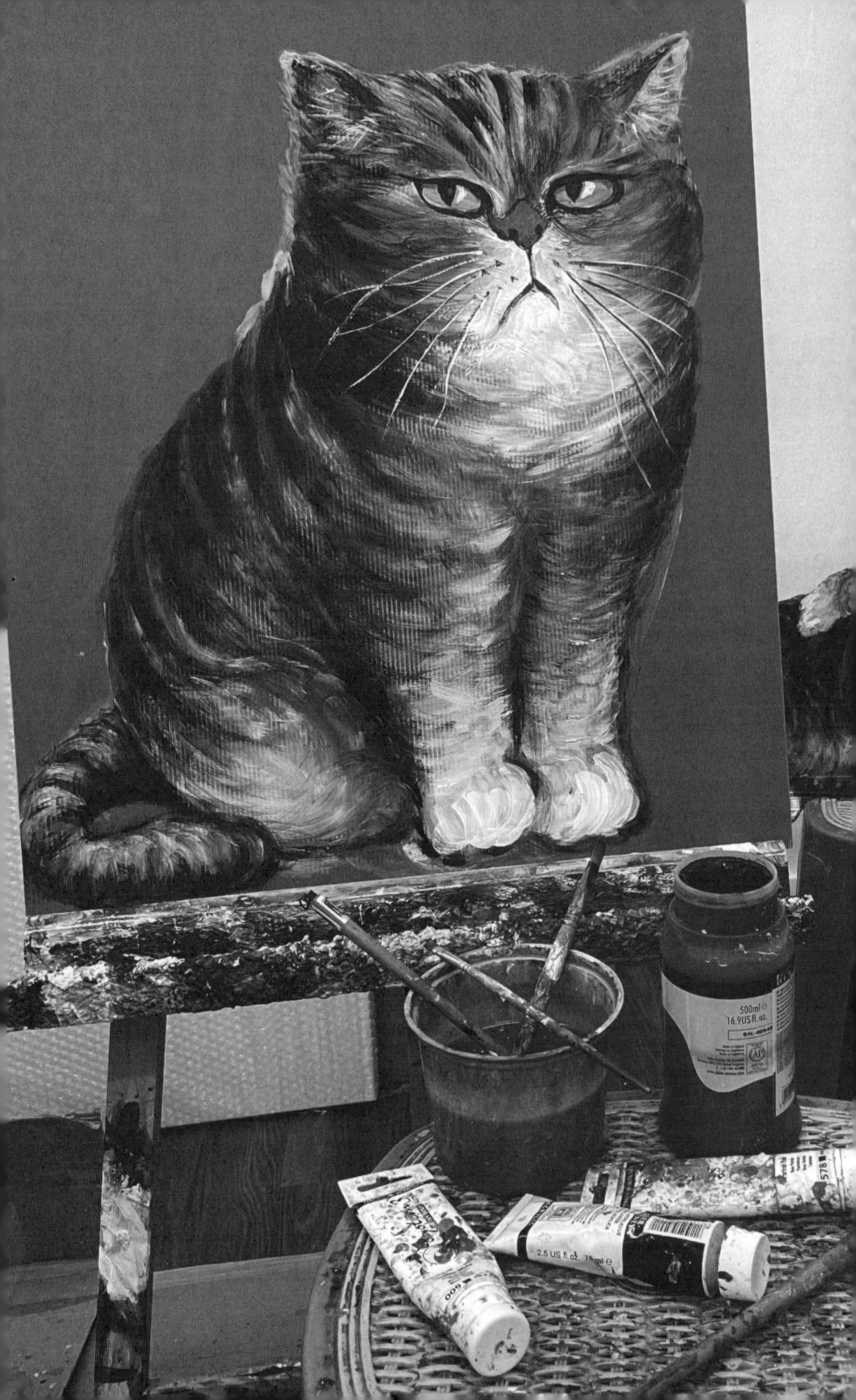
500ml
16.9US fl. oz.
2.5 US fl. oz. 75 ml

CHAPTER 6

The Art of Being Social

They all come together to support him when he puts brush to wall or canvas.

Without Social Media, I Am Nobody

There are people I know who do not believe in social media. They think once they allow themselves into the world of online friends, likes, and shares, their privacy and lives would never be the same again. Then, there are those who cannot imagine life without it. I belong to the latter group: for someone who was from the media world, I see it as a liberating development for the individual. Now that everyone can have a personal platform and can 'publish' his or her view, there is no need to beg the mainstream media, whether it is the TV station or newspapers, to do it. In fact, mainstream media monitors the social media closely. Social media is not just a bottomless reservoir of content; most news today breaks on social media. But for it to really work or have an impact, a person or an organisation needs to do it well, because there is an art to being social.

In early 2007, Barack Obama was a little-known senator running for president against Democratic nominee and household name, Hillary Clinton. Then, established and veteran politicians were weary of a new media they didn't understand; they had spent millions and years cultivating the editors and reporters of TV channels and newspapers.

Social media was new media, scary and unpredictable. On 4 November 2008, Obama made history as the first African American to win the election against Republican candidate John McCain, becoming the 44th president of the United States. Obama won by a margin of nearly 200 electoral votes and 8.5 million popular votes. Many factors contributed to his success, but a key contributor was the way Obama and his Chicago-based campaign team used social media and technology as an integral part of their campaign strategy, not only to raise money, but more importantly, to develop a groundswell of empowered volunteers who felt that they could make a difference. Obama's overwhelming victory turned even hard-boiled conservative politicians around on social media. Today, a politician's Facebook page, Instagram, or X (formerly known as Twitter) account are randomly used to make announcements and to comment; social media is now the platform politicians use to 'talk' to and be quoted by the mainstream media.

On a group level, more and more companies are relying on social media to engage and interact with their customers. If anyone knows how to get followers interacting, it's the American household name, Starbucks. Starbucks' Facebook account is designed to provide information. They upload a lot of eye-catching photos of their drinks, and plenty of fun and colourful videos. Their Facebook also contains tabs for their store locations as well as job opportunities.

Starbucks' X account is built for interacting with their audience. They try to connect with their followers on a personal level, building relationships and increasing their audience engagement. Starbucks'

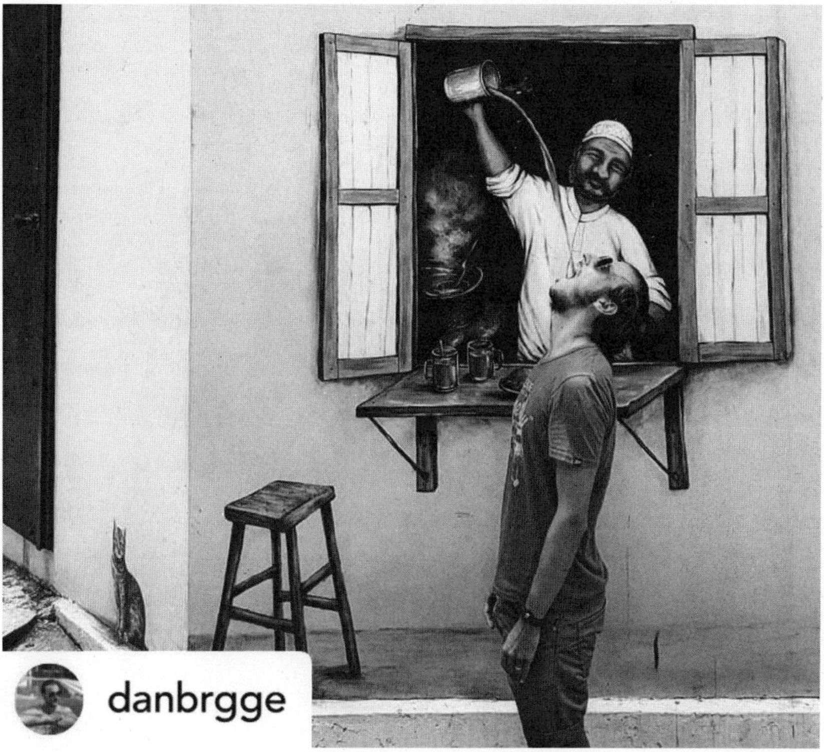

The multiplier effect of social media helped boost the visibility of Yew Chong's artworks.

Instagram account is filled with aesthetically pleasing images and videos of their drinks, and people enjoying their drinks. They also make it a point to respond to as many followers as possible, which is probably one of the reasons why they are so successful at engaging with their audiences.

Yip Yew Chong is a social media 'heartlander'; over the years, he has grown to understand how effective social media can be to his brand, and slowly integrates his art into these immersive platforms, tapping on their infinite possibilities. But he also understands social media is hungry, like an animal with an insatiable appetite. It needs to be fed… constantly.

"Once you slow down, the algorithm and followers will forget you." His face breaks into a knowing grin. "It is also double-edged. It can boost your brand but it can also 'cancel' you if you are not careful with your presentation — words or images. It is merciless. I use social media moderately and only for the sole purpose of promoting my art. I avoid posting about my family and friends or sharing mundane stuff. However, in reality, I can't just post my artworks without a back story. I do post about my personal life or family where they had inspired my art. It makes the artwork and back story more compelling. I also don't post every day, only when I have a new artwork or a good story. I focus on good content released in moderate frequency. It doesn't stop here. Engagement is important. Social media is for people to socialise, to connect, to gather, to share and exchange views. They gather at my post because of one common interest — my art. Hence, I think of ways to engage my followers, including answering all questions, throwing out teasers, and sharing their posts of my art. For all these, I plan, post, and manage all by myself." Yew Chong's base cuts across and includes all demographics: old and young, men and women, Chinese, Malays, Indians, and Eurasians.

"The media, mainstream and non-mainstream, help me to publicise my work," he says simply. "It's free advertising. If I can project myself consistently, and if the media also projects that consistently, I have a brand. Thinking back, if I had started doing art fresh after graduation, when there was no social media, I would not have survived."

As much as Yew Chong paints because he enjoys it, he understands that his supporters are important. He considers himself a performing artist, and like all performing artists, their audience is their bread and butter. "A performer feeds on the reception of his audience, and he is as good as how his audience feels. If the public does not respond to my art, the rest of the ecosystem dries up. People will stop commissioning me, collectors may stop collecting my work. So, I am a populist artist and I don't apologise for it. Populist is a bad word for purists, a bad word for artists who paint for a finer palate, a bad word for artists who paint for the learned eye. My paintings are for the layman. I strive for my art to strike a chord with the everyday man and woman. So, media, especially social media, is an extremely useful barometer for my art."

The artist is now keenly aware that he cannot be an artist who does not respond to questions or queries from the public. He tries to reply to every message or comment on social media, whether it is Facebook, Instagram, LinkedIn, or his website. He keeps the language simple, friendly, even in Singlish as the case may be. "Sometimes, people who enjoy my art leave a word of encouragement, nothing else," he says with a beam in his eyes. "I have to respond, thank them. Some names I recognise over time so I say a bit more. Of course, there are those who turn up on every occasion when I paint, and they bring their families along. They have become close friends. When I reply on the various social media platforms, it is important that they know it is my reply and not someone who replies on my behalf. They recognise my choice of words, my simple happy style. This is part and parcel of modern-day art, at least for me. Let me repeat, I cannot do without social media. When young budding artists ask me for advice, I tell them to learn and use social media. Publicise their art there, pair them with good stories, make full use of these free channels."

A relevant question at this juncture is, does including media, having to tend to its needs, take away the creativity and joy of making art?

"Ah." There is almost a sparkle in his eyes. "I must enjoy what I do; if I don't, I won't do it. So, the process must be something enjoyable, something I look forward to. For me, a part of creating art is to share art. Which is why I see myself more like a performing artist. And involving the media, social media, is now part and parcel of that process of sharing. Social media exposes my art to many people; it is interactive; the public comments, and their words further encourage me; their comments allow me to see things from their perspectives, allowing me to improve and change what I do. And what social media is especially good at is allowing my followers to propagate my art further, by creating their own art with my art. I find that especially rewarding, that I can be the source of their inspiration to their creative process, an inspiration to their joy."

Social media is so important to the artist that he is glad he only got into art full time after 25 years in finance. If he had entered the art world earlier, social media would only be in its infancy and he would not have benefitted from it the way he does now.

"In my mind, social media allows an artist to have his or her biggest exhibition without having to rent any space." He laughs. "In 2004, when a group of my friends thought of holding a joint art exhibition, our first challenge was finding space. Where? How big? What's the cost? When you are just starting out and don't have representation, the logistical demands alone could kill off a project. The hard brick and mortar considerations were real. Now, with social media, my works are perpetually on exhibition. So, if I had started earlier, with no help from social media, it would have been very difficult, I would have given up and gone back and continued with finance and accounting."

Even though Yew Chong enjoys the process of embedding media as part of his art, sustaining public interest — continuing to keep people interested — is probably the toughest part. "I don't want people to get bored; I cannot continue doing the same thing over and over again. For example, I have a painting on the Mid-Autumn Festival. Everybody wants to buy it. After it was sold, people asked me to paint it again for

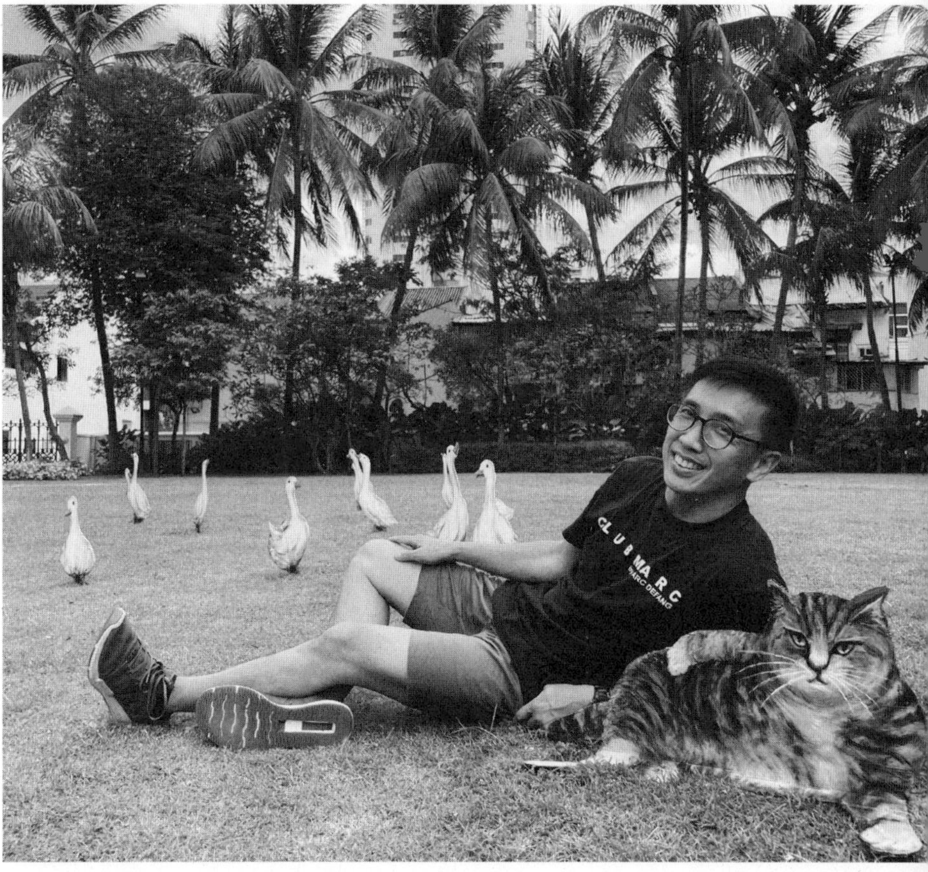

Grumpy Cat jagas *the chickens and ducks.*

them. And I told them and myself, no. People want it because it is unique, one of its kind. Perhaps many years down the road, I will paint it again. But not now. So, I must keep things fresh and unique. Once, twice, at most three times are enough. When people see the same thing for the fourth time, it's over. And I know this is how it is with the media. If you are old news or stale, you are dead in their eyes."

So, how does he know when something has expired, no longer fresh and no longer of interest? What does he do to keep things fresh?

"Surprise is always good." He rests his face on his palm. "When I had to reintroduce the chickens and the ducks to another location, at the Malay Heritage Centre, I knew I needed a new story. So, I introduce a cat into the picture, and make it all about the cat, even though the centre only requested for the fowls to be installed. I then called the cat the 'guard' of the fowls, one not to be messed with."

In a Facebook post, the cat ("I am just a piece of cardboard that happens to look like a big, fat, lazy, and sulky cat") announced the location of where the chickens and ducks would be that weekend. After the event, his social media continued with the theatre:

> *I sulk; you sulk. I smile; you still sulk. Never mind, you look cute anyway. Happy Sunday!*

Reinventing and keeping things fresh occupy the artist's mind at every turn. That Facebook post received more than a thousand likes. But it's hard work when you are a team of one: the producer, director, actor, and post-production team collapsed into one pair of hands.

A Recurring Support Cast

"My wife keeps the accounts. She is also the co-strategist of my art business." Yew Chong's fingers tap on the tabletop. "My daughter proofreads my key narratives and choice of words. My son takes photos of my artworks. That's the help from my family. I do research on the materials like paints and brushes and buy them by myself. When someone commissions a mural, I recce the place a few times, think through the realities on the ground and make a proposal. I present, negotiate, paint, deliver. When it comes to my art, I am a one-man show." He laughs.

Despite the audience he gets when he paints his murals, the reality is, painting is a lonely job. But the jovial fifty-something has a few tricks up his sleeves. Although every new mural is a fresh wall, he always brings along his 'friends', or what he likes to call, his 'support cast'.

"When I introduce an unusual and interesting character and find that this character works, I will use the character again," his eyes scan across the cast of characters of a mural on his phone. "And there are so many instances when I can use these characters. In fact, it is not because I want to use them, but because they are required. They contribute to the scene and are essential."

His support cast does not need to be human beings or even an animal; he considers the calendar, for instance, as a recurring cast member. "The calendar hanging on the wall, it is in every household, a common thing to have. In coffeeshops, they don't just have one calendar, there are many. Same with my old family home — so many calendars in the house. Same with clocks. Calendars and clocks are required because they help to depict the period, the era, which is the 1970s and 1980s. They contribute to the ambience. Imagine a wall of the 1970s without a calendar? It would look weird without it. By the 1990s, these calendars were out of fashion. For my first mural, the barber scene, I was scratching my head, what to put on the wall? When I decided on the calendar, I had to next decide the date. I thought my birthdate, 12, with a double digit, looks more balanced from an aesthetic point of view. A single digit looks scanty and stark. So, that date becomes the date on every calendar. There is no astrology in coming up with that date. For a long time, no one knew the date was my birthday. It was only after last year's show which was launched on my birthday that it became widely known. I did it for fun, not because birthdays are important. You know I don't celebrate birthdays. Yes, my art is about special days, the new year, mid-autumn, but in real life, these occasions are not important to me."

And then, there is the cat; it makes an appearance in most of his murals and paintings. "Like the calendar, it adds, and are like a time stamp to the murals. But unlike the calendar, the cat makes the mural lively, I always paint it in motion, moving, expressive. Of course, the fun part is to see observers hunt all over the mural for the cat. And once they find the cat, they actually stroke and pat the cat in relief. I want to say there is no hidden message. Some people think I am a cat lover and are surprised when I tell them I am not. I paint tabby cats because my family used to have one to catch rats in the old house. Mary was her name. The breed is one of the most common; they are everywhere on the streets."

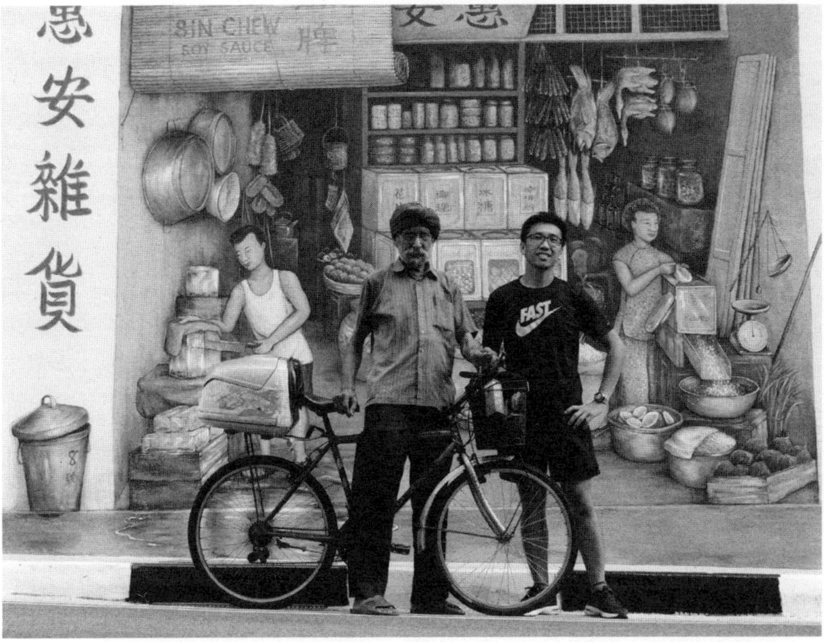

Mr Souran Singh cycled by the mural daily when Yew Chong was painting Provision Shop. *On the last painting day, Yew Chong invited him to take a photo.*

Of the human support cast, the most significant is Mr Singh with a green turban on a bicycle. "There is a back story to him. In 2015, when I was painting the provision shop mural in Everton Road, a Sikh man came by and watched me paint, every single day. Throughout the two weeks, he watched and I painted. We didn't talk. I was very focused on the mural and he just stood on the opposite side of the road, watching. Every day, he would watch me paint for a few minutes before he cycled off. He watched me paint twice a day, before going to work and when he came back from work. When I had completed the mural and was taking photographs, I saw him again. So, this time I invited him to take photographs with the mural and with me. I told him I would print out the photographs and bring it to him. He gave me his address and I went over when the photographs were ready. This little encounter created an impression. So, whenever appropriate, I would paint him riding on his bicycle in my paintings."

Unlike Mr Singh, there is one support cast with a sad story; she represents the unfortunate people of Singapore society; poor, destitute, and hungry. "I insert a poor old lady, begging, picking up crumbs on tables. Although my artworks depict positive and happy energy, I also want to be realistic, that amongst us there are always those less fortunate that we need to be mindful of. If the observer looks hard enough, he will see this figure, not prominent, but she is there in my paintings. It reminds me to count my blessings. Society is diverse. I don't try to hide this old lady, but I know most viewers don't see her because they are taken up by the main activities of the artwork. Most of the time, this lady is small, hunched, picking food from tables. I did however, paint her begging in a hawker centre fairly prominently once."

Does he have a reference in real life?

"I created her because I want to remember Dai Soh, the tenant from the old house," he says calmly. "I still remember one occasion vividly. She was sitting at the back of the house, staring at me when I was eating ice cream. Her eyes seemed to long for it so I shared the ice cream with her. Somehow, those eyes and how she sat make me want to remember the less fortunate among us."

In many murals there is an old-fashioned clock, and this member of the support cast is always at ten past ten. The short and long hands of the clock come together to form a happy face. "I recall the advertisements of watches and clocks; they are always at ten past ten.

It's a happy face when the face of the clock is round. There is no other significance, it is not my birth time nor does it mean anything auspicious."

I want to know if there are any other muses he has, a part of the art he includes even subconsciously. His face lights up, as if I have touched on a secret he has been waiting to unleash. "Flying birds in the sky." His voice is almost a shout. "Like the cat, they add movement to a still painting, movement to the sky. Most of my murals with a skyline have flying birds. I don't like to paint clouds; they distract from the activities of the painting way too much; flying birds are my way of adding movement without it being too distracting."

A favourite group of support cast is also the children, and they are painted far apart from each other, running, playing, shouting. "They form the extreme movements and 'noise' of the paintings." His eyes are excited, darting up and down, thinking, remembering. "In my painting, *Preparing for the Haj*, the boys are shouting at each other from different windows. In my HDB painting, a boy is cycling and waving at two other boys from the second floor. Children playing and running about are what we see every day. They are, by nature, active and lively. When I add them to a mural or painting, the viewer identifies with the painting straightaway. Children make the paintings and murals realistic and lively. There is something delightful about seeing children running after a train, for example."

Perhaps less obvious as a support cast but more as a theme is multiracialism. It is a part of Singapore society we witness every day, in the malls, supermarket, on the streets, in public transport. "No one tells me to include this and I try not to force it in," Yew Chong stresses.

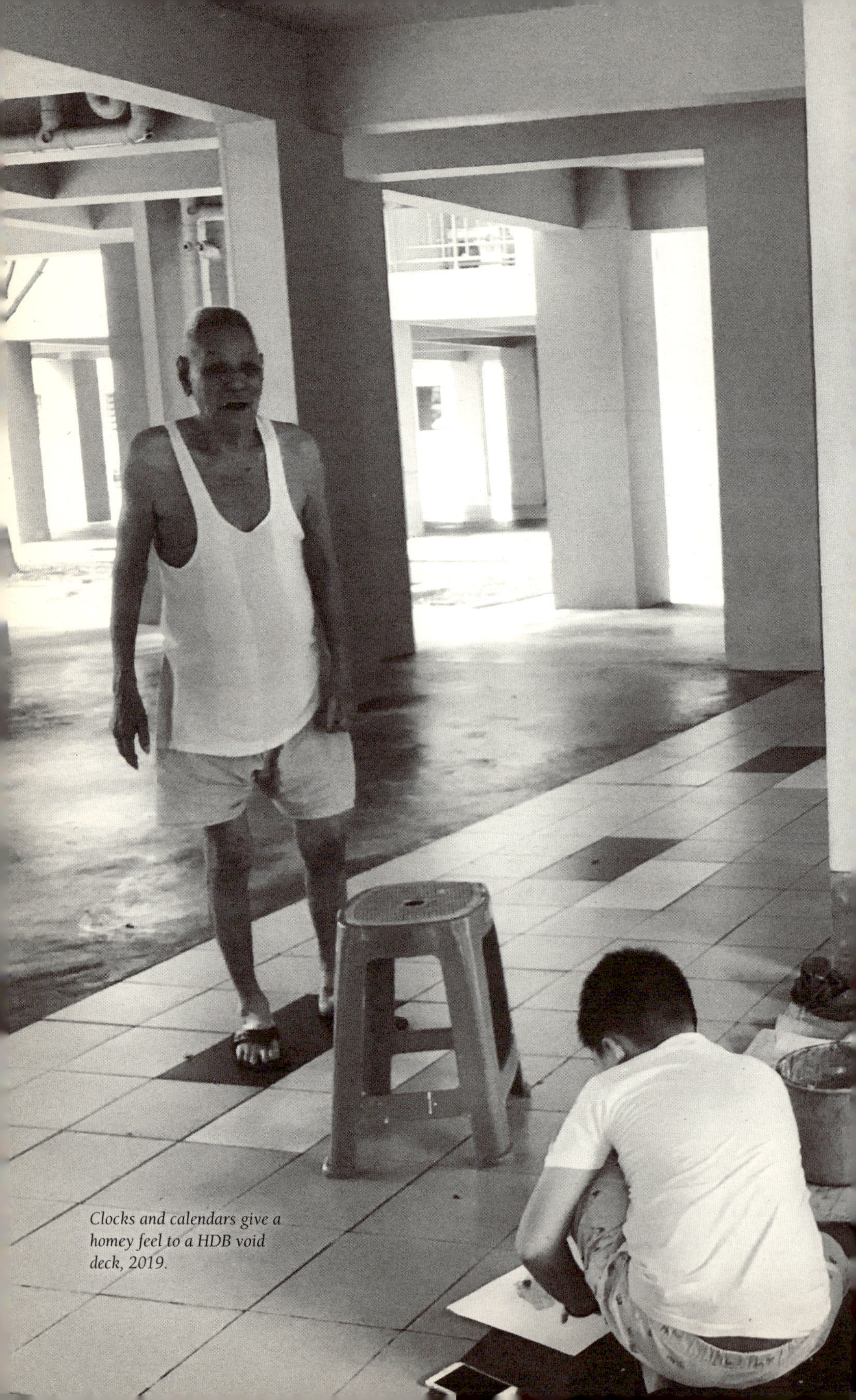

Clocks and calendars give a homey feel to a HDB void deck, 2019.

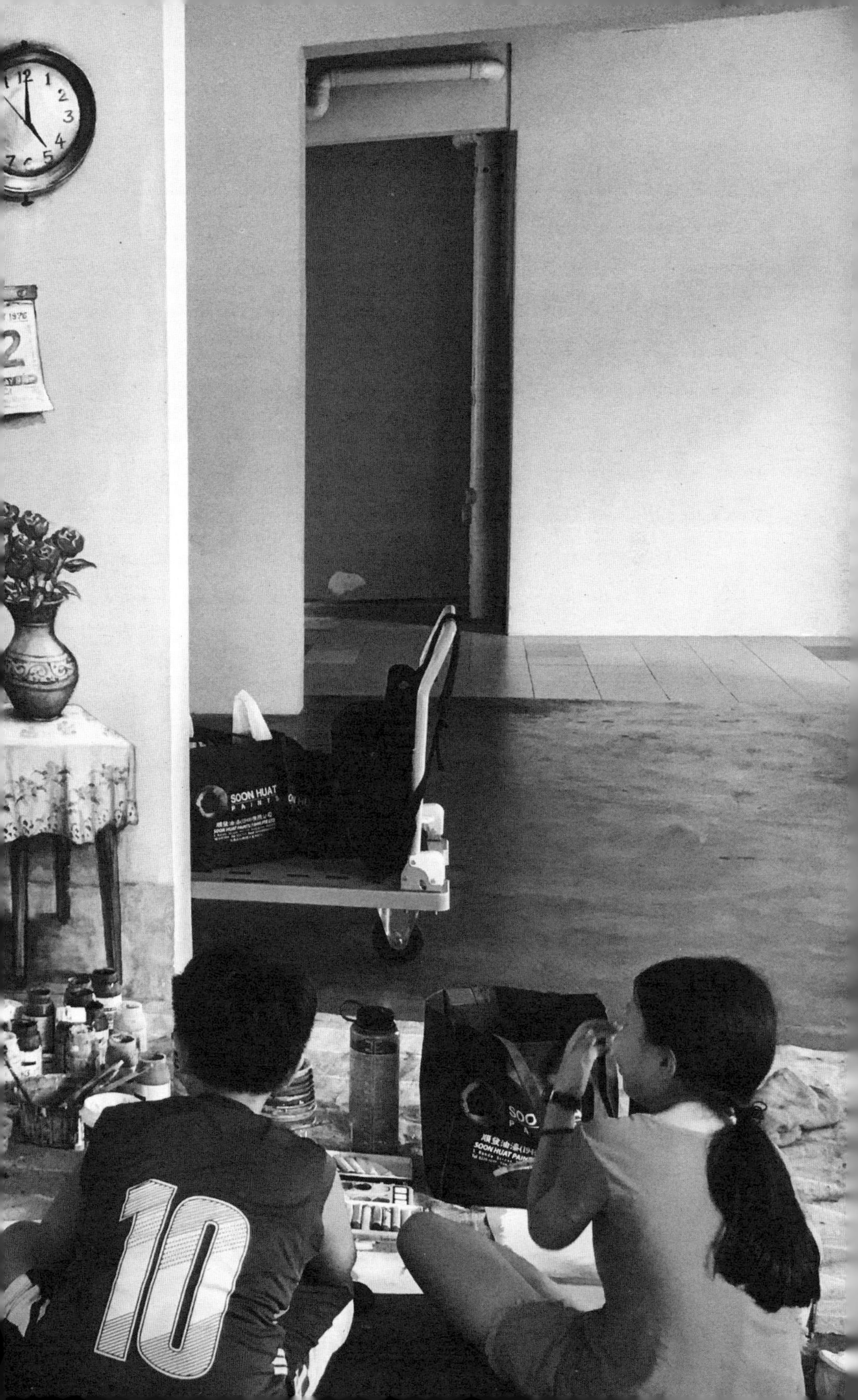
SOON HUAT PAINTS
10

"I allow this theme to come out naturally. And this brings me to another recurring cast, religious buildings. Multiracialism comes through in the forms of religious buildings or places of worship, and you see a mixture of them, a church next to a temple, and a temple next to a mosque. We don't think of it because we are so used to the mix of cultures and races here, yet when I paint them this aspect of Singapore society comes to the fore. Various religious buildings and their architecture also add vibrancy to my work. They are now quite a signature of mine, as these are lively public places where people meet."

Apart from recurring cast and themes, the artist also has recurring techniques of painting. One technique he employs frequently is the light bokeh effect, where the light comes from the back. This backlit style allows for long shadows to form, shadows cast from figures on the road, buildings, or trees. The light with long shadows makes the objects more 3-D. It also adds to the overall mood of the painting.

Always there but not always noticed is Yew Chong's ability to paint smoke; white smoke, from firecrackers during Chinese New Year, incense in a temple, chimneys of rooftops, to the stove of a hawker, they are in the air and add a layer of realism to his works like spices do to a dish. "Smoke is something I almost always use, like birds and cats; smoke adds to the movement of the artwork. When I paint a hawker without smoke, it doesn't work. The moment I add smoke, the painting moves, comes alive."

There are others, like the chickens and roosters, bird cages and bamboo blinds, his unmistakable road signs, TV antennas from old roof tops, his propensity to add zinc roofs to his art; they all come together to support him whenever he puts brush to wall or canvas.

"They are familiar friends that keep me company." The artist allows a knowing grin. "These friends are my tricks in the bag; even when I am painting something entirely different, introducing them anew keeps me grounded, like anchors; they are the touch points of my brand, my signature."

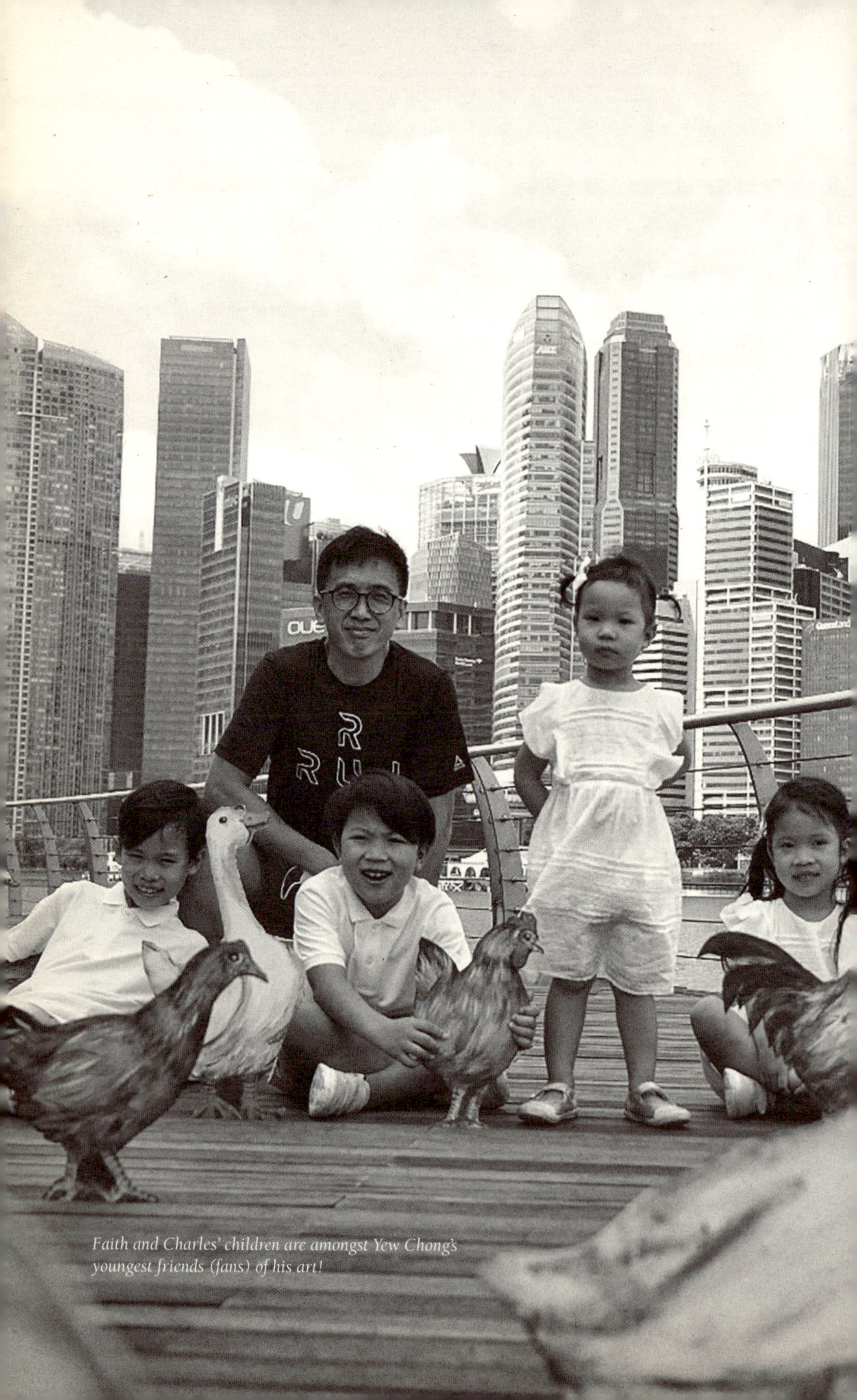

Faith and Charles' children are amongst Yew Chong's youngest friends (fans) of his art!

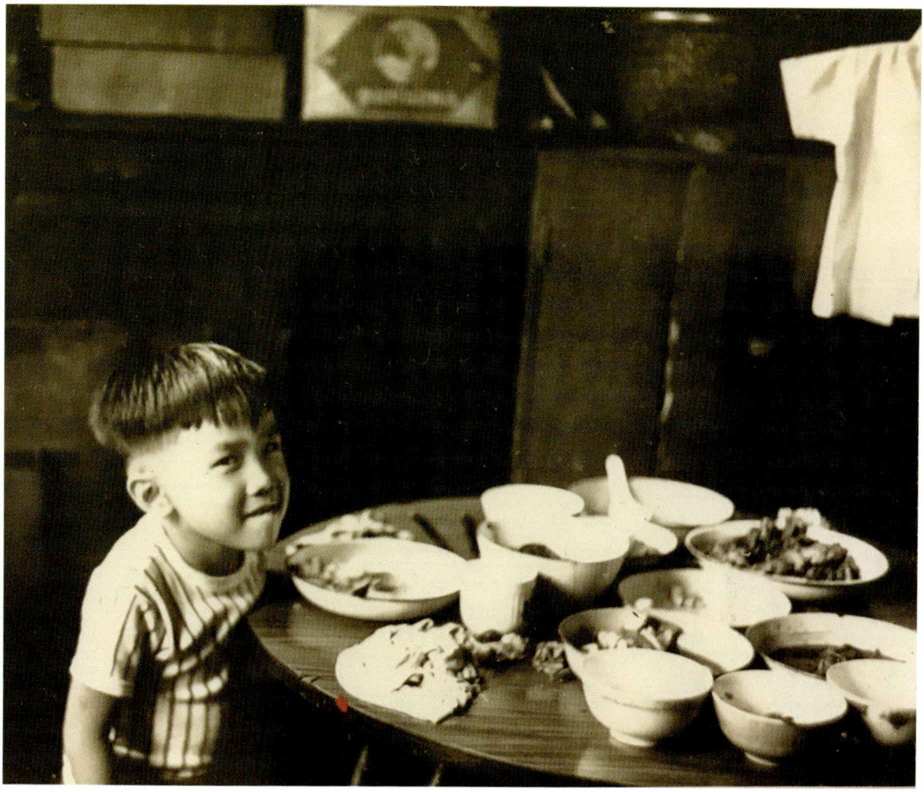

Old Chinatown home, 1974.

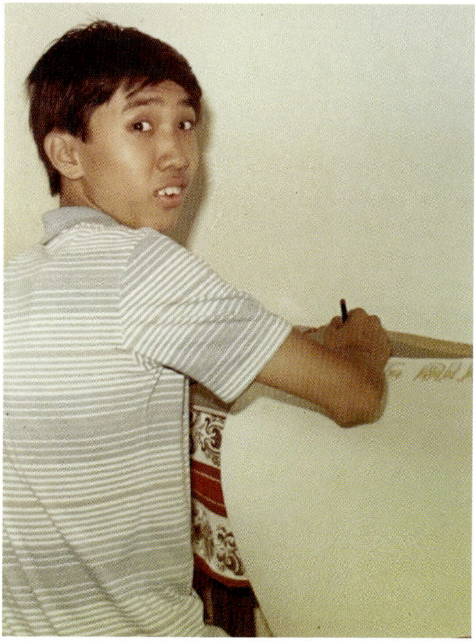

Drawing on a sewing machine at new Chinatown flat, 1984.

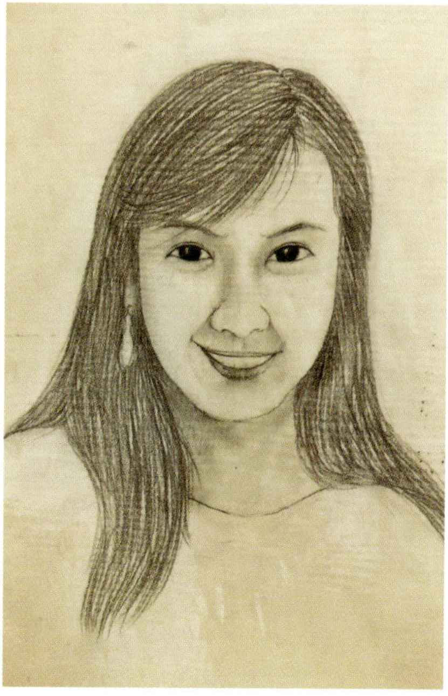

Portrait of girlfriend and future wife, 1991.

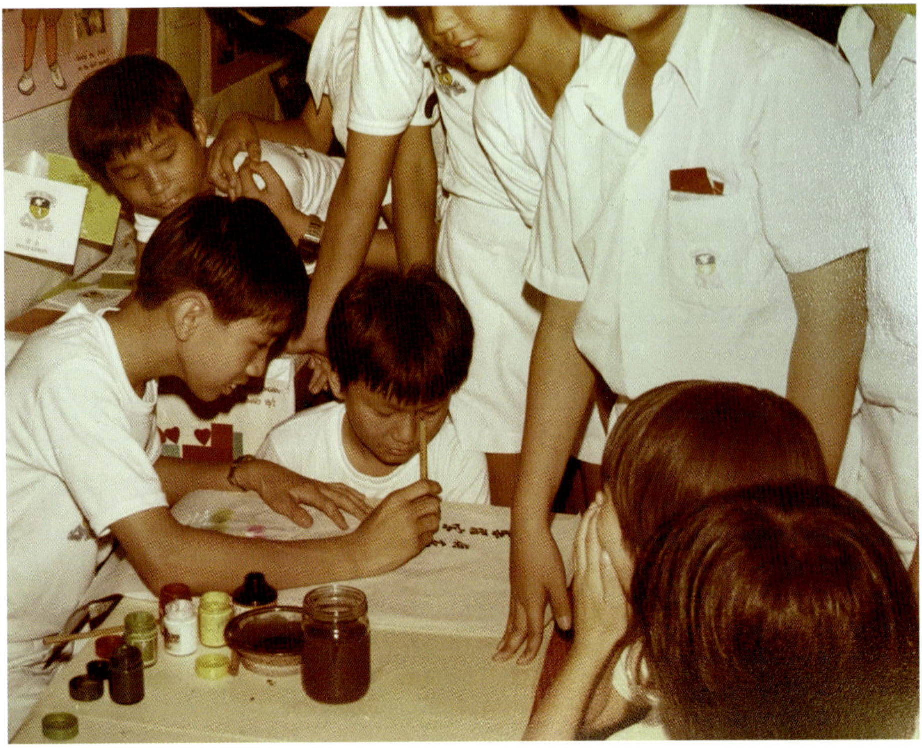

Pearl's Hill School, 1981.

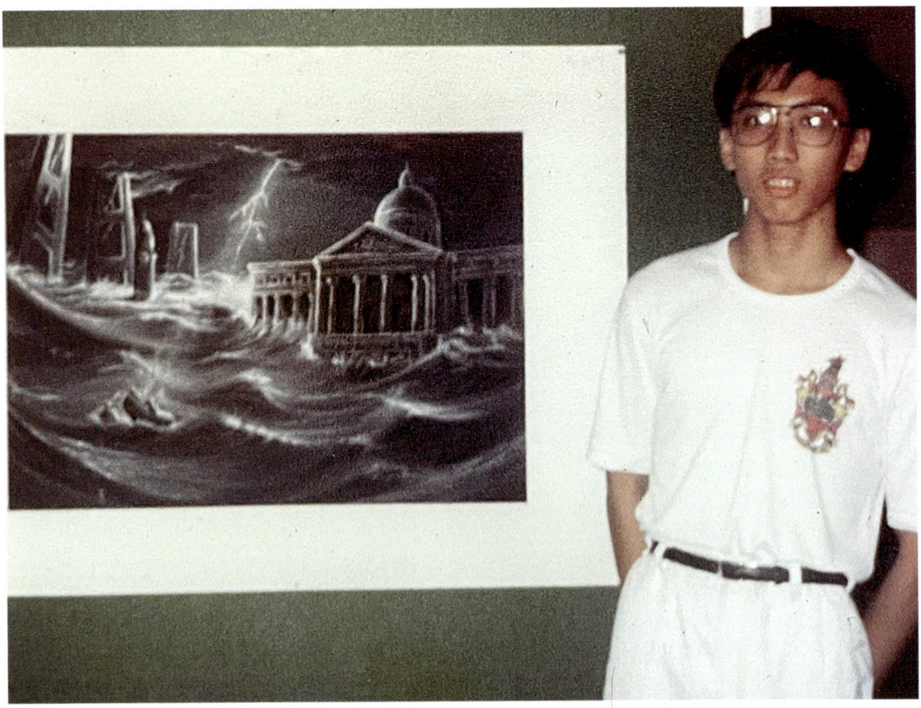

Painting on *Climate Change*, Raffles Junior College, 1987.

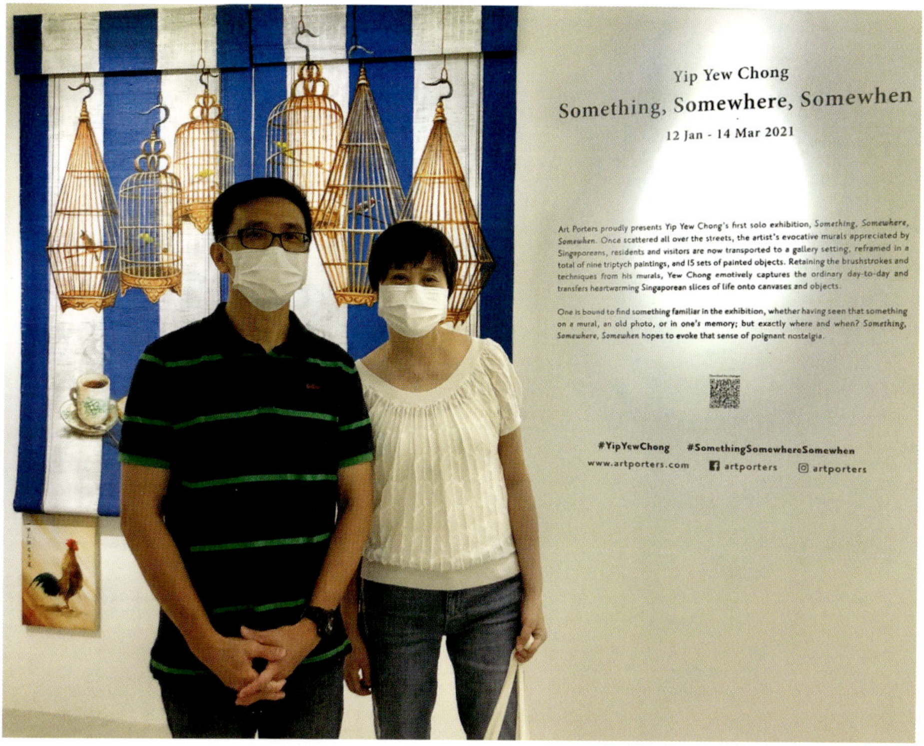

First solo exhibition at Art Porters, 2021.

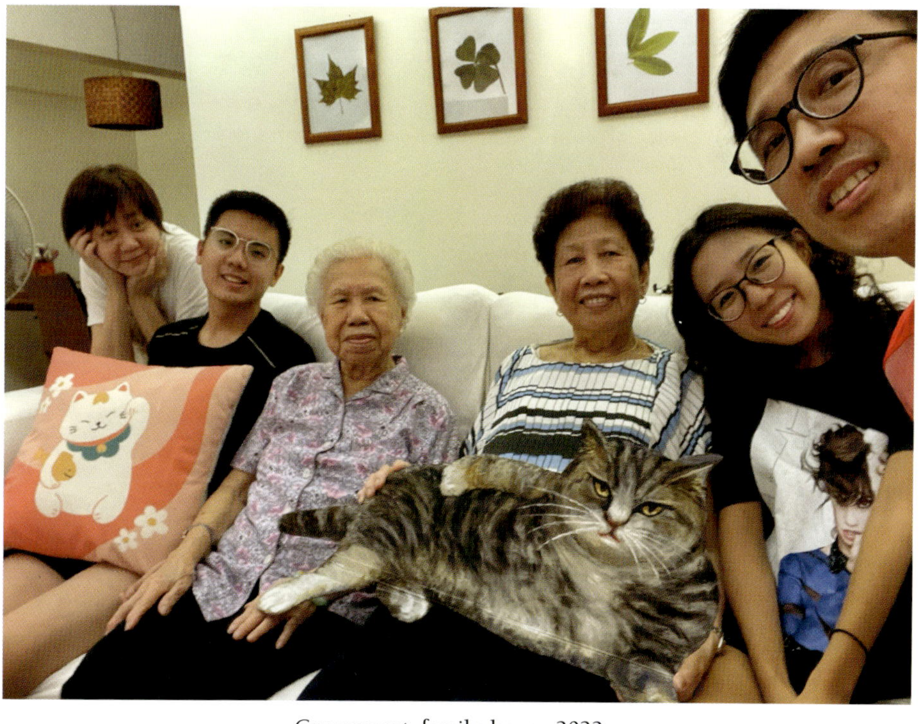

Grumpy cat, family, home, 2022.

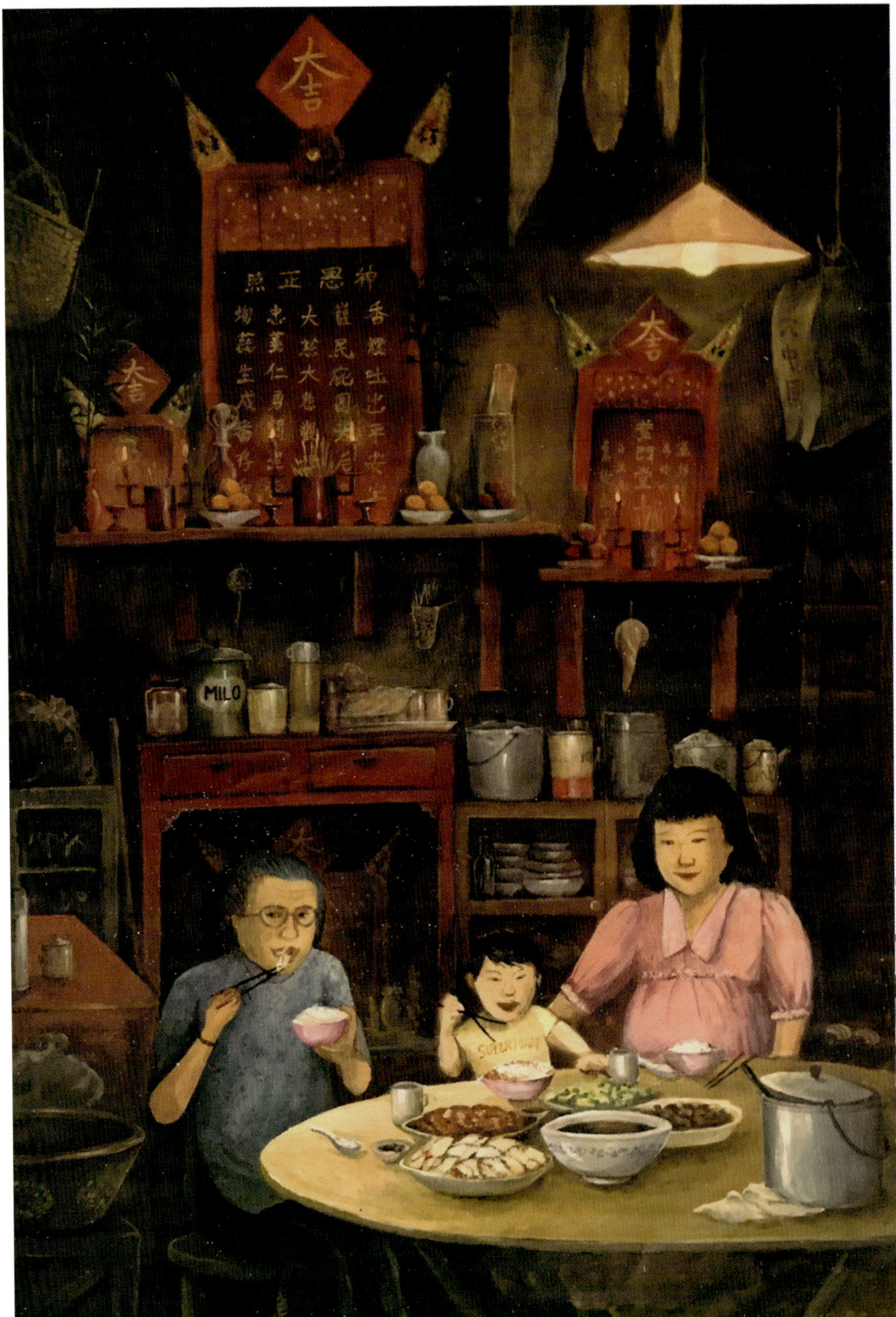

In 1992, Yew Chong painted this artwork of his childhood home using acrylic paints bought by his then-girlfriend. One of his first acrylic paintings, he submitted it to the UOB Painting of the Year competition.

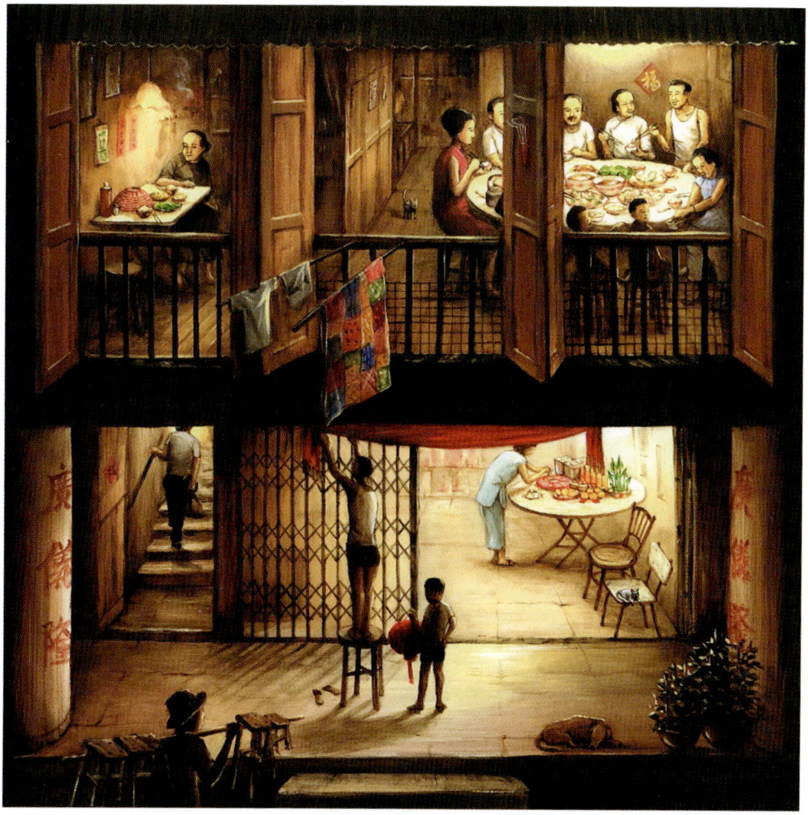

New Year's Eve, 2019.

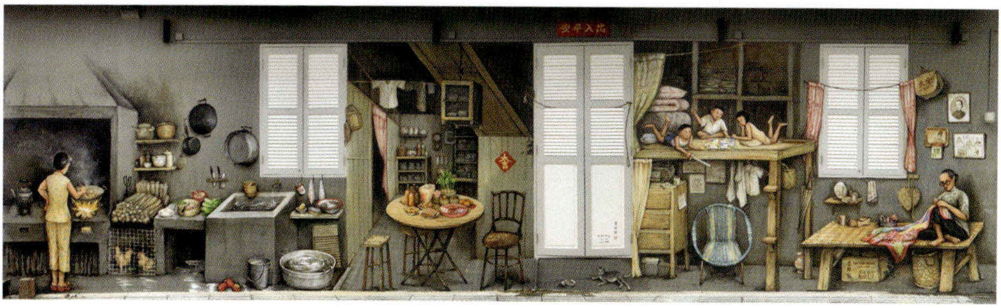

My Chinatown Home mural, 2019.

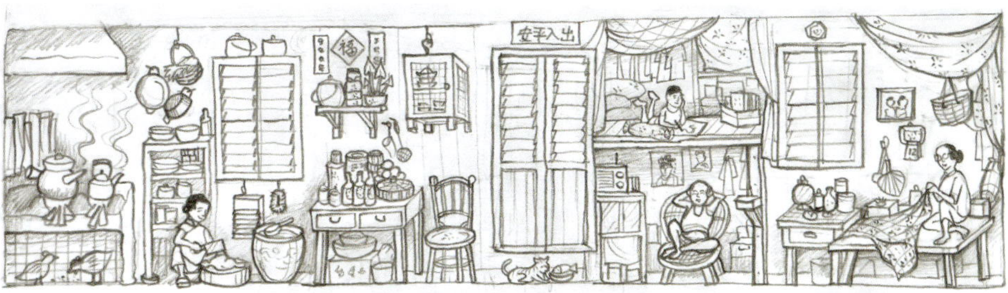

Original concept sketch of the mural.

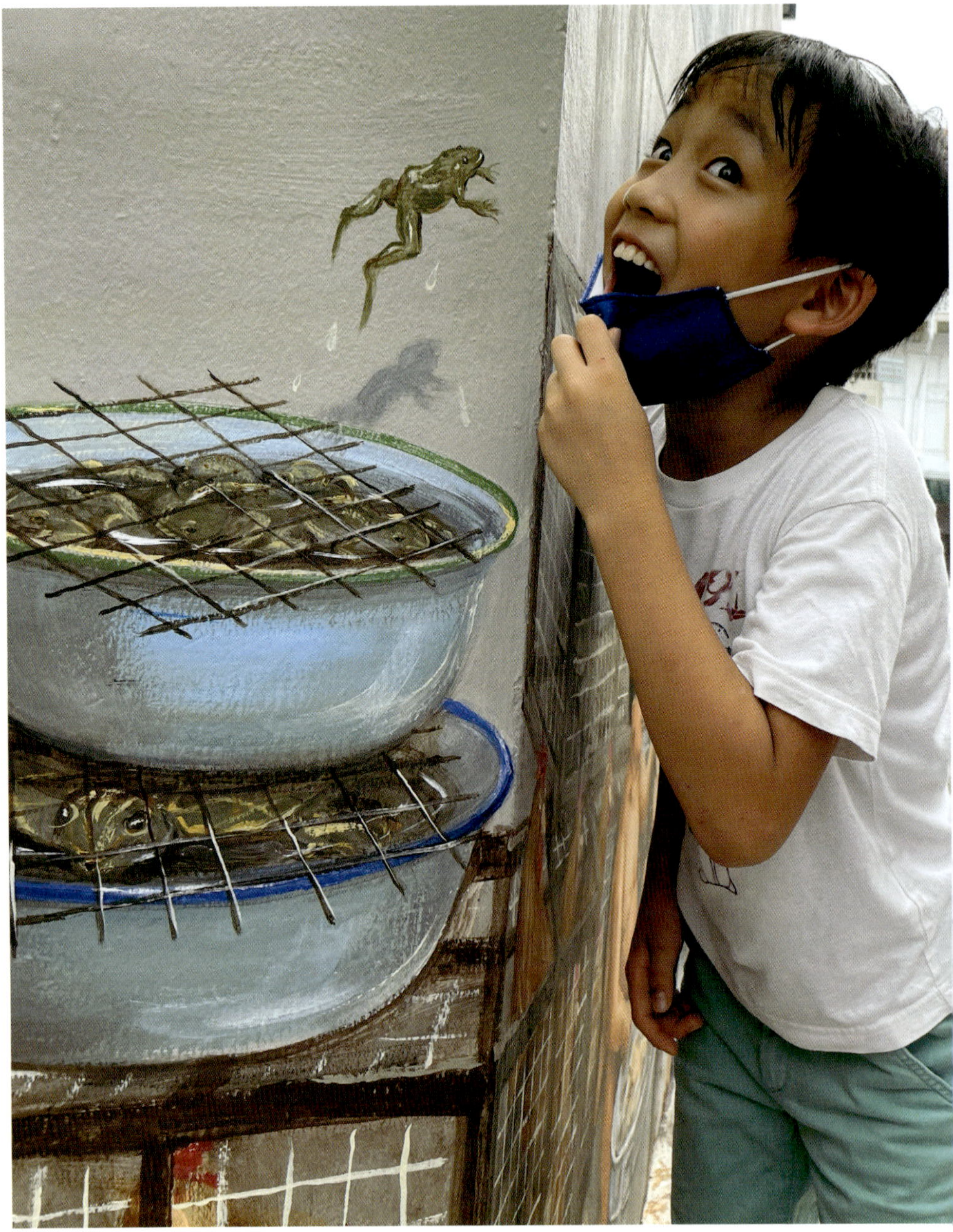

Chinatown Wet Market, 2021.

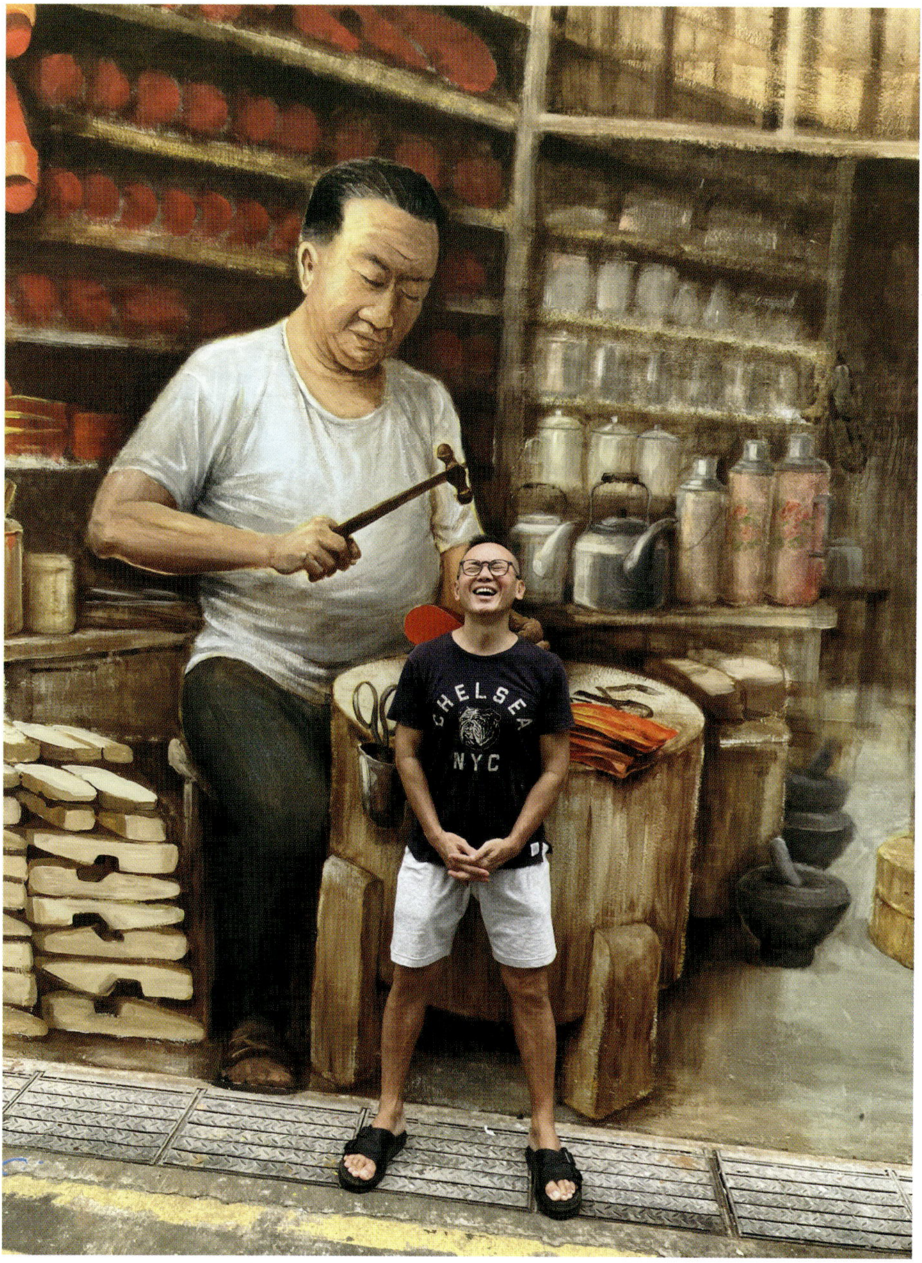

Clog Maker, 2023.

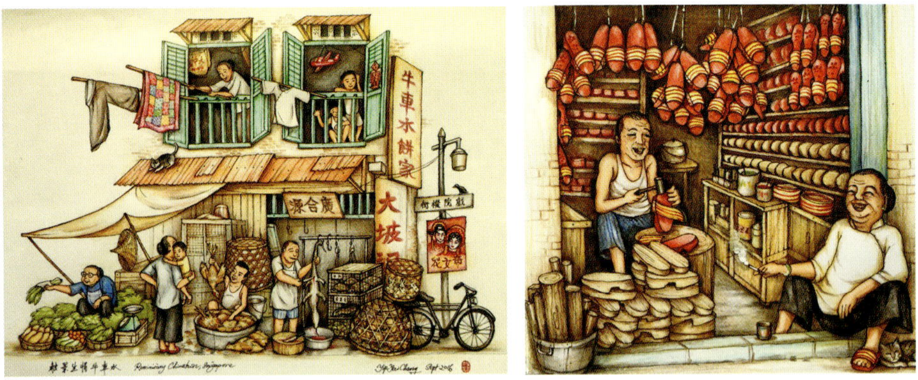

Original concept sketches, 2016.

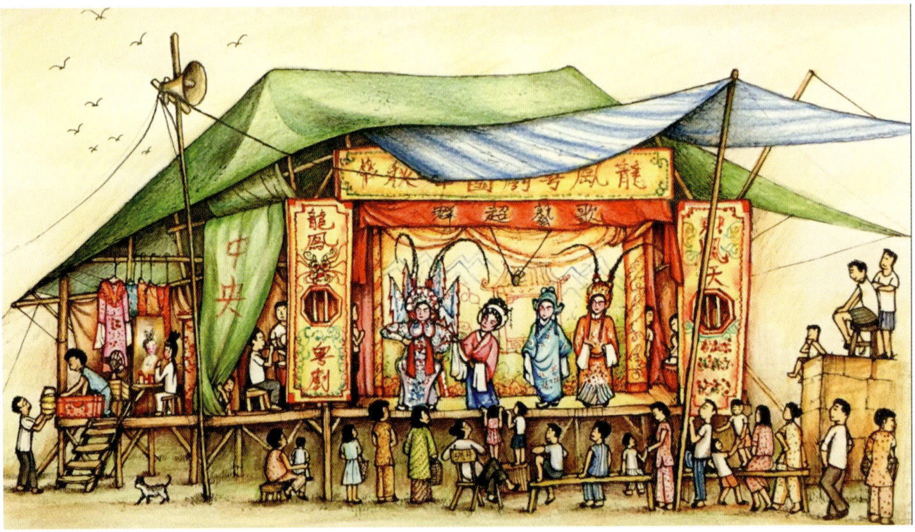

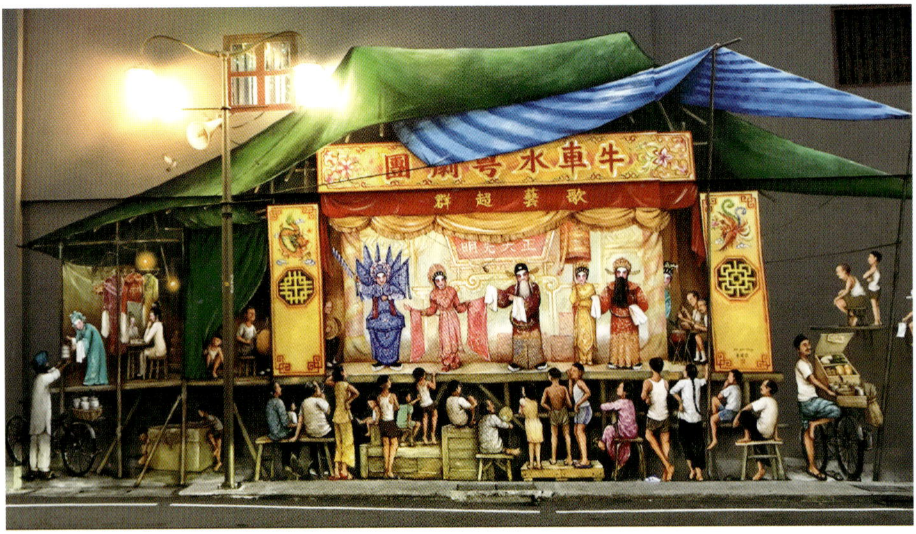

Cantonese Opera mural, 2019.

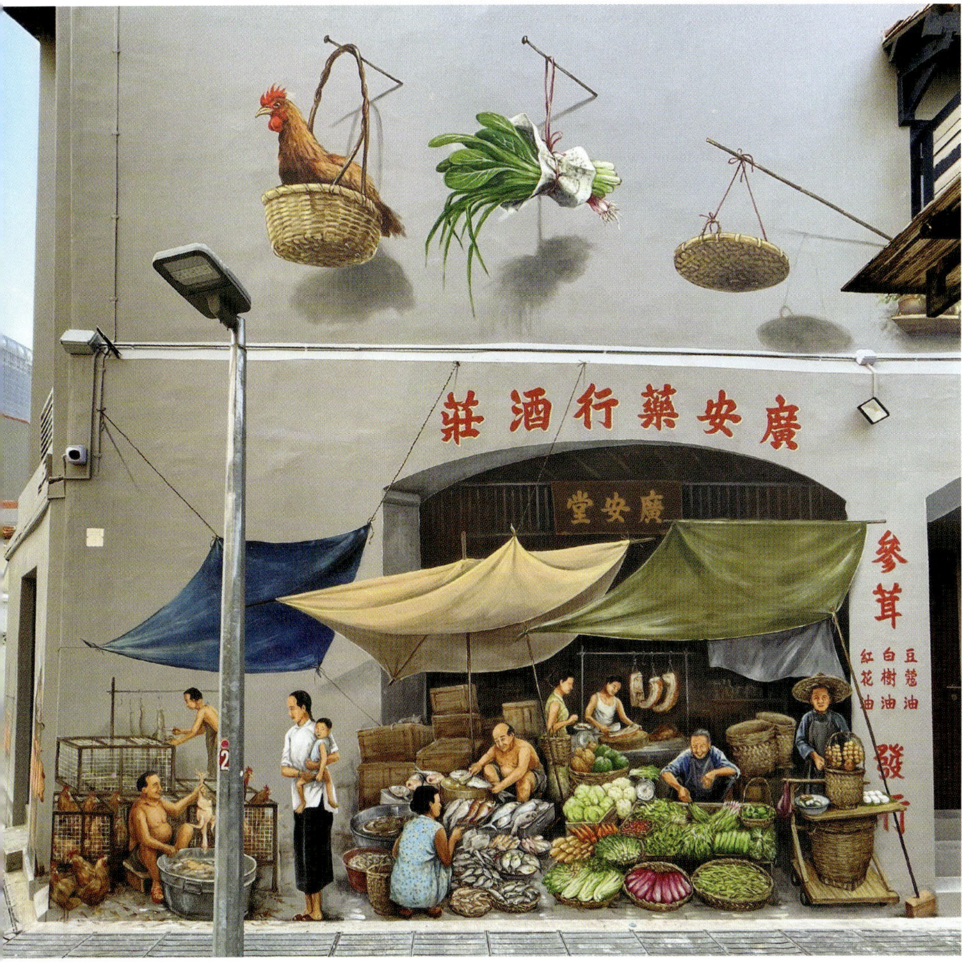

Chinatown Wet Market, 2021.

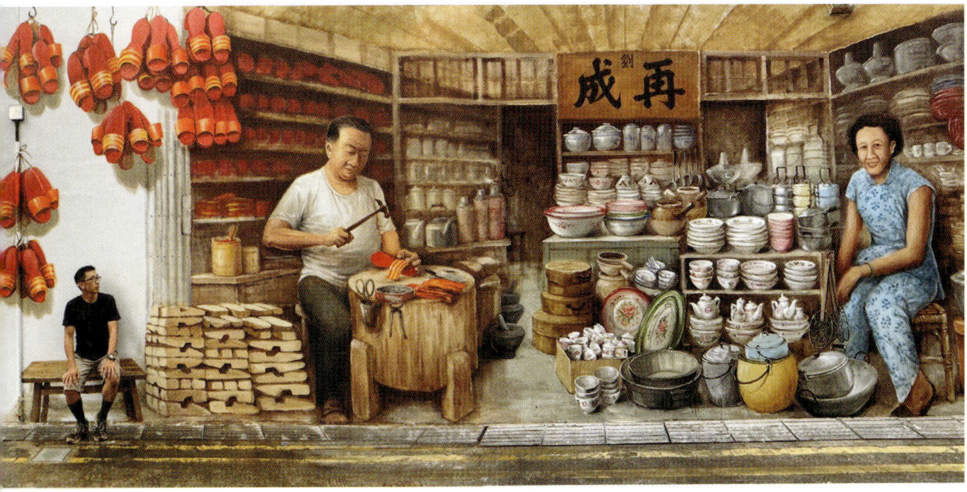

Clog Maker and Kitchenware Shop, 2023.

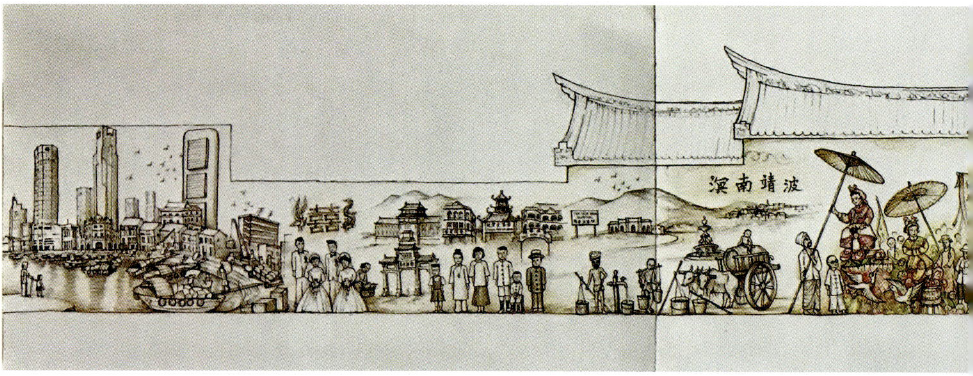

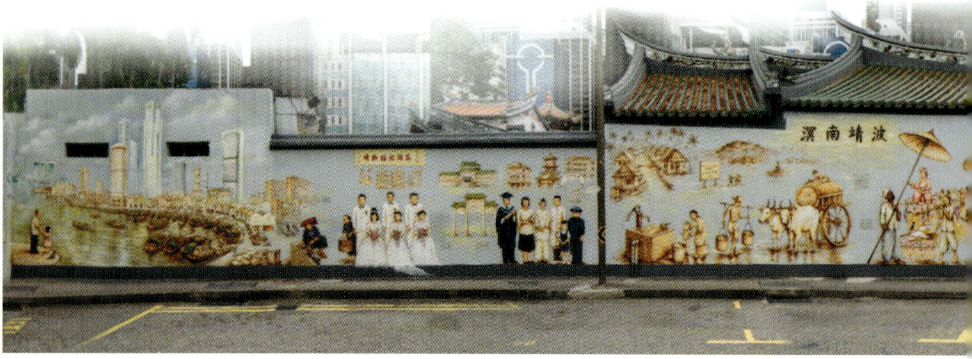

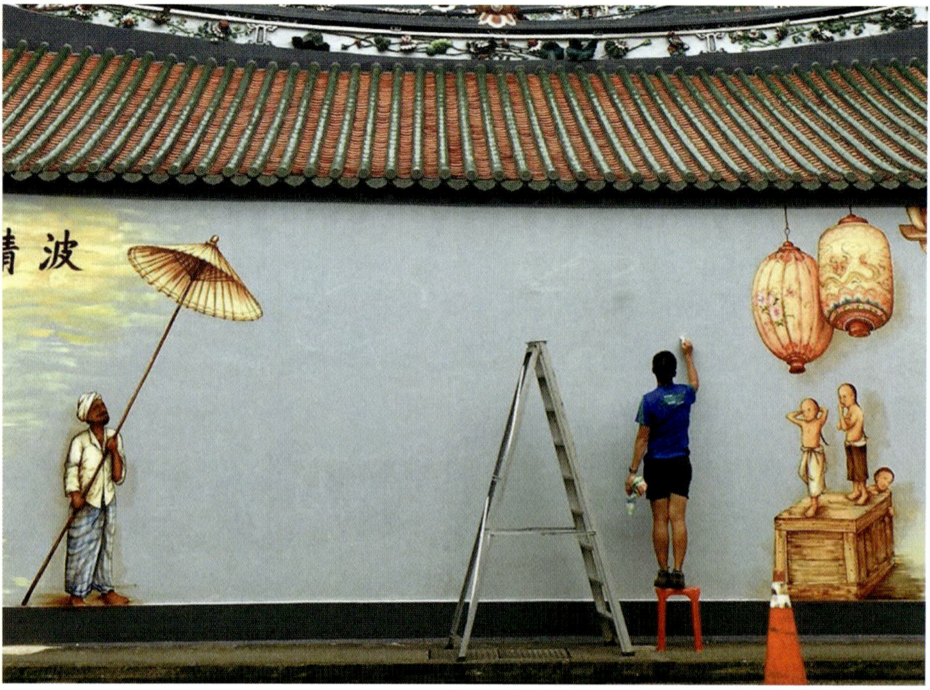

Left & right pages: *Thian Hock Keng Mural*, 2017. Bottom left photo by Pamela Ho.

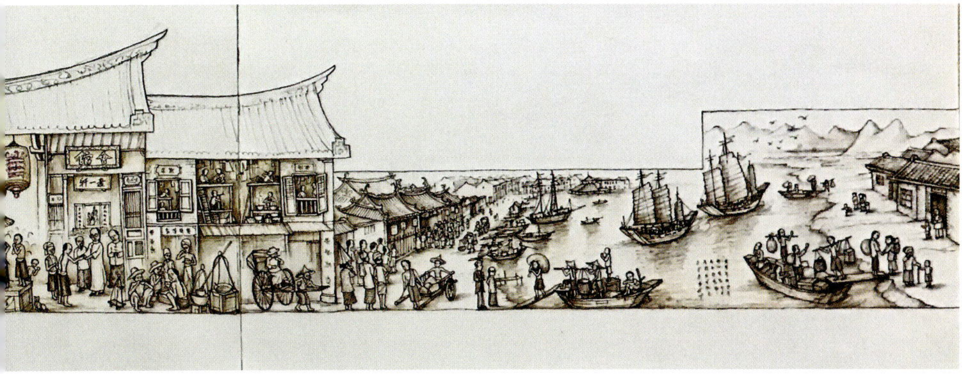

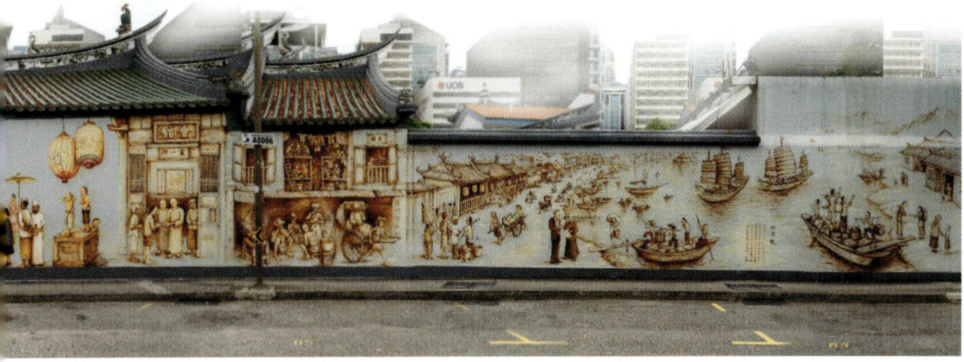
UOB

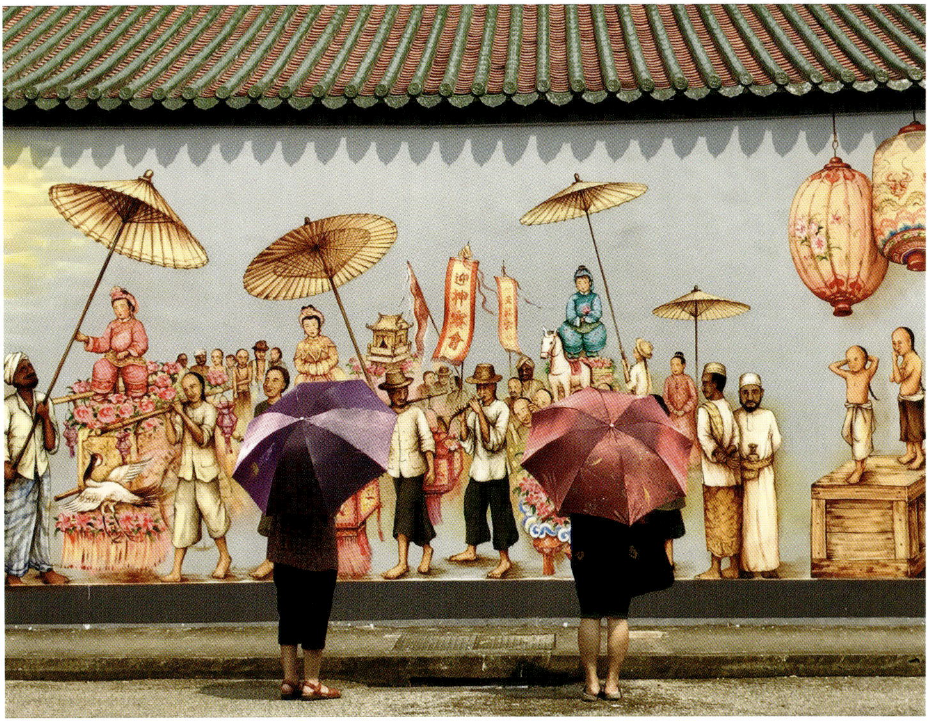
迎神賽會

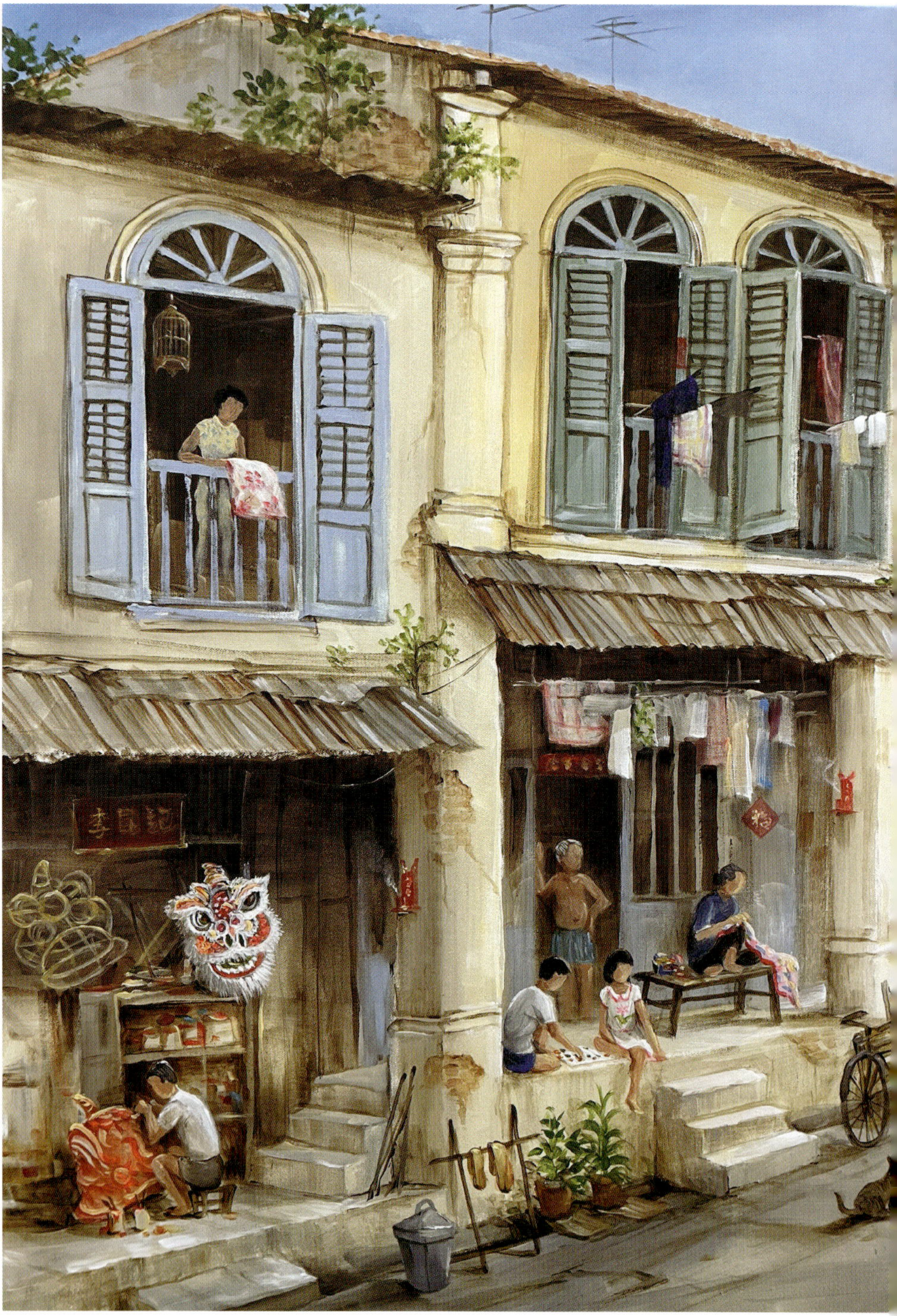

Ann Siang Hill, 2023.

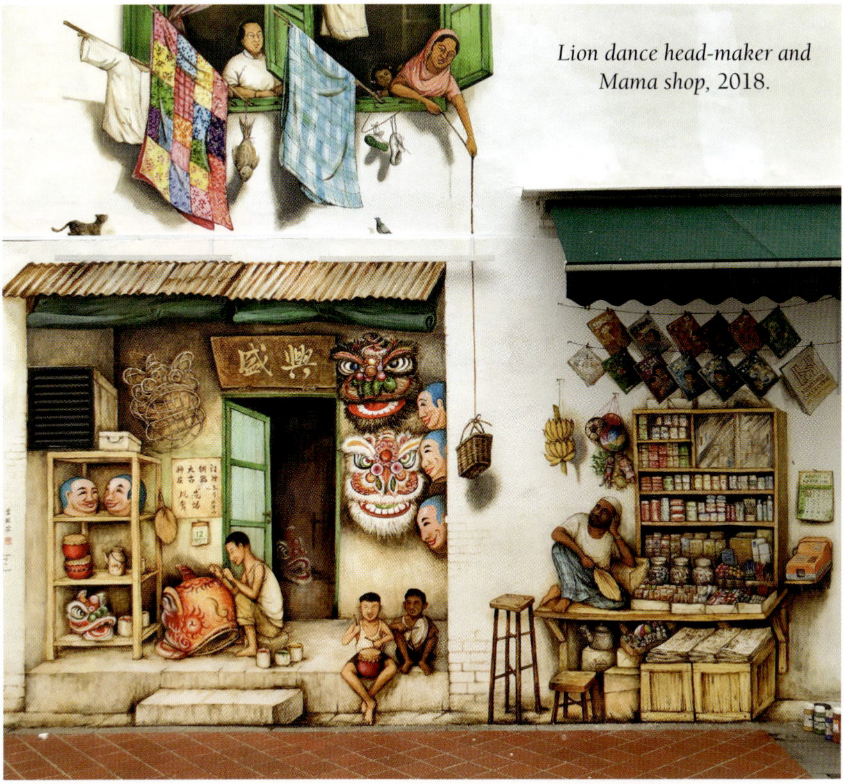

Lion dance head-maker and Mama shop, 2018.

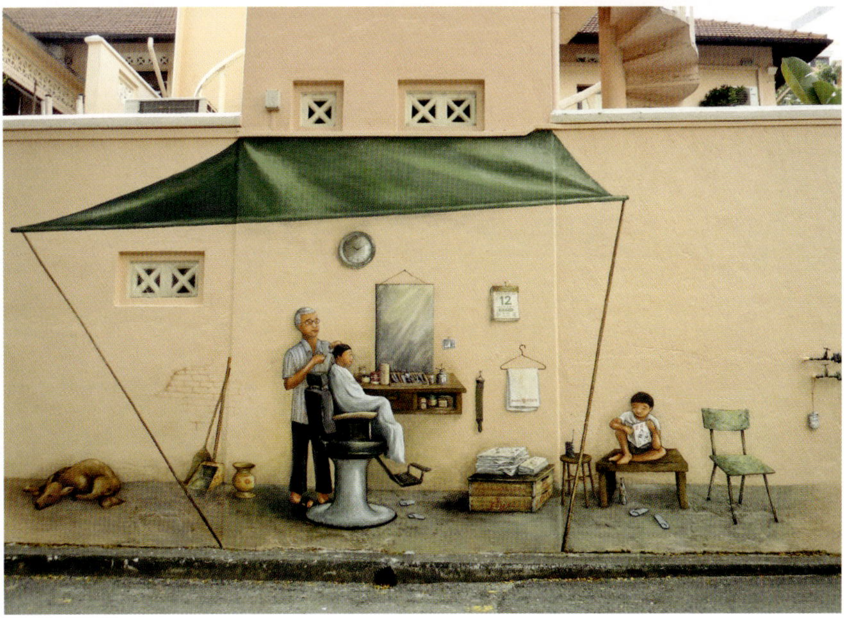

Barber, 2015.

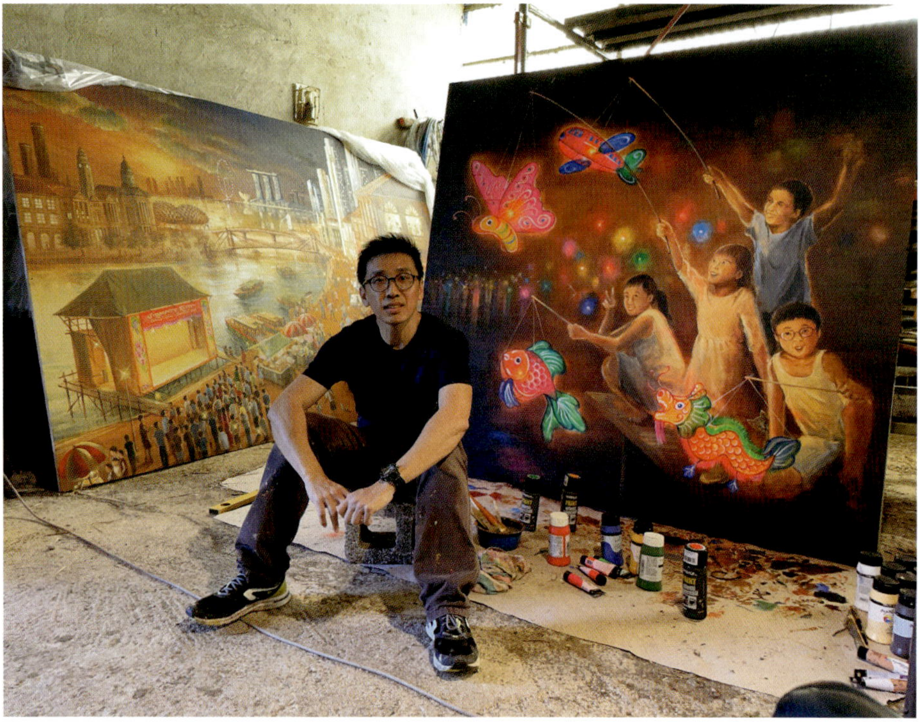

Cicerale, Italy, 2022.

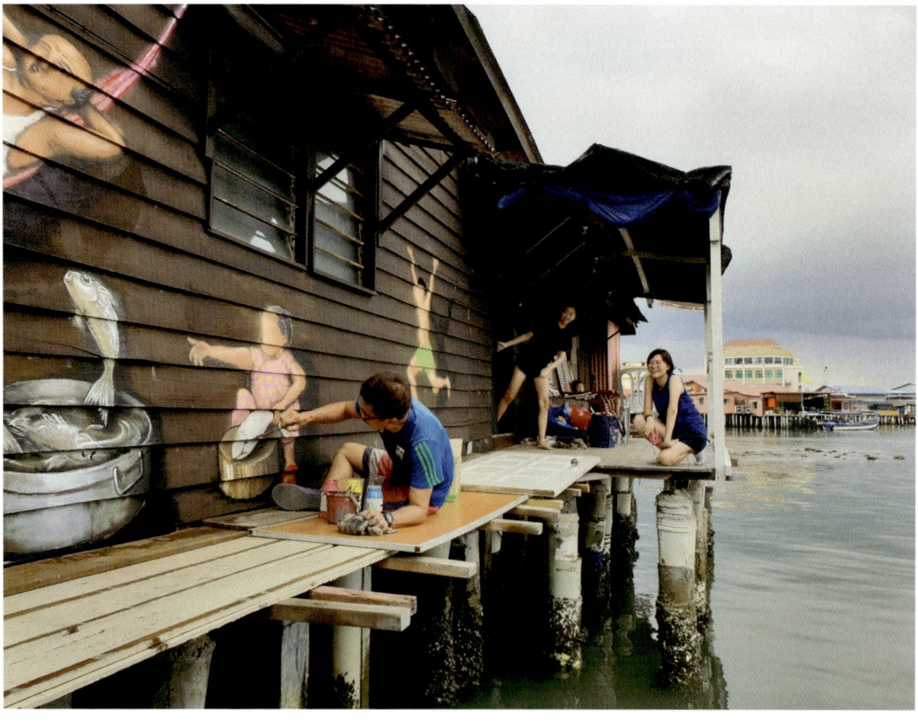

Chew Jetty, Penang, 2018.

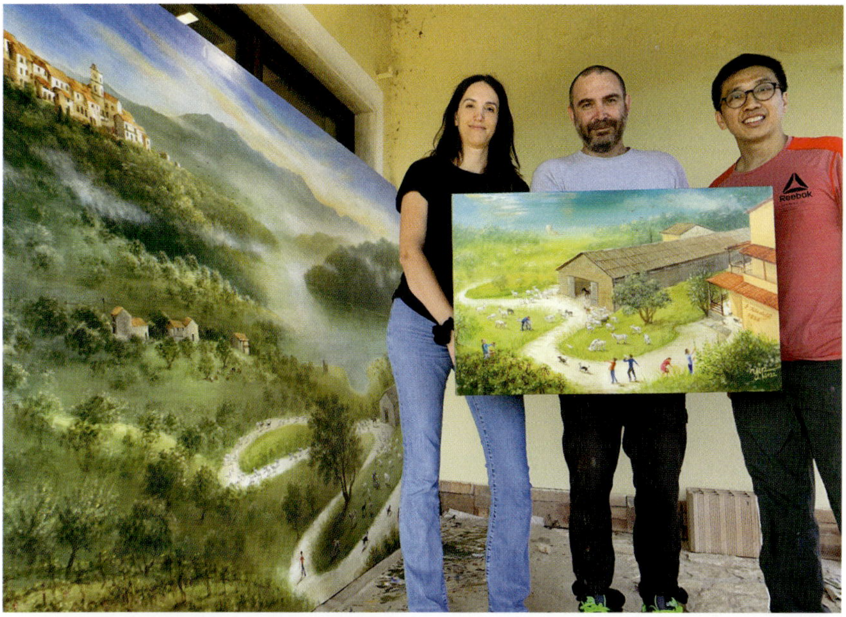

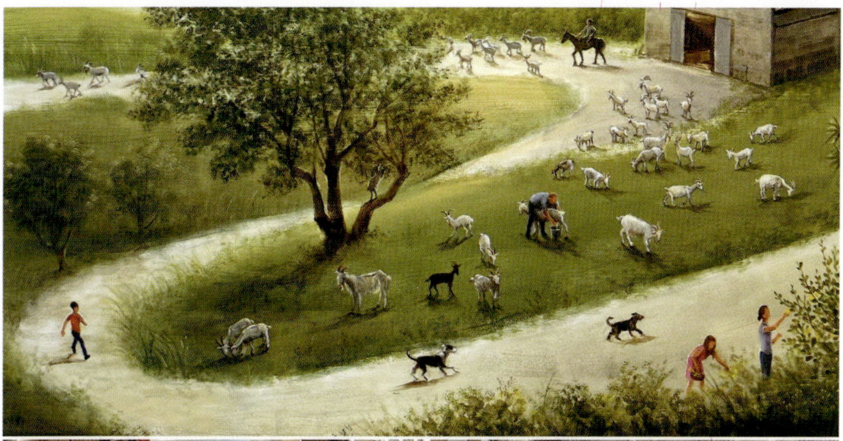

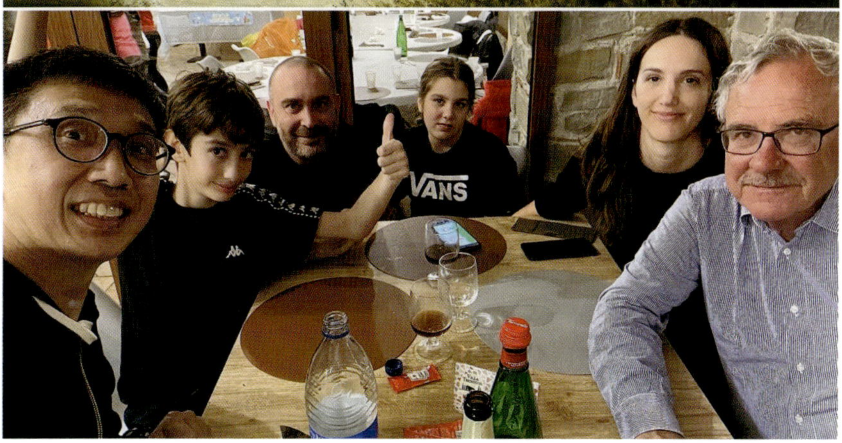

With host family in Italy, 2022.

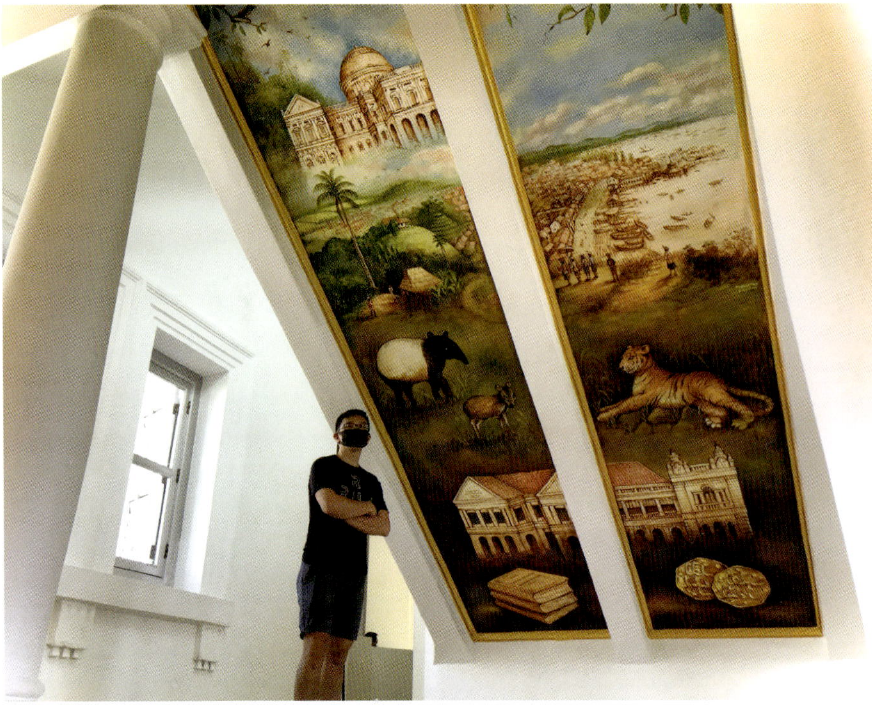

History of the National Museum of Singapore, 2017.

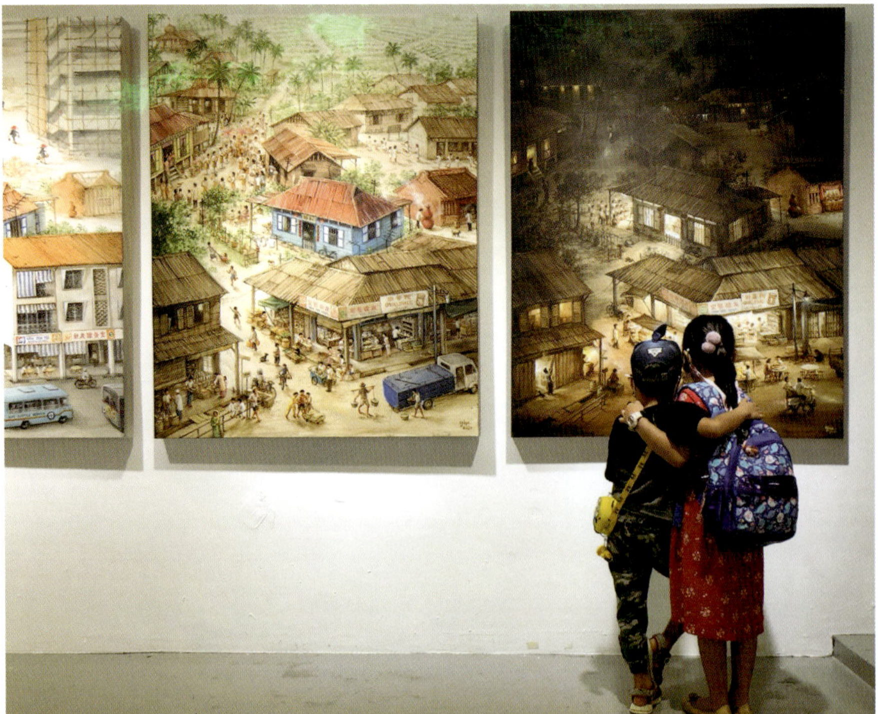

Jalan Singapura, 2020.

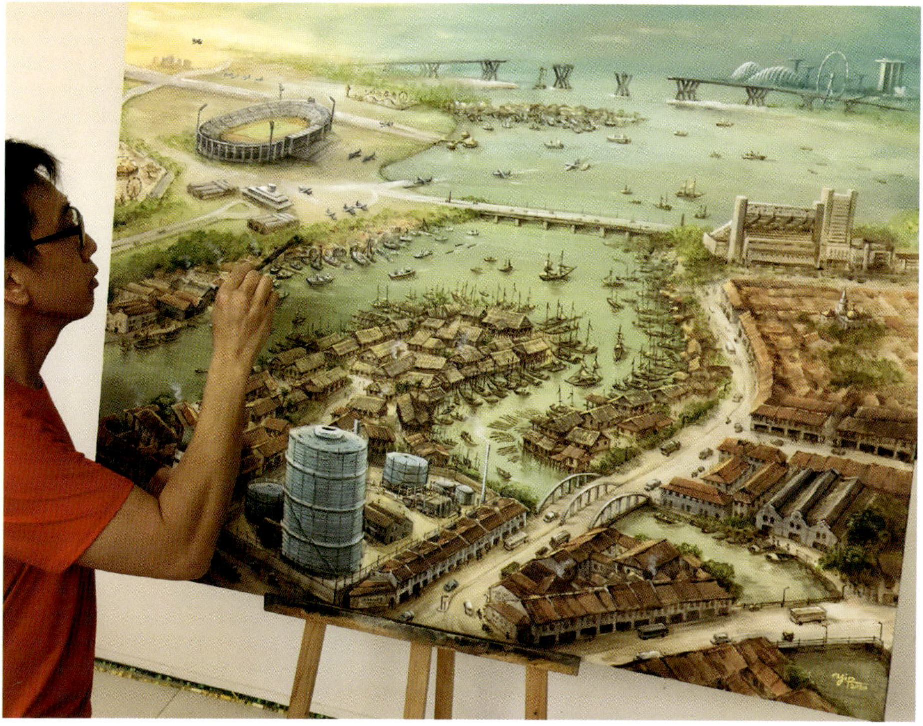

Kallang, 2020.

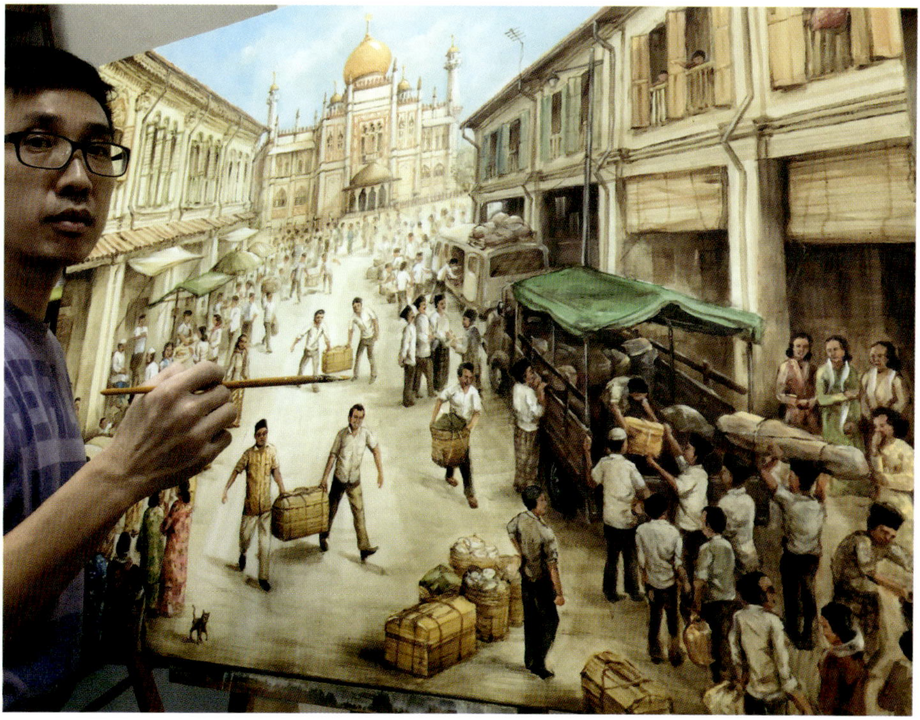

Preparing for the Haj, 2020.

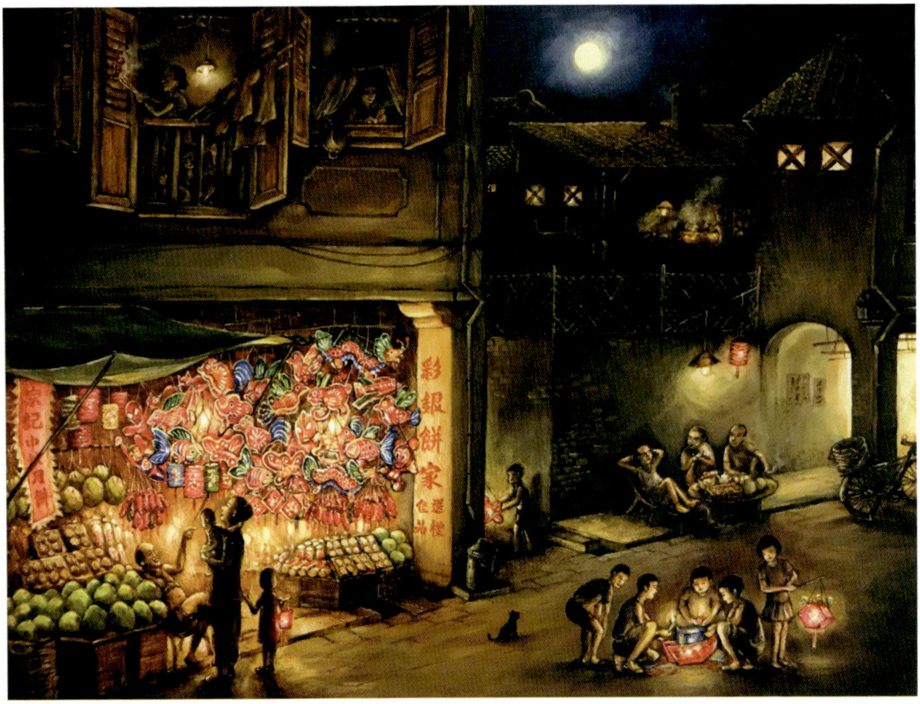

Mid-autumn Night, 2017.

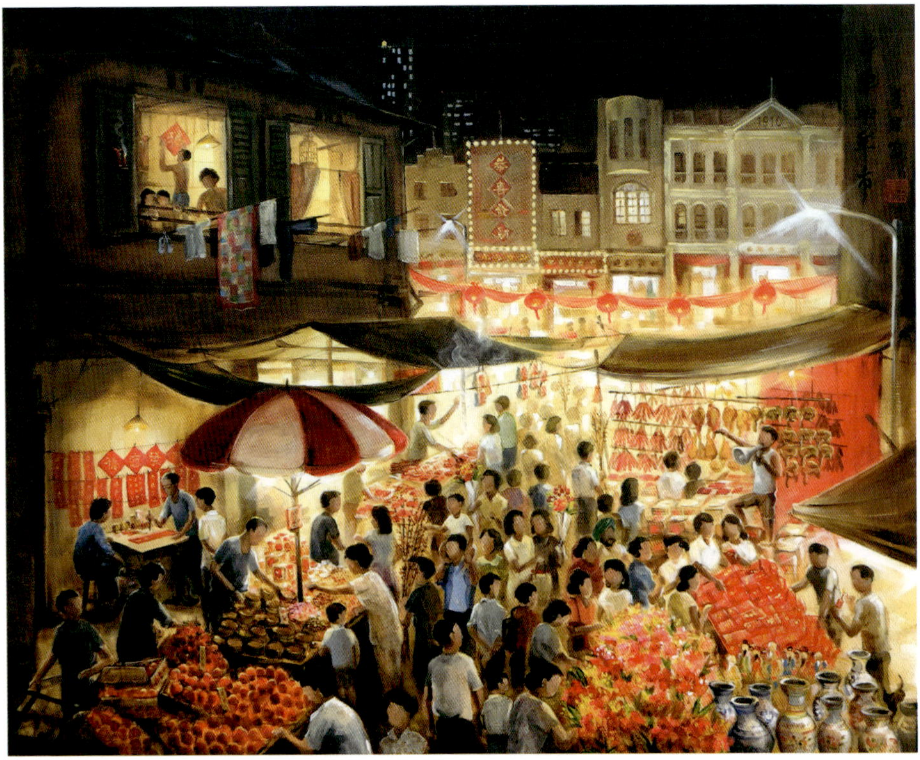

Chinatown Lunar New Year Bazaar, 2023.

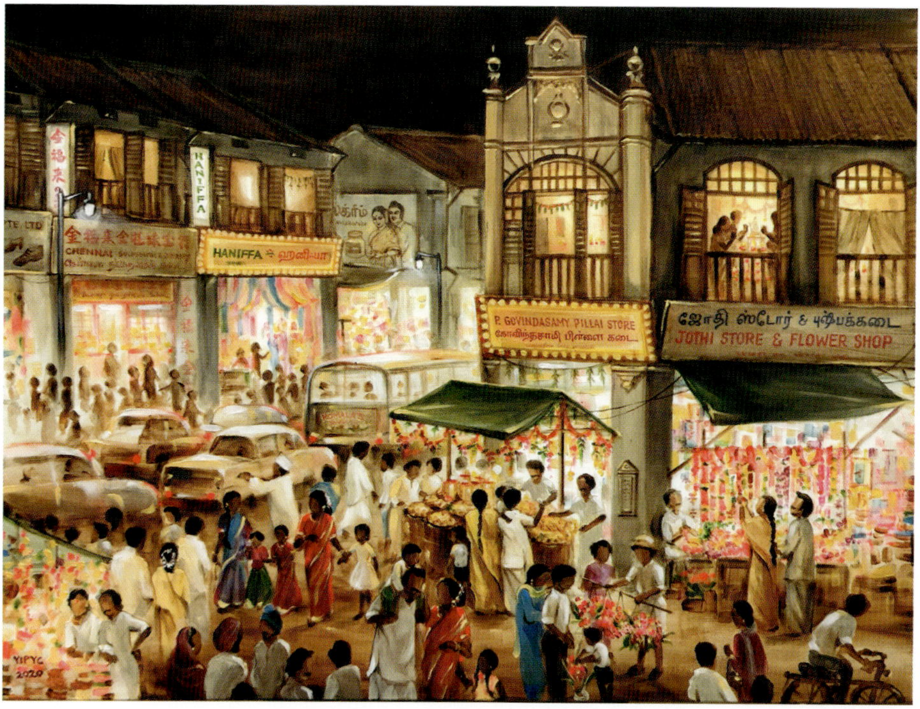

Deepavali Eve at Serangoon Road, 2020.

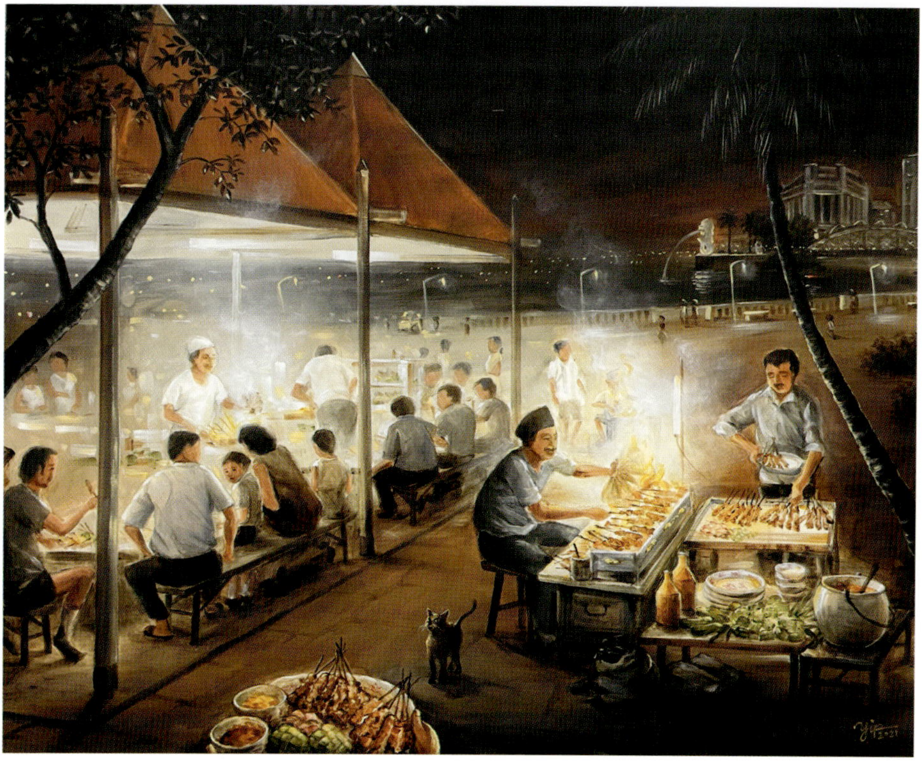

Satay Club, 2021.

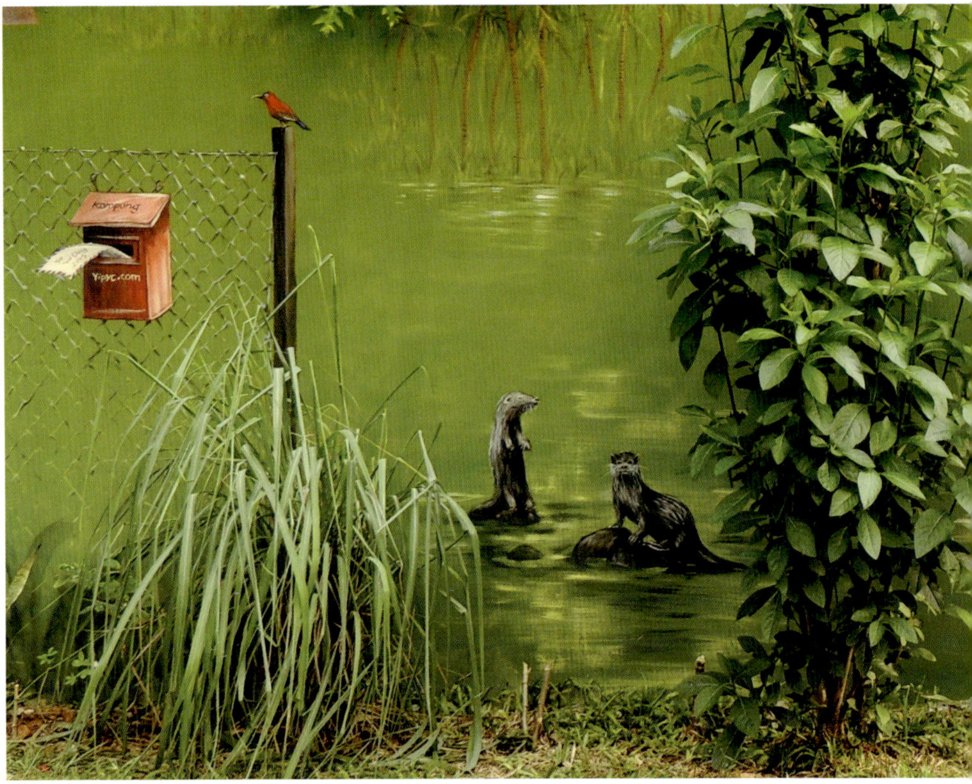

Yew Chong's first commissioned mural, *Kampung*, 2015.

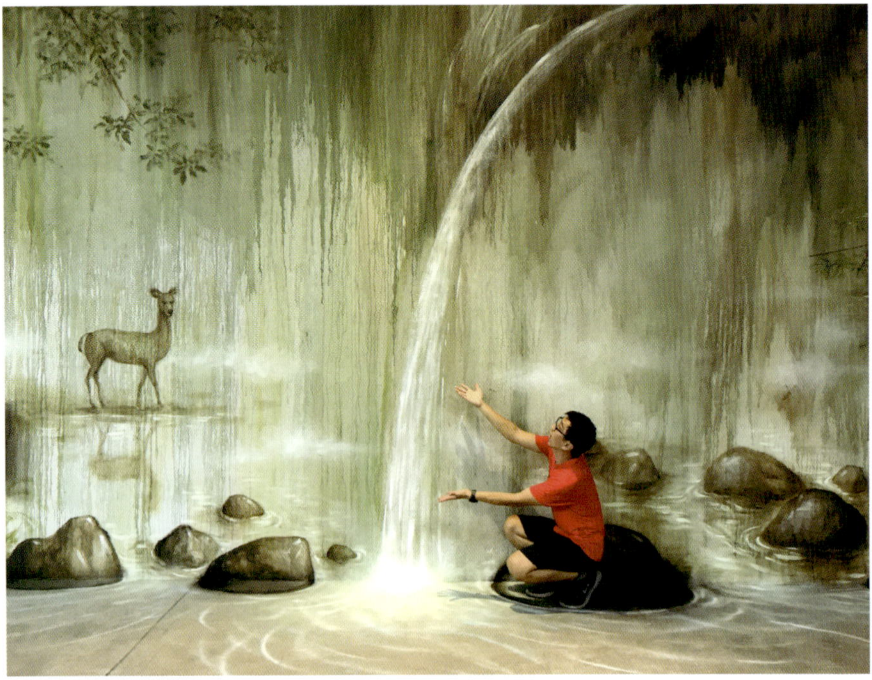

Hutan Lipur, Kuala Lumpur, 2018.

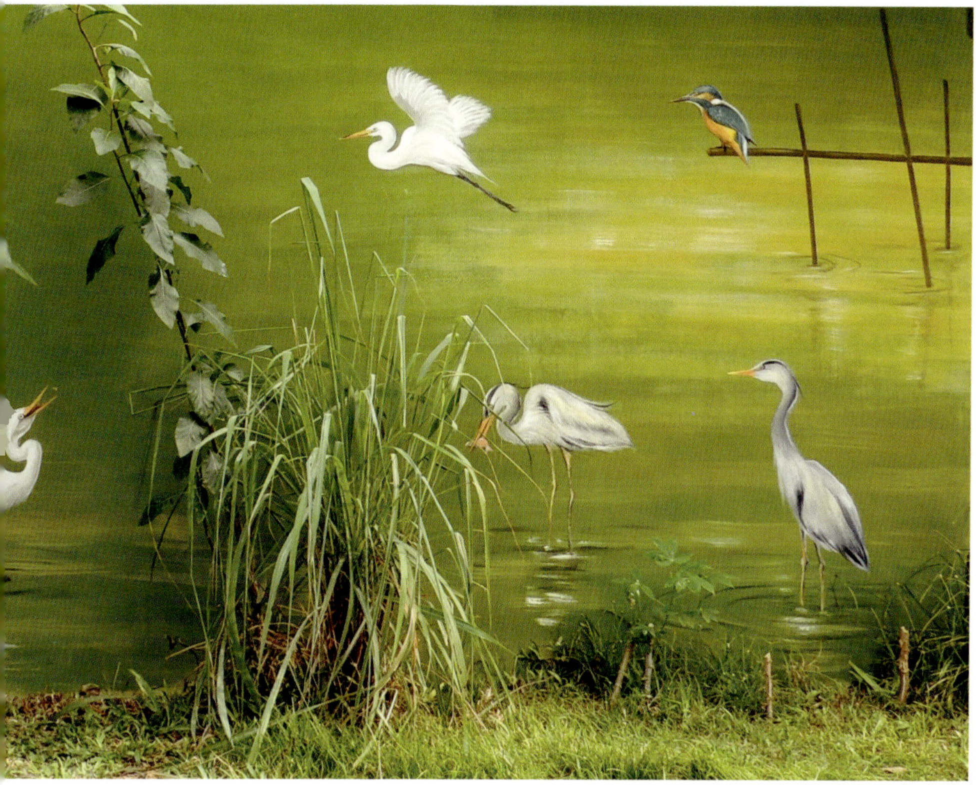

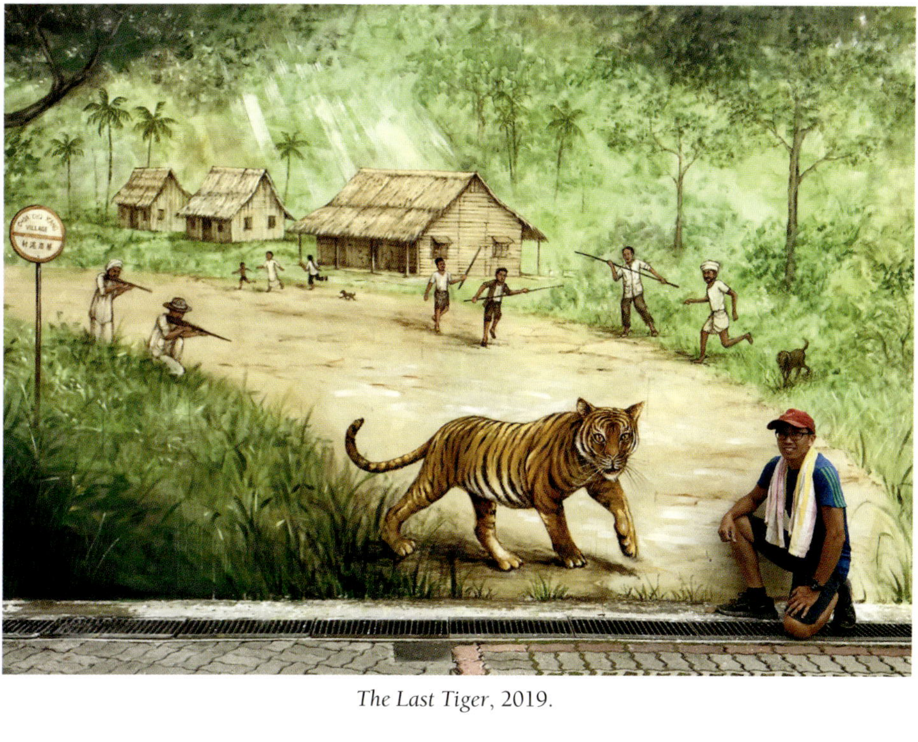

The Last Tiger, 2019.

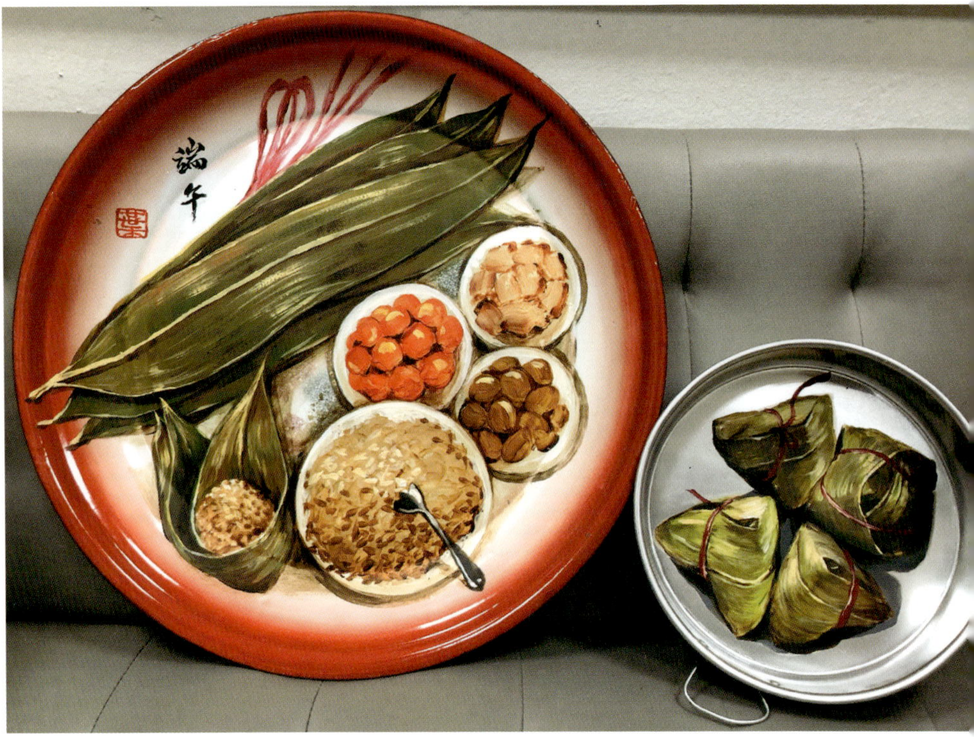

Dumpling Festival, 2020.

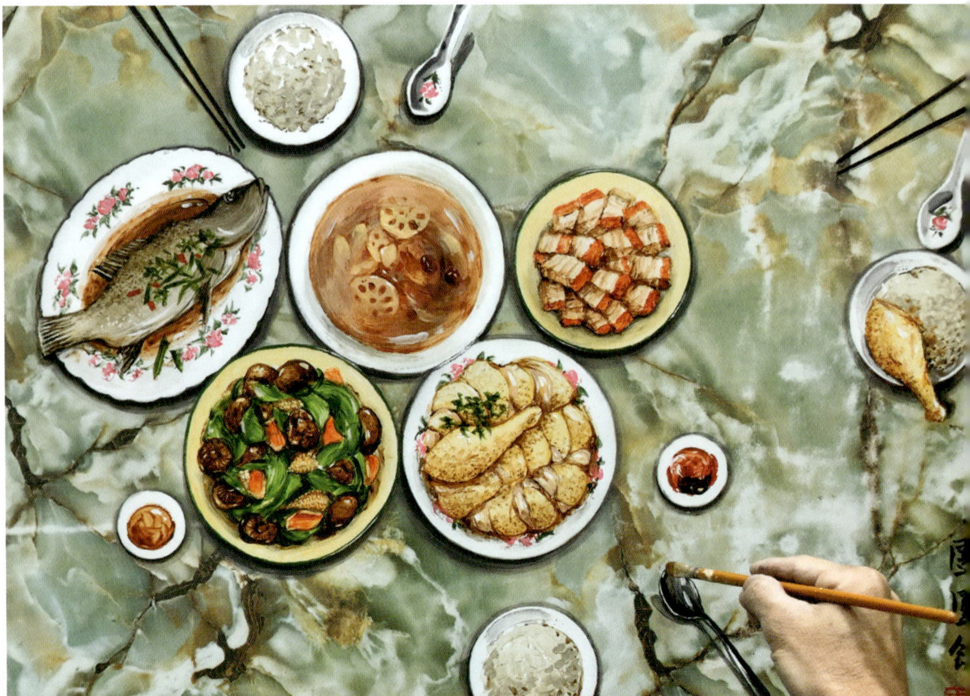

Reunion dinner, 2020.

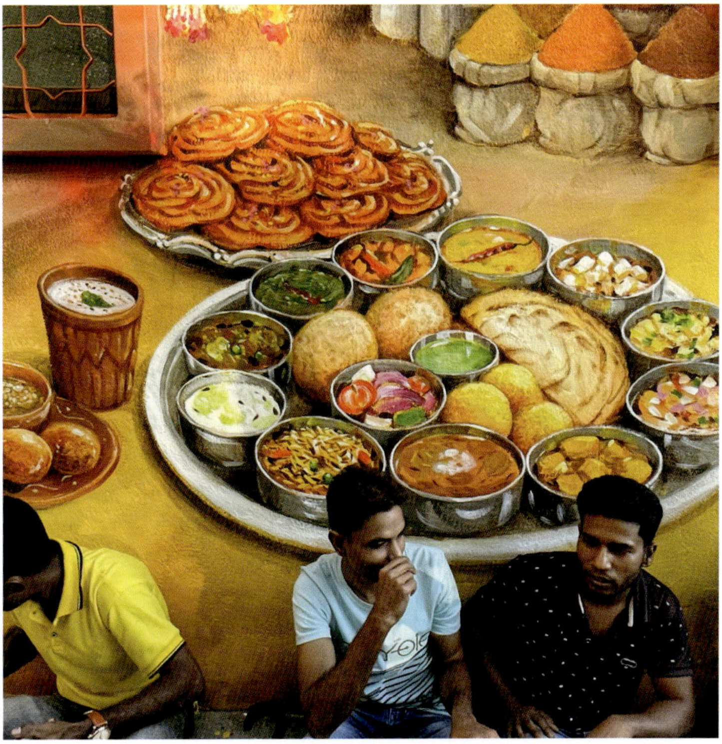

Mural at Arya Samaj, 2023.

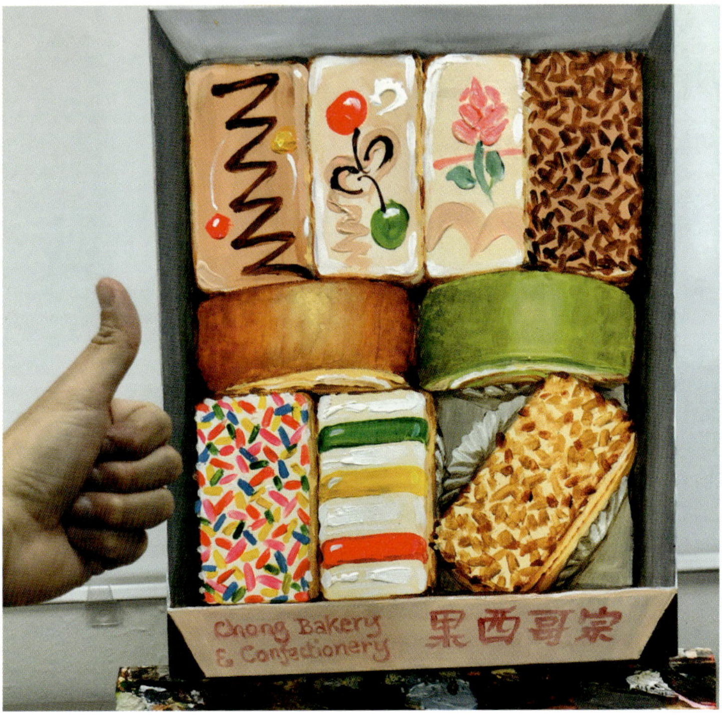

Chong Bakery and Confectionery, 2020.

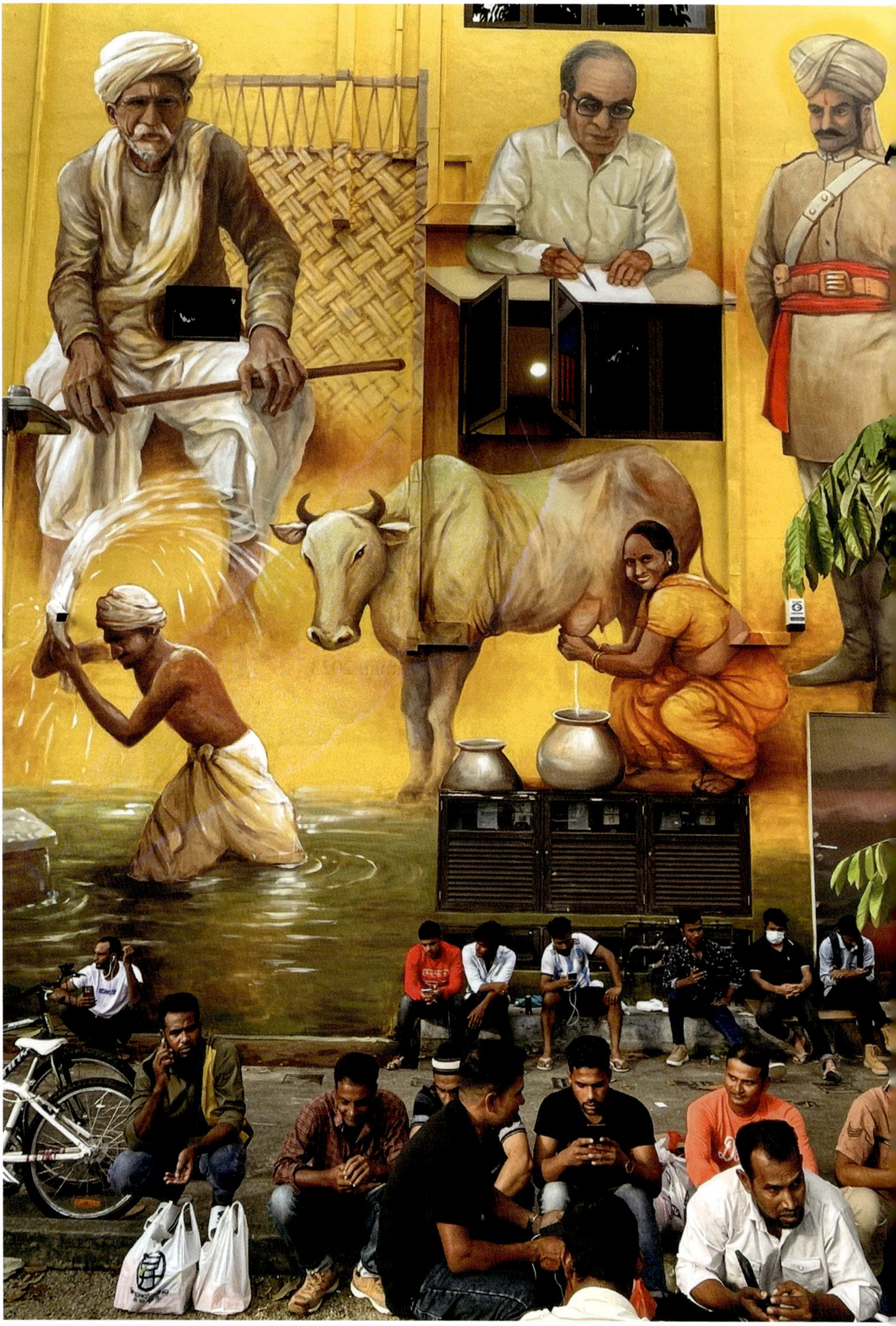

Mural at Arya Samaj, 2023.

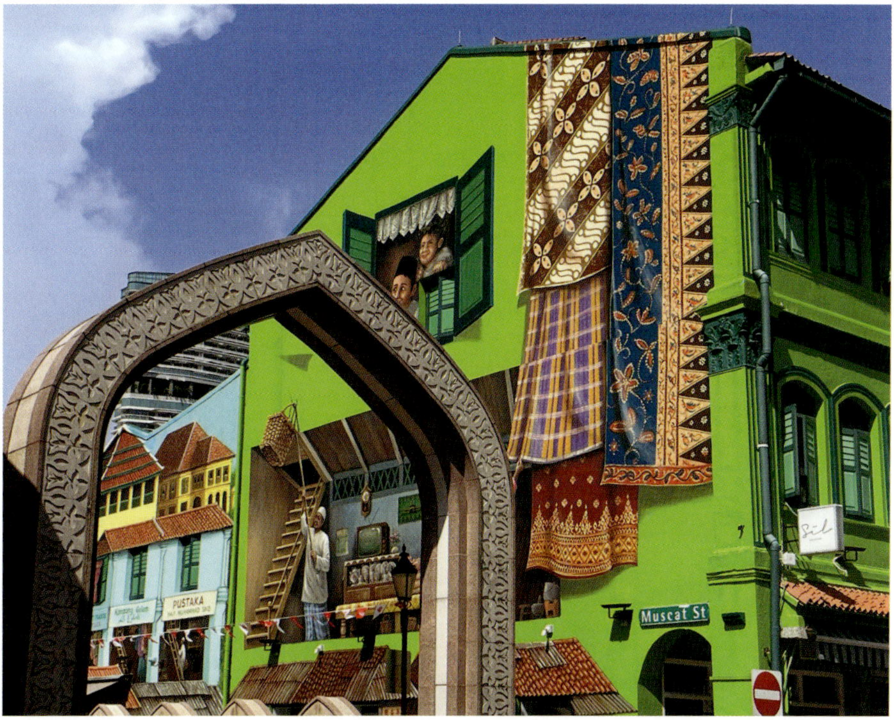

Kampong Gelam mural, 2023.

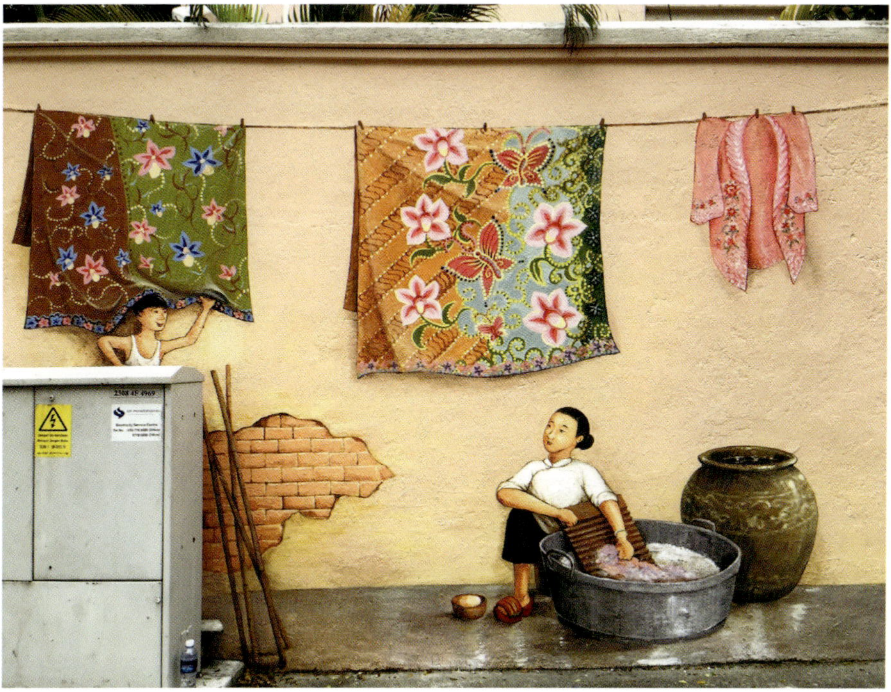

Amah, 2015. Yew Chong's first street mural.

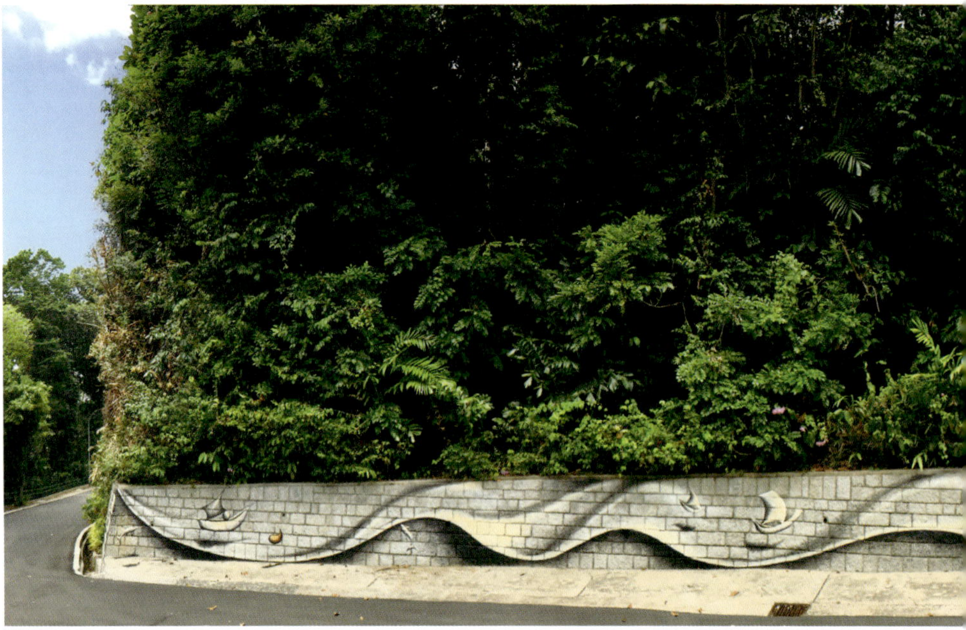

Waves of the Strait, 2019.

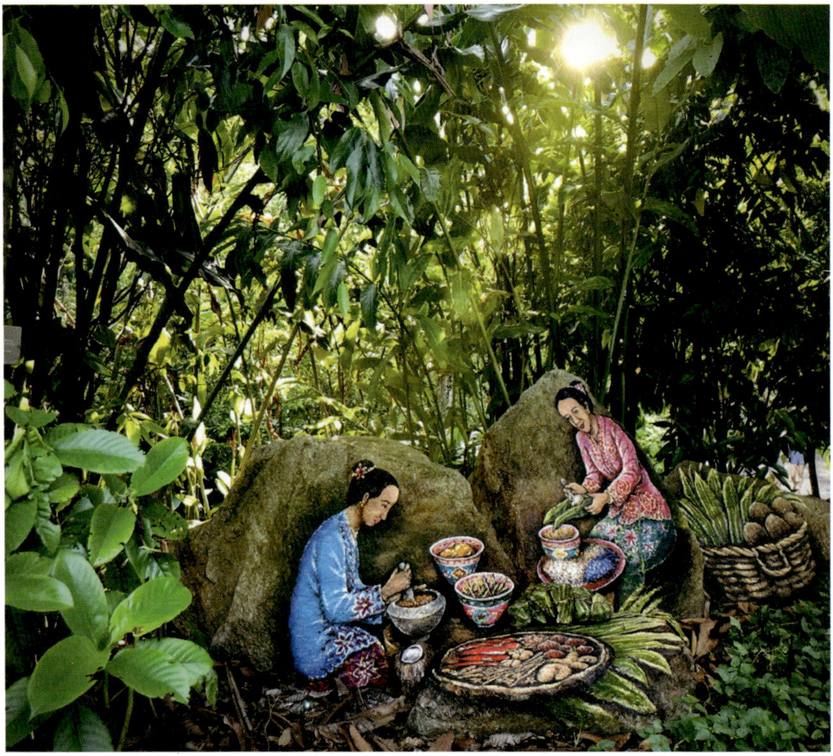

Botanic Gardens mural, 2018, in memory of Serene Koh. Serene commissioned the mural as a gift back to the Botanic Gardens for providing a healing space while she was convalescing from cancer. Serene passed six months after the mural was completed.

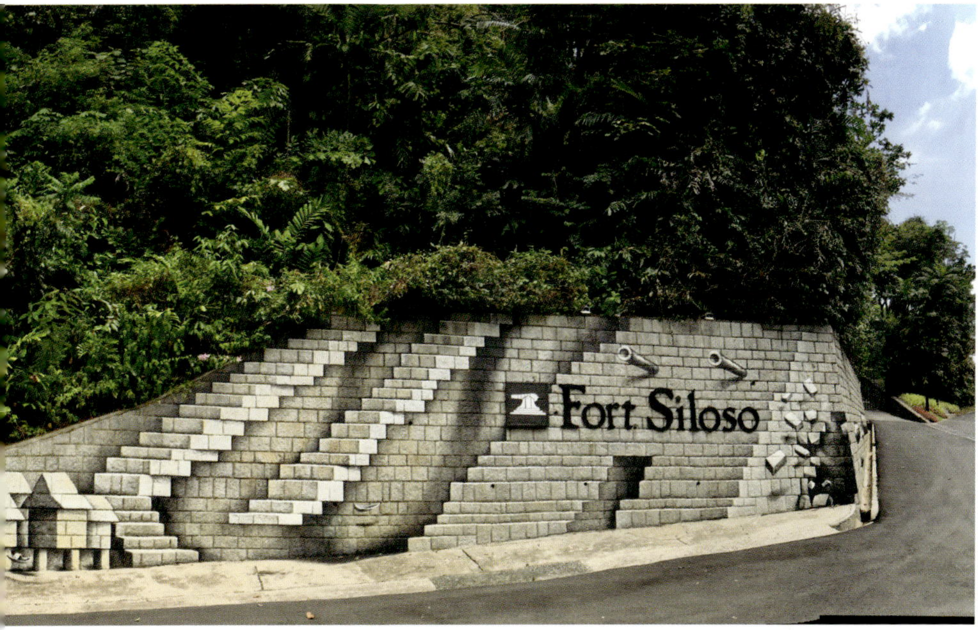

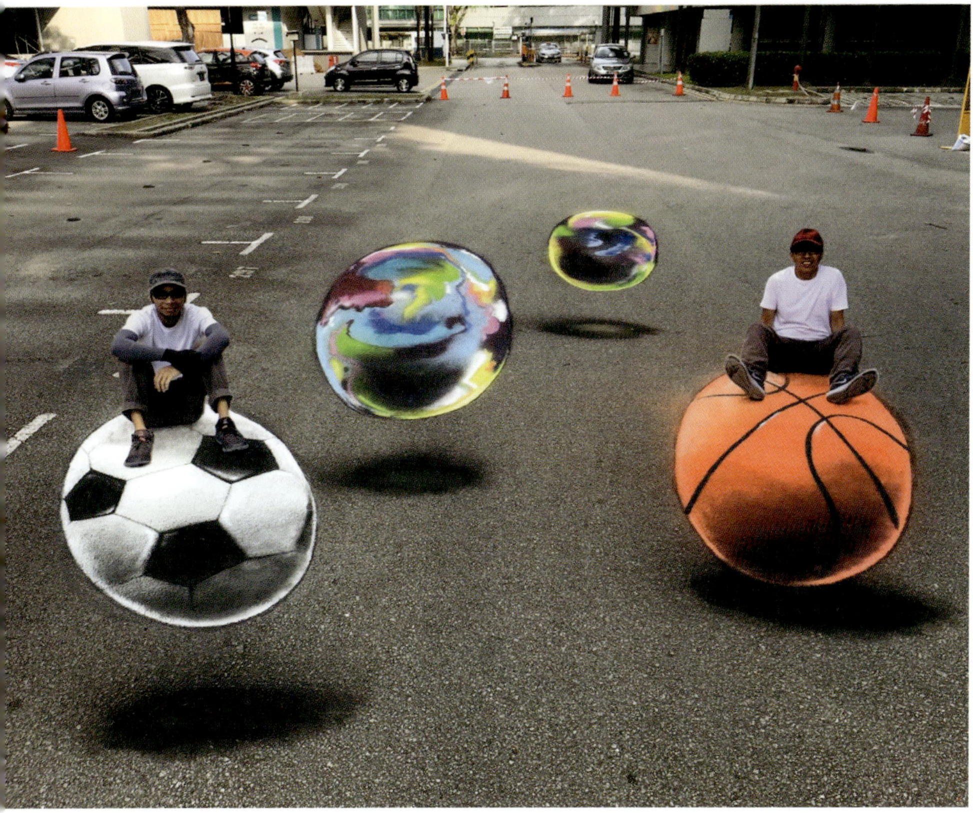

JTC Launchpad trial mural with TraseOne, 2019. Yew Chong painted this on his 50th birthday.

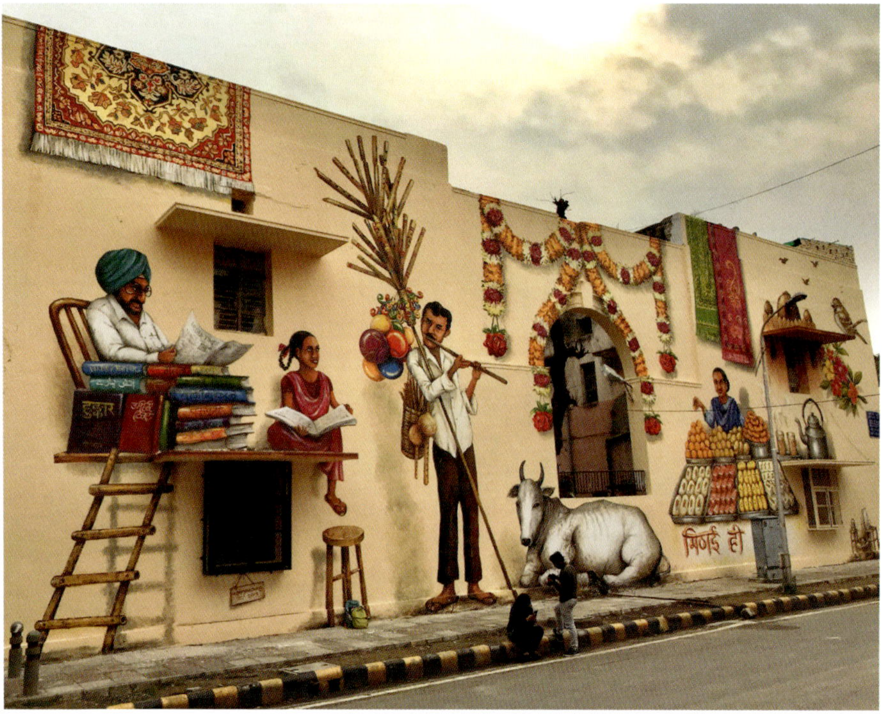

Impressions of Lodhi, New Delhi, 2019.

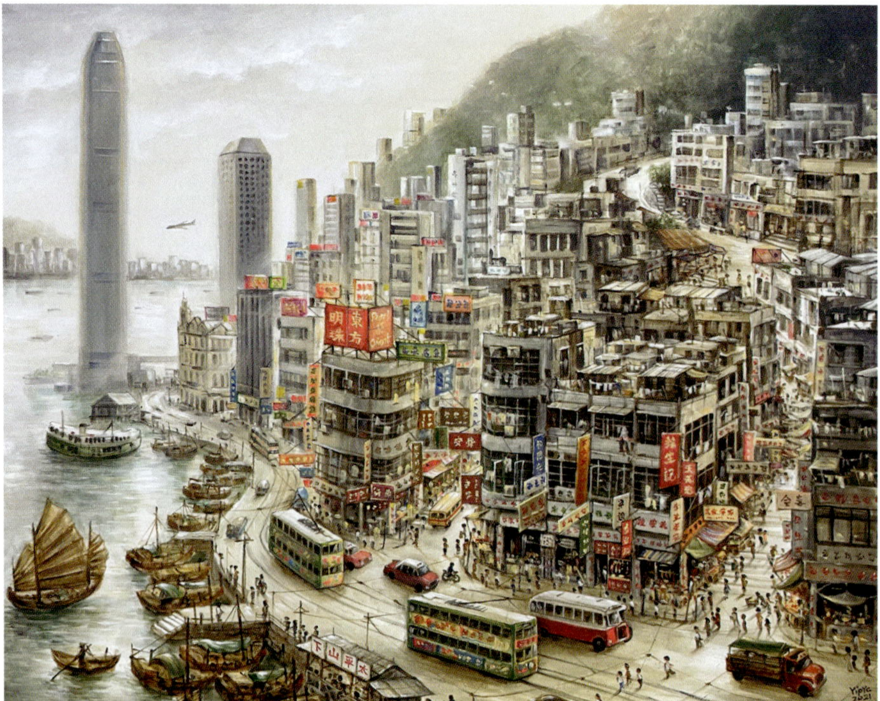

Below the Victoria Peak, 2021.

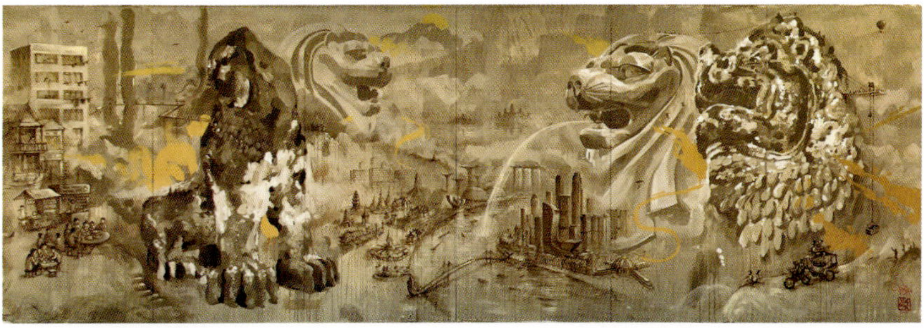

Cambodia-Singapore, 55 and Beyond, Phnom Penh, 2020. With Fonki.

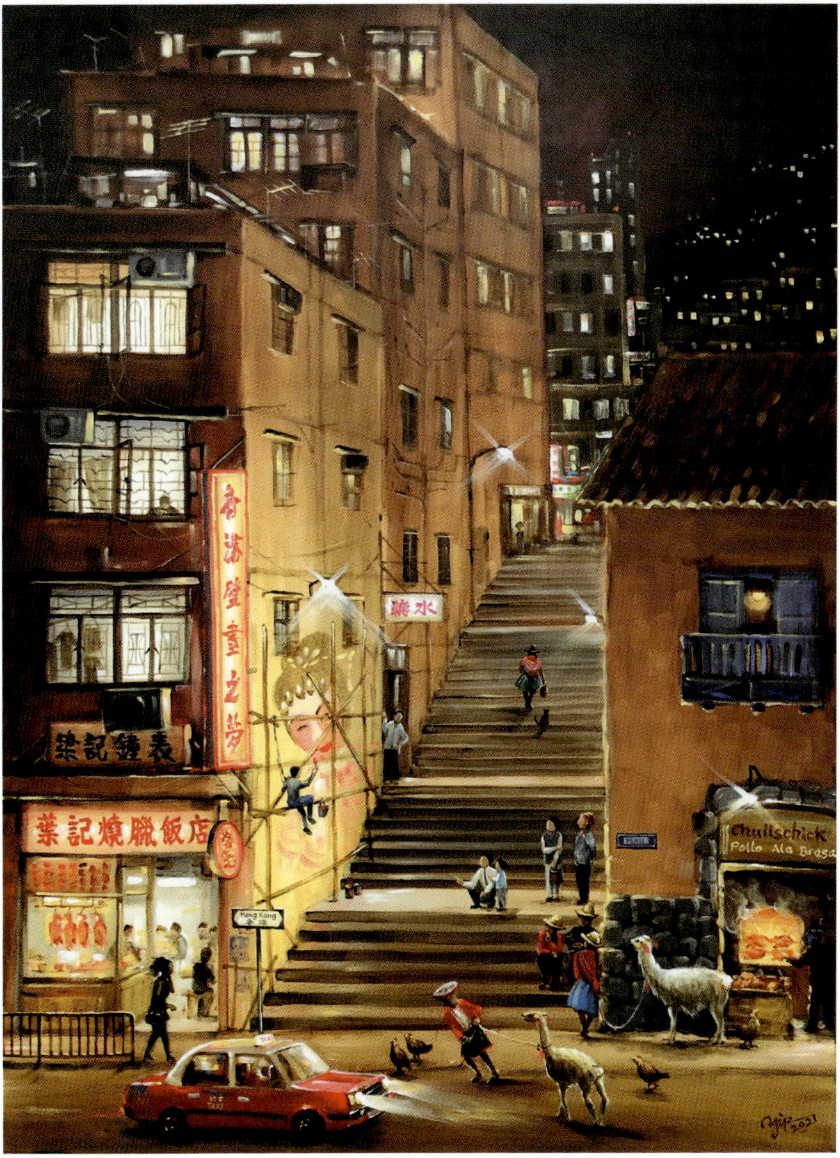

Peru in Hong Kong, 2021.

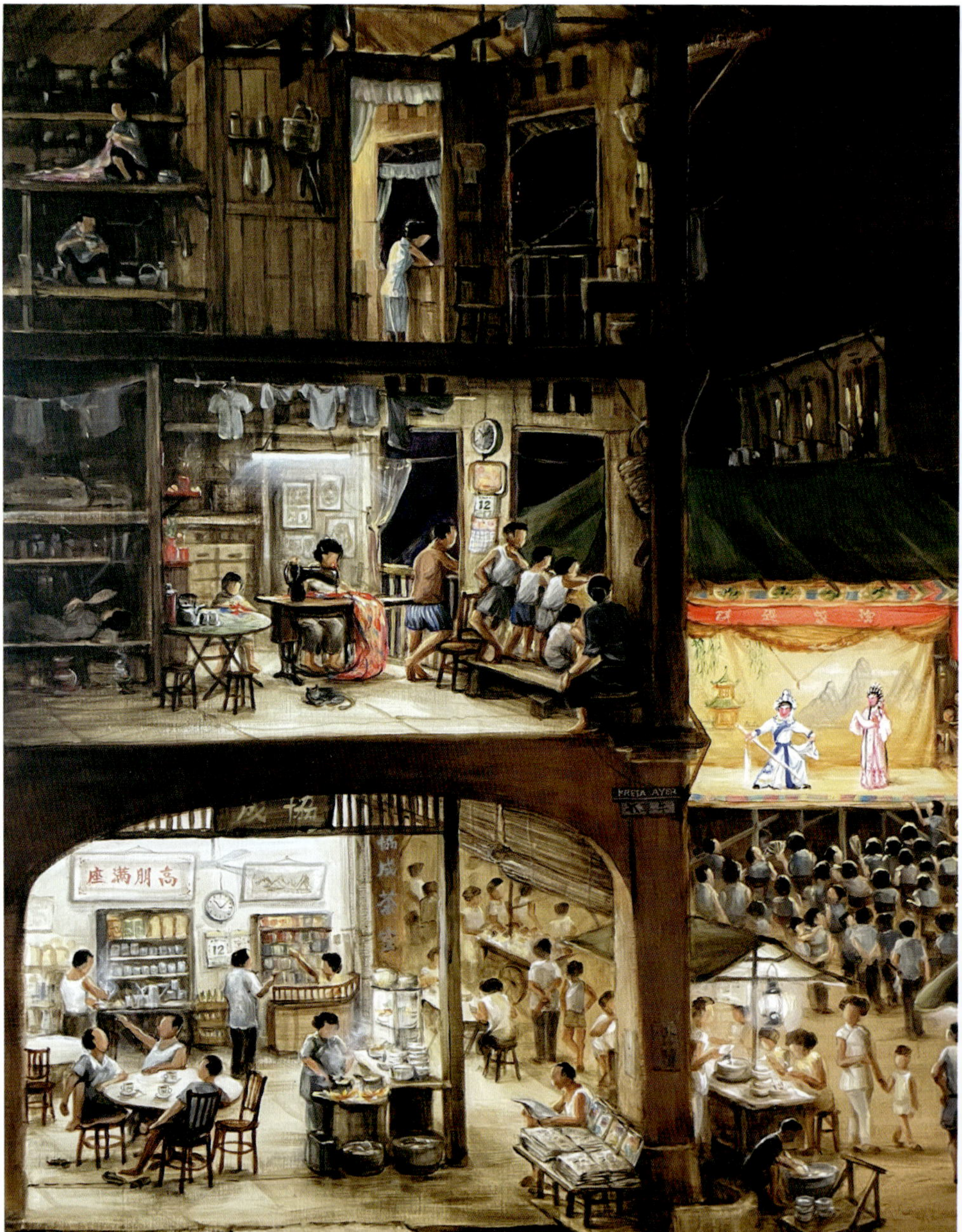

"Watching opera" of *I Paint My Singapore*, 2022.

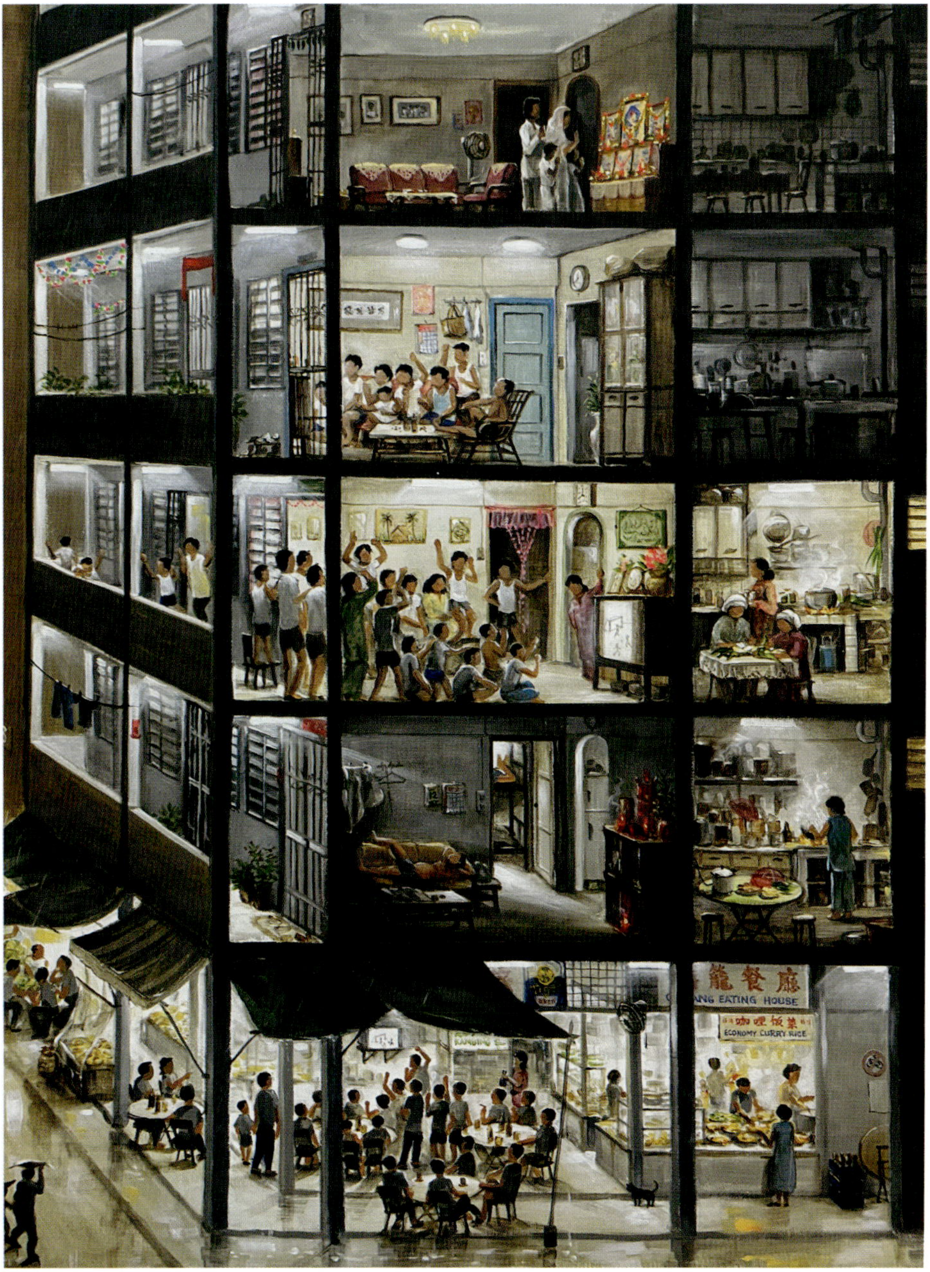

"Watching Malaysia Cup" of *I Paint My Singapore*, 2022.

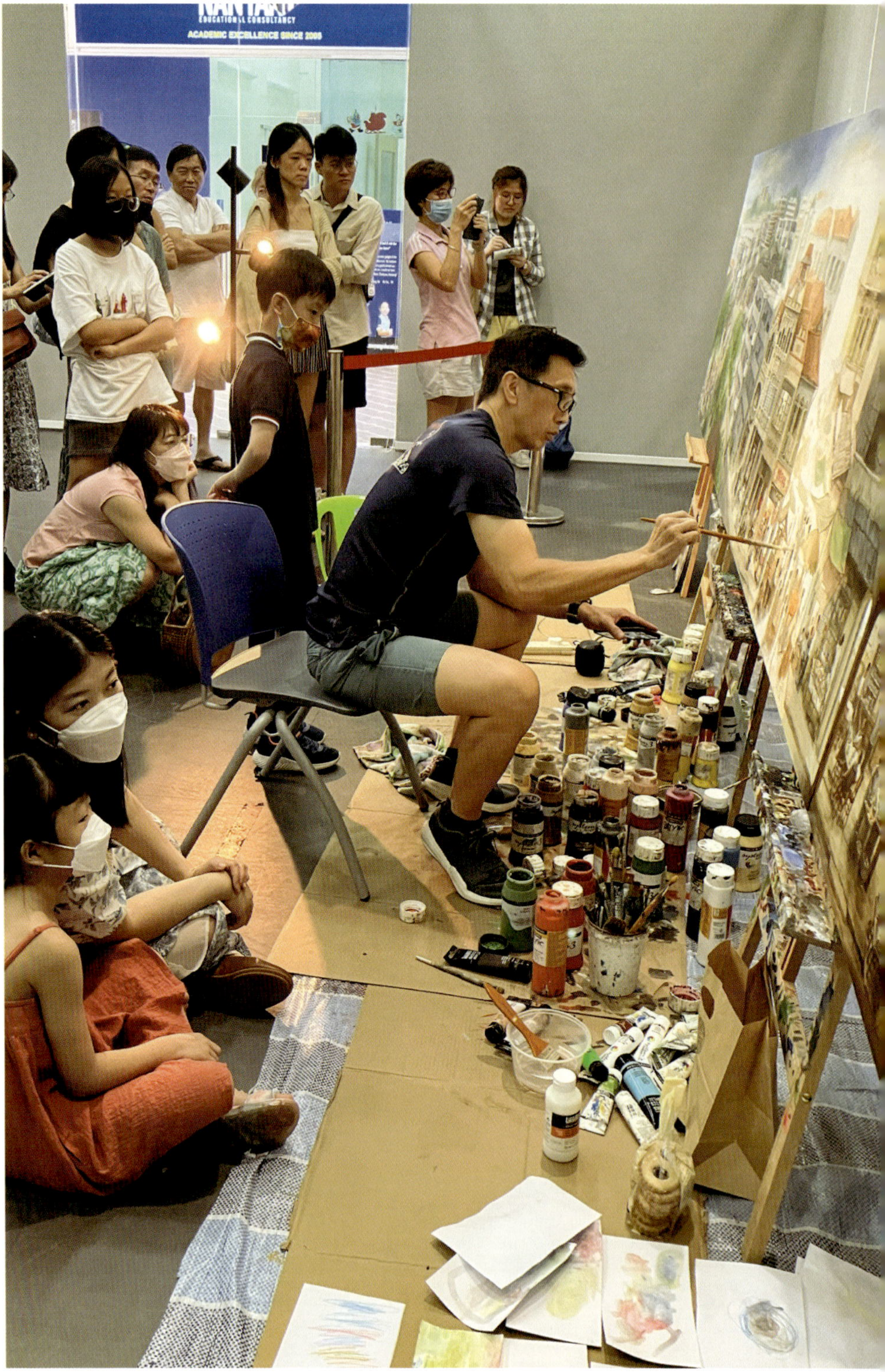

Painting the final panel of *I Paint My Singapore*, 2023.

CHAPTER 7

A People's Artist

His art is open and friendly; it literally allows me in.

He Is Genuine, So Is His Art

I first met them when we posed for photographs with chickens and ducks at Yew Chong's installation in Marina Bay. Then, they popped up again when he restored his mural at Tiong Bahru. "This family is one of my greatest supporters," Yew Chong texted. "They show up at every event of mine, and when I restored the mural at Tiong Bahru, they were there for seven hours; they brought food and drinks and also a birthday cake. If you want a good profile of the people who follow me, talk to them."

I want to understand why some Singaporeans are so taken by Yip Yew Chong. They are young and old, rich and not so rich, boys and girls, men and women, self-employed and professionals, Indians, Malays, Chinese and Eurasians, Singaporeans and foreigners; in other words, the people who like his work and support him cut across almost every demographic. I take up Yew Chong's suggestion and contact Faith.

Faith and Charles run a consulting company and have four kids, ages nine, seven, five, and two. When she finds out I am writing a book on Yew Chong, she invites me over to her apartment for dinner. "You can meet my family, and we would be more than happy to talk about Yew Chong and his art," she texts back.

Her apartment, on a high floor, has a panoramic view of eastern Singapore, including the prized sea view. I arrive to a boisterous welcome from the four kids; each has drawn a picture for me to express their joy that I have come to interview them about the artist they idolise. When we finally settle down in the dining room, all four, including the two-year-old, sit obediently; I can see excitement dancing in their eyes.

"We were looking for interesting places for our babywearing photoshoots, and these kids you see here were the models," Faith begins, standing behind the two-year-old. "We needed places that told stories, especially the rich cultural heritage of not just the locale but also the country. I found out about Yip Yew Chong and his murals from a blog I read. So, we set out to look for the murals. It was September 2015, and Yip Yew Chong had just completed his murals, *Ah Mah* and *The Barber* at Everton Road. We didn't know then that we would all become devout fans."

"I was just one year old." Matthew, the seven-year-old, laughs, showing a row of milk-white teeth.

"And the murals turned out perfect for the shoot," Faith sounds enthusiastic, but maintains her soothing, calm voice. "Not only were they colourful, they told stories of Singapore's past, how it was back then. They provided a suitable backdrop for the products. These advertisements would be used in the US, Europe, Australia and Asia." She pauses and looks at her youngest in front of her. "But we didn't get a chance to meet the artist because he was only painting part-time then, only on the weekends. We, and I mean every kid in this home, and the two of us, 'followed' him from mural to mural, across Chinatown, and slowly across Singapore. By the time we finally met him, which was last year when he painted the mural on Temple Street, we had had all four kids, and everyone was a fan of his."

Marcus, the oldest, tugs at my hand. "We go to see *The Letter Writer* every year during Chinese New Year, because it is in Chinatown." His almost round face breaks into a beam. "We have seen 36 murals!" he says with a boast in his voice.

"Yes, the kids have visited 36 of his murals in Singapore," Charles' voice is low, but carries the same excitement as his son. "There are many places they enjoy visiting, the zoo, the bird park or crossing over to Sentosa Island, but nothing beats a trip to Yew Chong's murals. It's many levels of interest for the kids, his murals have inspired them to draw and paint; then, it is a history lesson of the subject matter the murals depict, and also a geography lesson of the places they were painted. Honestly, not just for the kids, but the two of us as well."

"What touches us is," Faith pauses and composes herself. "We take photographs of the kids with his murals. Over the years, as we explore more and more murals, we also see how the kids, each one of them, grow up. The first mural, the eldest was two; he is now nine. The murals don't change, the kids do, taller. But one thing stays constant, the happy faces of the kids. They are always happy in the pictures around his murals."

I turn to the kids, all looking at me with unblinking eyes. "What is it about Yip Yew Chong's art that attracts you to them? One by one. You first." I look right at Marcus and smile.

"When I see *kor kor* Yew Chong's art, it is very realistic." Marcus pauses to breathe. "It has a lot of details, and each detail has a story behind it. A story from the past." He stops and tries to remember, either what he has prepared or picturing the murals in his head. "It is so realistic; it is like a time machine. I can go back and relive the past again." He pauses again, then decides his answer is okay and nods at me.

Matthew is impatient and decides to speak, "The murals are realistic, and it has a lot of details that tell us what his childhood is like. And the older generation can also tell the younger generation this is where they grew up."

Marcus looks at his brother. "So, so yes, I agree with him."

We all laugh.

When I look at Macayla, who is five; she just smiles at me.

"Go on," Faith encourages. "Tell *kor kor* Tai Ho what you told me. You said so much before he came."

Macayla continues to smile without saying a word.

Faith turns to her youngest, Matthea. "Why do you like *kor kor* Yew Chong's paintings? Tell me what you told me earlier."

She looks directly at her mom and smiles with her baby teeth. "… because I like."

We all laugh again, and suddenly all the kids talk at the same time. "One at a time," I remind them.

Faith looks at me now. "The kids, all of them, stayed with Yew Chong when he restored the mural at Tiong Bahru, for seven hours, from late morning through the afternoon to early evening. They saw how hard he worked and that made them appreciate his art even more.

I think that made them realise that anything good requires hard work."

"We didn't know that seven hours had passed," Matthew chips in, thrilled that he can relive that day with me. "We thought it was only… 30 minutes."

"I thought we were going there for an hour," Charles laughs. "We ended up with no lunch; it was like a picnic with no food that did not end."

I turn to the kids, "Why did you stay so long?"

"We want to help him pack up," Matthew offers. "And he was patient, so we want to be patient too. When he needed help, we helped him, like throwing away his paints and helping him hold his ladder when he was climbing. We like him because he is very friendly."

Faith carries Matthew up from the chair; it seems Matthew has said something she wants to emphasise. "Even though he has achieved so much, he is still so approachable, friendly, and so sincere."

"He is a people's artist, very popular," I add. "Widely followed on social media and mainstream media."

"Yet so unassuming," says Faith. "He entertained and talked to everyone while he painted. He would have finished restoring the mural if it wasn't for the crowd and the fans talking to him, taking pictures with him."

"For the younger generation, his art allows them a glimpse of the situation of Singapore in the past," Charles decides to join in again. "They never experienced what their parents did; the murals helped them understand what their parents went through, how things were like. Yew Chong is firstly a storyteller, then an artist. A lot of the stories tell of what his childhood was like. For the older folks who had lived

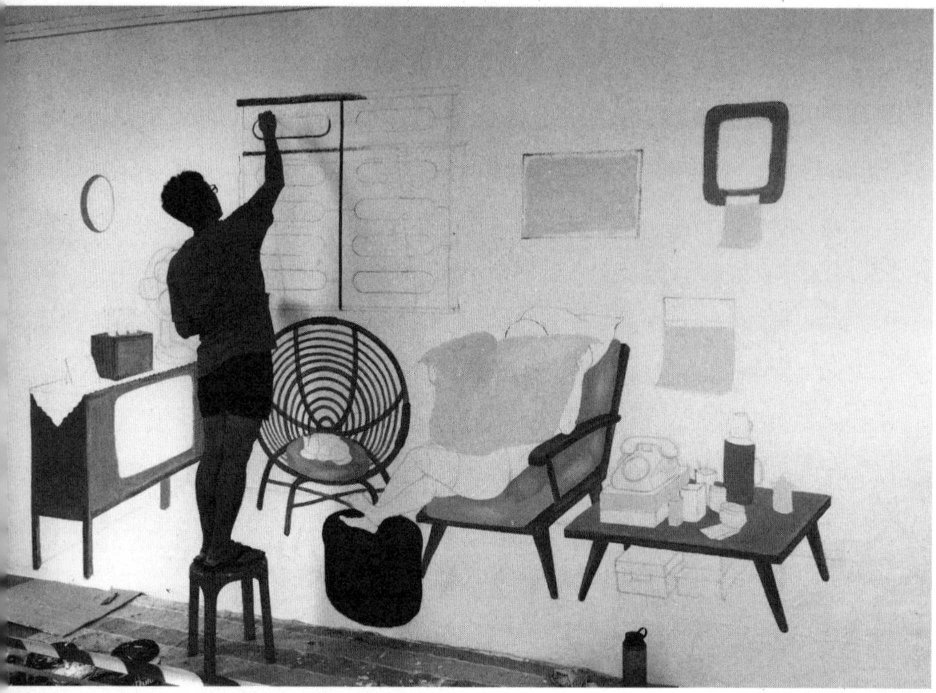

Creating home *mural in Tiong Bahru, 2016.*

through these experiences, these images invoke certain emotions. You won't see these now, so seeing these images make them happy. Young or old, we all relate to his art."

"It's so important to remember our past," Faith reinforces. "We are where we are today because of what we have in the past."

Charles said *relatable*. This is the question I want the family to answer. "Why do you think his art is so relatable?"

"He knows what to include in his art that relates to the layman." Charles has probably thought about this before. "Details of this and that that other artists may find too ordinary and unimportant. But he wants to include them because that was his life, like the calendar, the clock, the kitchen with the stove, the cat, things that invoke the everyday of the recent past. This honesty, his sincerity in revealing even the most mundane, the most ordinary, make it very relatable. He is genuine, and so is his art. You can just feel it. Not just Singaporeans, but foreigners find the art relatable too."

"Before the pandemic, whenever we visited his murals in Chinatown, we see tour groups there." Faith smiles. "The tourists asked so many questions; they took so many pictures."

I look at the drawings the kids have done for me. "This is your

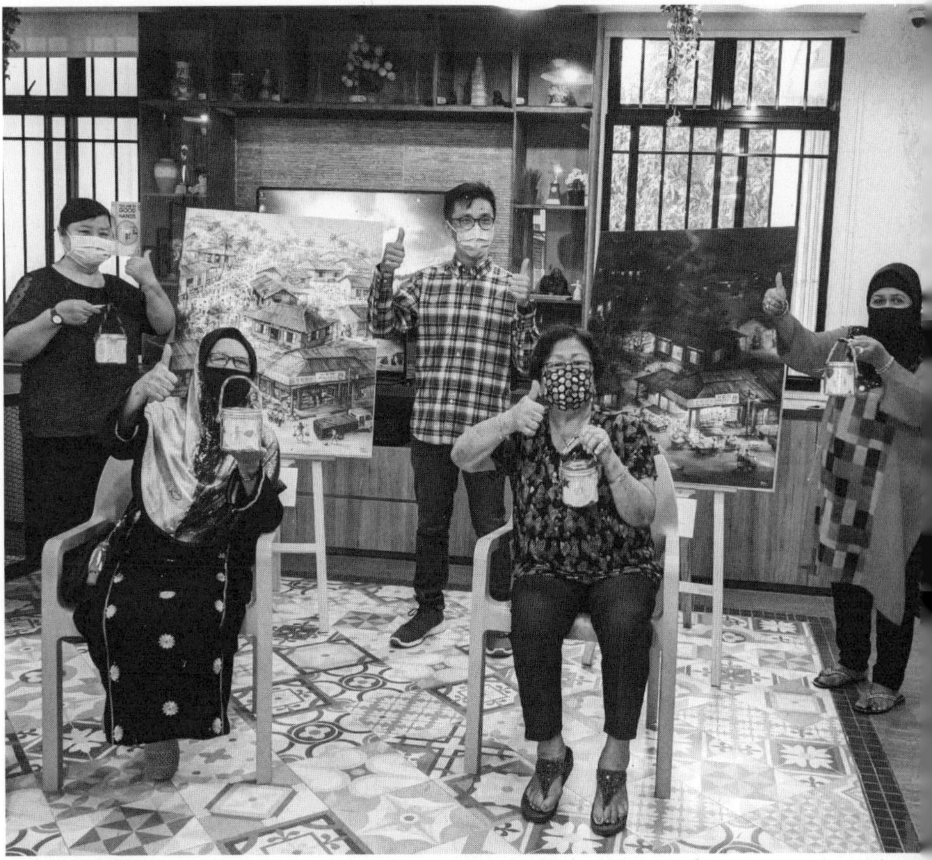

The artworks can serve multiple purposes. Replicas of the artworks toured various senior care centres as part of an art therapy program.

drawing?" I ask Marcus. "Is it inspired by Yew Chong?"

"Yes!" he shouts. "I want to be an artist like him when I grow up."

"Me too!" his younger brother shouts louder.

"After they met Yew Chong, whenever they go out, they bring their sketchbooks." Faith's eyes are dancing now, like her kids. "We are happy they take drawing and painting seriously."

Happy. An apt word to describe the young family. The children insist on showing me their bedrooms, where there are more drawings and artworks on the walls. As I marvel at the art, I tell myself, Yew Chong would be proud to know what an influence he has on them.

Effortlessly Includes Every Race

Singapore's Chinatown is the only Chinatown in the world to boast a Buddhist temple, a mosque, and a Hindu temple along a single street. Perhaps being a native of Chinatown, Yew Chong effortlessly includes every race in his art. "I grew up in Chinatown, on Sago Lane, then Smith Street; most of my art are inspired by my memories of Old Singapore, 30 to 40 years ago. Then, Singapore looked like this."

I have asked Yew Chong for lunch to verify some facts, and after lunch, we walk around his murals, and today, I find myself talking about race. We are right in front of a mural that looks like it is split right in the middle, the *Lion Dance Head Maker* on the left side, and the *Mamakshop* on the right. Lion dance is Chinese, the *Mamakshop* Tamil. An Indian boy and a Chinese boy are playing drums outside the *Lion Dance Head Maker* shop. Is he conscious of this racial mixing? Has he done it deliberately to be politically correct?

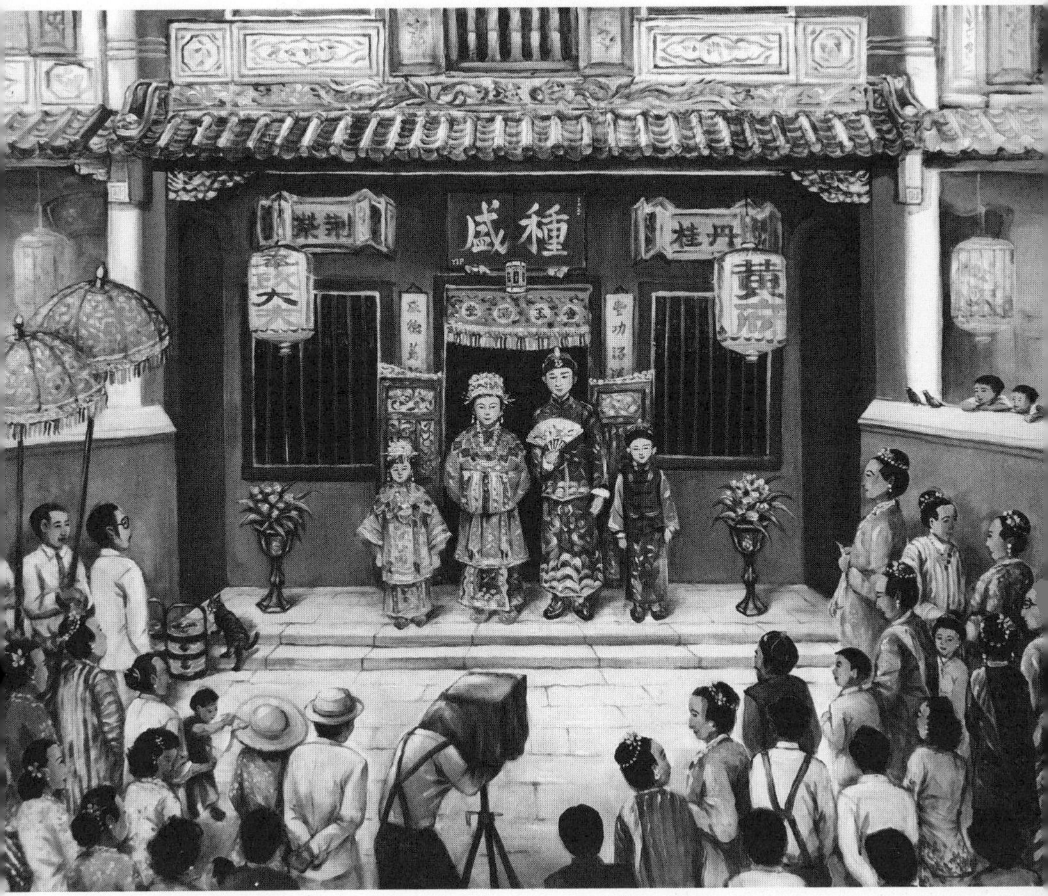

Peranakan wedding, 2020.

"Oh, they are real people!" he says with a laugh in his voice. "Whether it is the paper mask seller, or Abdul Kadir, this Tamil Muslim manning the *mamakshop*. Look at the sweets and knick-knacks, I used to go to his shop and buy them. He taught me my first Tamil words — *kaalai vanakkam* — which means good morning. My art often depicts multiracialism; I draw what I see everywhere. This is how we live in Singapore. I've painted all the races in my murals, including Eurasians,

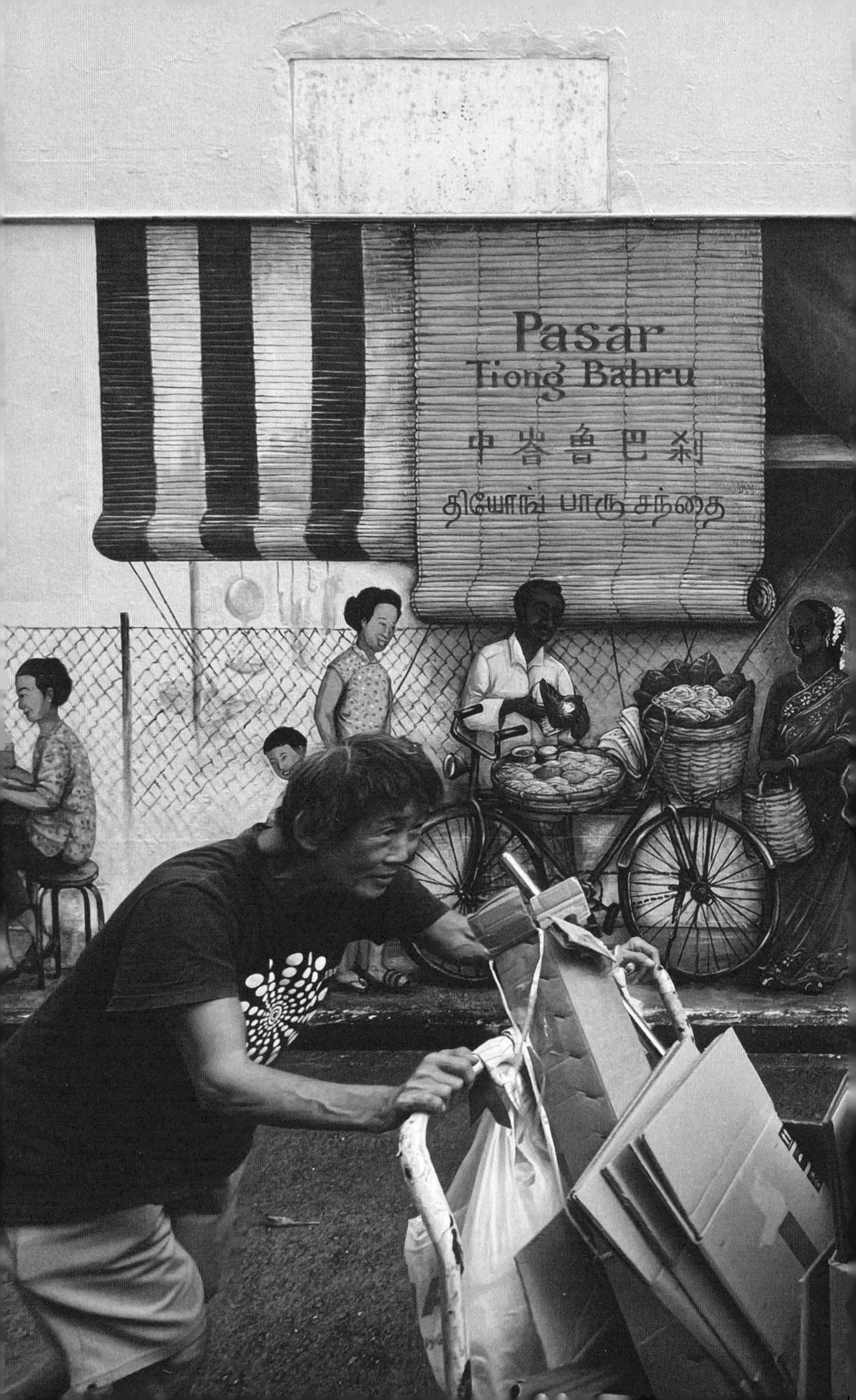
Pasar
Tiong Bahru
中峇鲁巴刹
தியோங் பாரு சந்தை

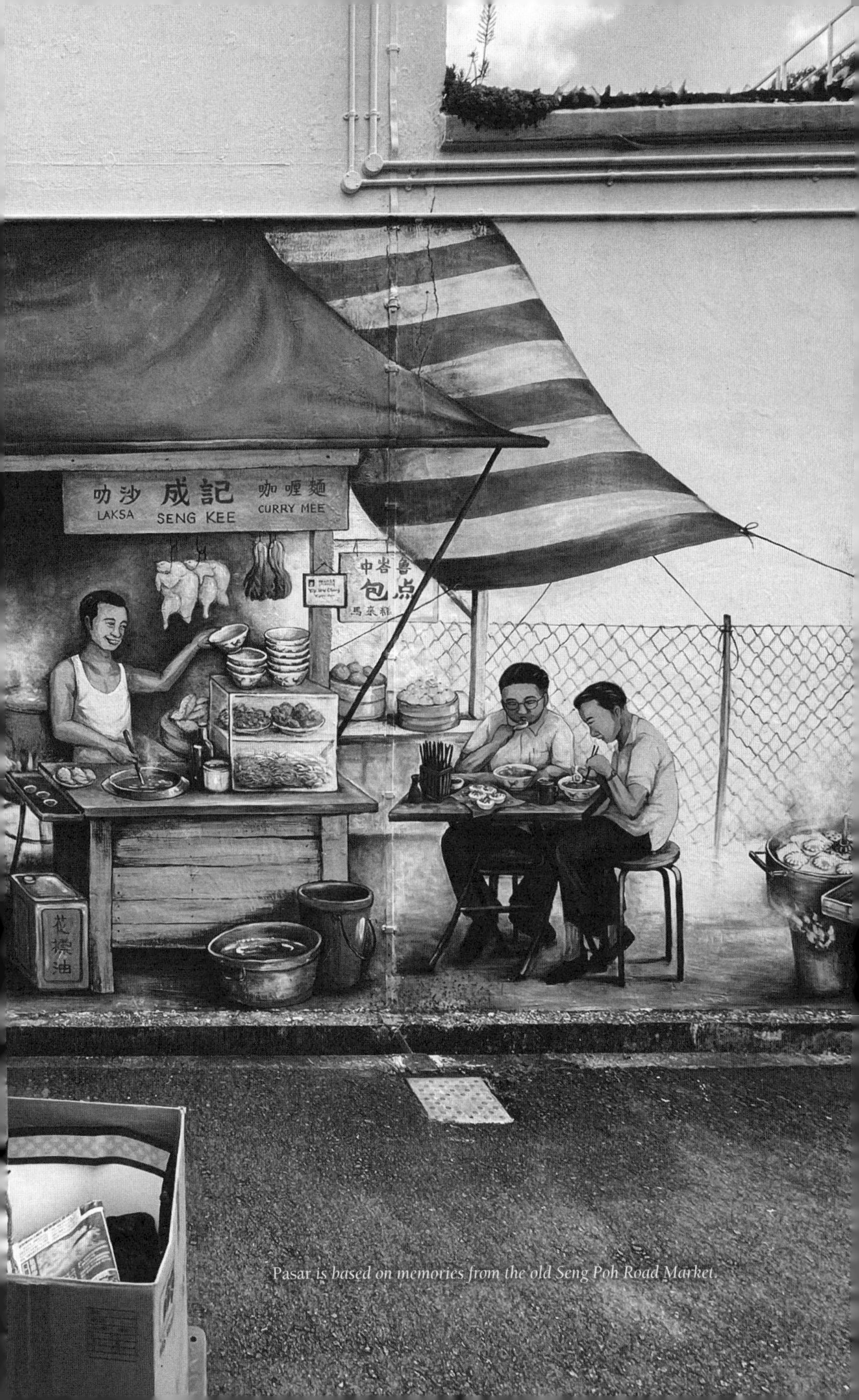

Pasar is based on memories from the old Seng Poh Road Market.

Caucasians, and Sikhs. It isn't done to be politically correct; it is done to depict reality. For example, Chinatown is a misnomer. It is multiracial, not monoethnic as the name suggests. Chinatown was coined in the 1970s for ease of tourism promotion."

Yew Chong's easy inclusion of different races has not gone unnoticed, especially to those once described officially as 'others'. Percival Shepherdson is a retired chef in his 70s. He has taken an interest to know family history, cultures, foods, and religious practices of various races in Singapore. He frequents museums and art exhibitions, and is a fan of the mural art in Penang. When he discovered Yew Chong's art, instinctively, he felt a sense of home. "Even though I am Eurasian, I have associated myself with the Chinatown area for almost 50 years. I enjoy Chinese culture, food, and the sights and sound. My wife of 45 years is Chinese. When I first chanced on Yew Chong's art, I felt so good because it depicts us without separating us."

Shepherdson is now another fan; he never misses a mural or an exhibition. Like Charles and Faith, his family and friends are now followers of the artist. "I can feel that he paints with feelings, depicting the actual scenes, and the paintings bring memories of the past, be it home environment, daily activities of the street scenes, or the surrounding area. Each time I see the mural, I can see myself in the scene, and I can associate with the paraphernalia items in the paintings."

Aishah Jaffar was Yew Chong's colleague at Reuters. She remembers him as a passionate traveller who loved to share films and videos of his travels. "We both left Reuters but kept in touch, and I remember he loved going to Penang, Malaysia and would talk about the murals he saw there... Pre-Covid I always invited friends to my home for Hari

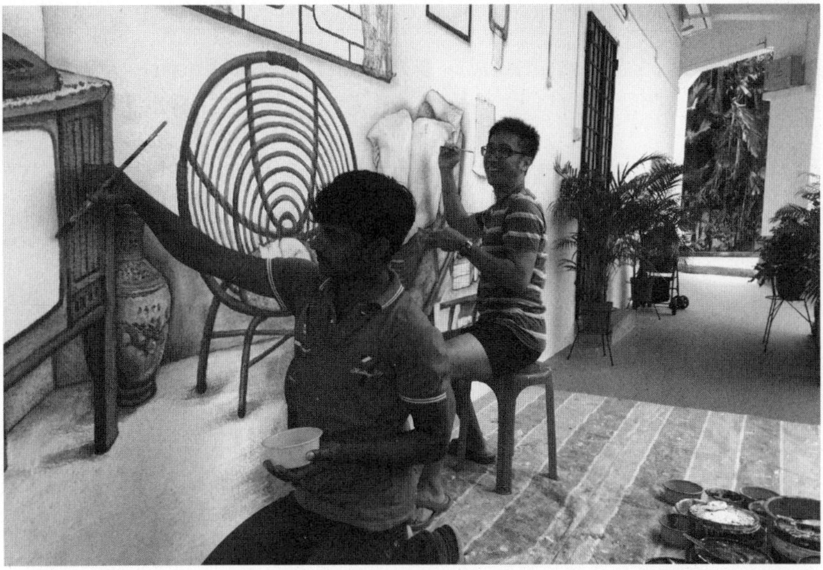

A migrant worker came by and requested to pose for a photo with a brush in hand. Best actor award for him!

Raya Puasa. On one of these visits, he stayed longer even after everyone had left, and we chatted. We talked about many things but one that stuck was him wanting to paint a mural in Chinatown. Lo and behold, there are so many of his murals there now. I feel so happy for him."

Aishah is familiar with Yew Chong's murals and paintings. Even today, when she is in a restaurant in Chinatown, around Kampong Gelam, or Tiong Bahru, she steals a little time for the murals, to remind herself of her friend, and his ability to connect with Singaporeans. "I think it's the authenticity of the works, the colours, and they seem to draw you to see things with his eyes and his heart."

They have both grown older over the years, but somehow Yew Chong's energy and spirit make him 'ageless'. If she needed to describe him in one word, it'd be 'storyteller'. "Yew Chong's strength is his storytelling; he is a giver… you feel his generosity. His art kind of reaches out to you to tell a story. When you talk to him in person, you get drawn into his stories, could be his travels, his past experiences. It is the same with his art, it feels familiar, warm, and in many ways, brings comfort. It also has elements of playfulness, which is very much like him and his cheeky personality. If you know Yew Chong, you will somehow like him or like something about him. And his art is the same, it draws you, and you will find something familiar, and you can't help but have a good feeling about it."

So, is that why people feel happy when they see his art?

"It's the subjects he chooses, and the stories behind them," she says, trying to be specific and precise. "The way the subjects are depicted, and the honesty in them. I remember he once told me his figure drawing isn't that good. I told myself then, it is not the drawing; it is the honest style that people appreciate, a kind of 'Yew Chong realism'. And he paints things that seem to be the things people love; he has a knack of doing that. In a way, it's genius, being able to connect with so many human beings in one common way."

Noriko Ohashi has lived in Singapore for three and a half years. When she arrived in August 2018, she volunteered as a Japanese-speaking guide at the National Museum of Singapore. As a docent there, she got to know of Yew Chong's works.

"I was fascinated by his artworks which depict the history of Singapore and the lives of Singaporeans not long ago; I quickly became a fan," she speaks slowly and carefully. "Today, two of his works are still there, *History of the National Museum of Singapore* and *Moving Memories*. Not long after, my friends and I looked for his murals over all Singapore. And whenever I heard that he was going to be doing his murals live, we went to see him, again and again. In the last three years, I have managed to find most of his artworks in Singapore."

Like the others I have spoken to, she finds in the artworks aspects of the man that speak to her. "I think the best thing about his works is that we feel his own kindness and warmth from the art. His art is open and friendly; it literally allows me 'in'. For example, if there is a chair in his mural, I sit on it and become part of it. And with so many murals that I get to experience and interact, I feel part of Singapore life through his art. It is a special, happy experience, I must say."

Noriko recalls an incident in 2021, one that she will remember for a long time because of how the artist include the audience in his artworks. "He was painting a large mural in Chinatown at the end of 2021. I went to see that at least five times while he was painting. He kept painting, whether it was hot or it rained. Sometimes, he would stop working and talk with the people watching him. He listened and asked for their opinions; even the children he asked how he should paint the animals. I was impressed to see how his art had the inputs of his audience. He did not do it for show; he really listened. Slowly, I got to know him well, like his other supporters. Today, I feel like Mr Yip and his fans are one family."

And apart from the charm and nostalgia the murals invoked, Noriko feels the murals are distinctly Singaporean. "Japan is an island nation with a single ethnic group; it is not easy to come into contact with many races and cultures. I feel great respect for the Singaporean peoples' open-mindedness and acceptance of all kinds of people, all shown in the artist's art. So, his art represents the multiracial, multicultural Singapore that I have come to know and love. When I go back to Japan with my daughters, I will want to stay connected to Singapore, help other Japanese know more about Singapore and how unusual a place it is. And partly thanks to Yip Yew Chong's art."

Affirmation of Community History

If there is one man who knows Yip Yew Chong's murals well, he must be Kelvin Ang, someone I introduced briefly in Chapter 3. Kelvin works at the Urban Redevelopment Authority (URA), the government's department for city planning, land use, and conservation. He is the Director of Conservation Management, in charge of looking after Singapore architecture for future generations. When an artist wishes to paint something on a building in the public domain, he will have oversight of it.

"As a regulator, when an artist wishes to place art in a location that is seen by the public on a daily basis, then the public perception is an important part of our consideration," Kelvin explains what comes under his purview. "This is especially so in a conservation area where there are pre-existing values of memories, and of heritage. If an art does not adequately address these pre-existing values, then the art may not be well received by the community. For us, how the community feel is important."

Kelvin and his team engage the community through the People's Association and its network of grassroots organisations like the Community Clubs, seeking and listening to their thoughts and feelings when an artist submits an artwork for consideration. "For conservation areas, residents are particular. They do not see art just as decorative; they also see art as a tool for education, and a tool for communication, not just for pleasure."

Even today, with Yew Chong's murals so well received and publicised, there are still areas in Chinatown where his plans are yet to be realised. The custodians of these areas are not convinced that there should be art on their walls, Yew Chong's art or anyone else's. These owners may not be equipped with enough knowledge on mural making and mural maintenance to be comfortable living with the art.

"Typically, when a proposal comes to the URA, we look at the hygiene issues first: architecture, location, content (cannot be obscene or vulgar for instance), then it's up to the community," he pauses. "As a regulator, we do not have a strong role, or we shouldn't have a strong role. The community's decision must be respected because it takes time and resources to maintain a mural. I would like to add that the entire exercise is a very useful tool for community formation."

Pinning down to Yew Chong's works in particular, I want to know how they have influenced or affected the communities that they are in.

"From the URA standpoint, our observation, after the artworks have been installed, whether it's from volunteers, old residents, or shopkeepers of Chinatown or Kampong Glam, they have been almost always very positive. Especially for former residents, because his artworks deal with Singapore's recent past, from the 1950s to the 1980s, where people still live in the old city, the murals provide a window to their past in a very engaging way. The artist has the ability to create murals that people are able to put themselves into. It is a short circuit of time and space. Because he also paints a lot of scenes that are of the everyday person, he gives honour to the experience of the men and women in the street who built up this country. It is almost an affirmation of their own past. And that is a very powerful thing for the community. By recognising the individuals, and they are very recognisable actually in Singapore, he recognises the everyman where people can place themselves into. And because he is also able to represent the multiethnicity of Singapore, it is a very necessary antidote to how cultural discourses are now being discussed. In history books, we don't read about the everyday life of people, it's always about the big dates and disasters. So, his is an antidote, about the everyday beauty of people and their lives. These are my observation of his works in the heritage streets where the URA has a say."

Wearing his personal hat, Kelvin also volunteers with the grassroots in Tiong Bahru. And he has some good stories to tell, especially at the beginning, when Yew Chong was not that known yet.

"Residents were very protective of Tiong Bahru and they questioned him, 'How can you paint this scene, the fortune teller, when it wasn't there?' One of the senior residents, a lady in her early 70s, was very sure there was no such person and didn't want him to paint things that were not true. Yew Chong came back with a photograph of the fortune teller, black and white photo of around 1969. We then showed the photograph to the lady. When she looked at the photograph, she admitted that she had forgotten. And that one photograph allowed the community to rally together and say, this is our memory. It was almost an affirmation of their community history. To this day, to me personally, I think the Tiong Bahru murals are some of the most successful interventions with regards to how art plays a role in not just making a space beautiful, but serves as an educational tool to visitors, and an affirmation tool for the residents. So, it fulfils multiple objectives."

Does Yew Chong's art bring a smile to the faces of residents where his murals are? I relate to him an incident, when Yew Chong was explaining his mural to me in Chinatown. A woman in her late 60s walked by. She stopped and stared and stared at the mural for a very long time. We decided to talk to her. When she found out that the artist himself was talking to her, she became very excited and told us how much joy the mural had brought her and her friends and family. I suspected and told Yew Chong that this lady might not have ever been to an art gallery, let alone a museum, but was able to enjoy art on the street of Chinatown. It was, I said, a joyous gift he had bestowed to ordinary men and women of Singapore.

"Definitely," Kelvin says with a thought in his voice. "You have brought up an important point. We shouldn't segregate art in the museum and art in everyday life. Not everyone wants to subject themselves to the 'rules' of a museum, but it doesn't mean they are not interested in art, or music. This lady you speak of, she may not want to visit a museum, but if you ask her, 'Do you want to go to this place (don't call it a gallery or museum) to see Mr Yip's work?' She may say yes because she has seen his works. I use it as an entry point. So, making art accessible in everyday life is very important."

He pauses and wants to go back to the point about bringing a smile to the residents. "Every time when I walk past the back lanes in Tiong Bahru, people do stop to look at his work and smile. It is one of the places where everyone is happy that the murals are there. I am so glad that's the title of your book."

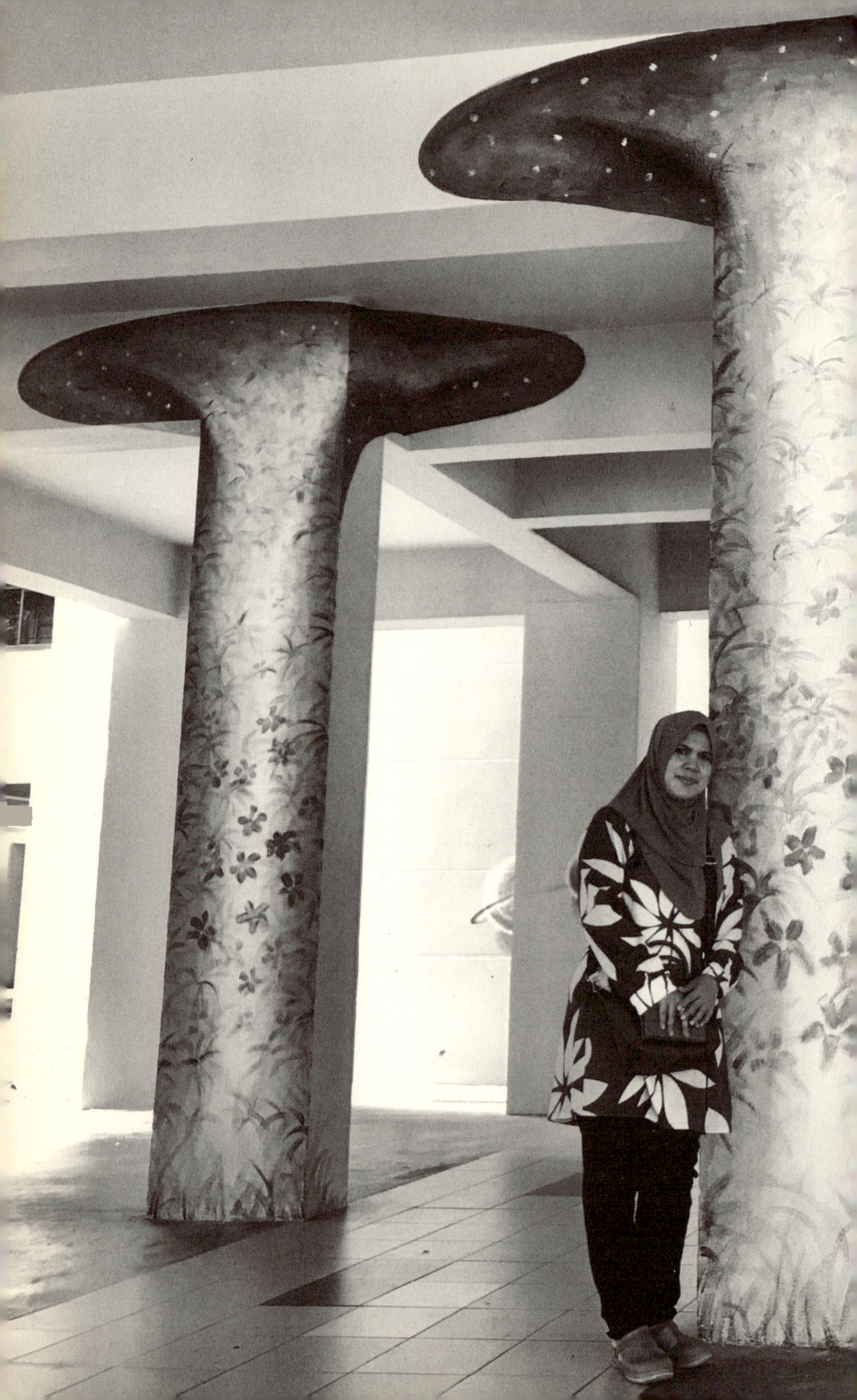

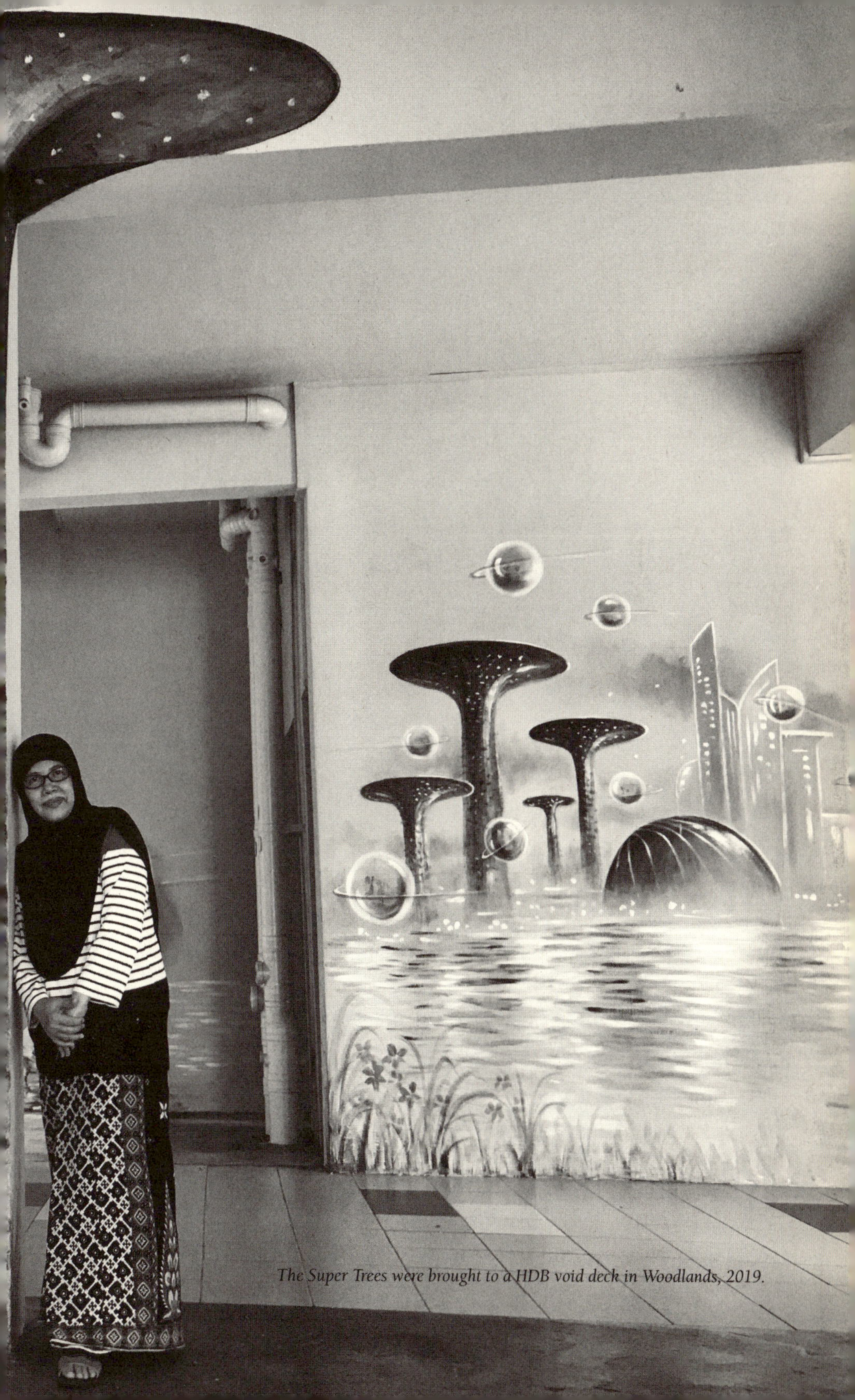

The Super Trees were brought to a HDB void deck in Woodlands, 2019.

Talking about segregating art, I am curious what his views may be of Yew Chong's genre, which is essentially imagination based loosely on reality. It does not fall into a known genre, and purists are not keen on art that is not of an accepted genre.

"Yew Chong needs to ask himself, what continues to be the intention in creating the art he creates," Kelvin's voice anchors in. "Does it fulfil that intention or reward he gets from it? As long as that intention is fulfilled, he should take strength from that, because he is only answerable to himself. There is more than enough art in all other styles and types for everybody else, but there is only one him, as there is only one of every other artist. He or she will do what they like to do best. Of course, each artist must be rewarded or recognised in many ways that are sufficient enough to keep them going. The ultimate test is the test of time. In 10 years, or 20 years' time, how would we look at this art? With everything in the creative world, there is a cycle. It could be a fad, or it could endure. Would we say, oh let's keep it in the storeroom, or oh, let's do a retrospective? So, I hope Yew Chong can see his art from that perspective; let history be the arbitrator, let time speak in 10, perhaps 20, 30 years' time."

My mind goes back to Van Gogh, and how he only sold one piece of art while he lived. The purists then did not think much of his revolutionary style; there was no name for his genre. Today, the entire era has been happily classified as impressionism, and today, impressionists do pretty damn well.

Kelvin adds, "For someone who has made the recent history of Singapore come to life for the present and future generations, his work definitely has a role, even if it is a style you cannot pin down."

It goes back to a point many people I have spoken to have raised. He is a people's artist; in his art, he tells stories and has painted in a way that the layman and woman can relate to; ordinary people see themselves in his art. If he, at 54, were to now go to school to study art, graduate, and start painting for the trained eye, for the purist, and lose his most important audience, the ordinary men and women who have embraced and supported him, that would be unfortunate. He has struck a chord with the layman and woman, connected with them; he should never lose that.

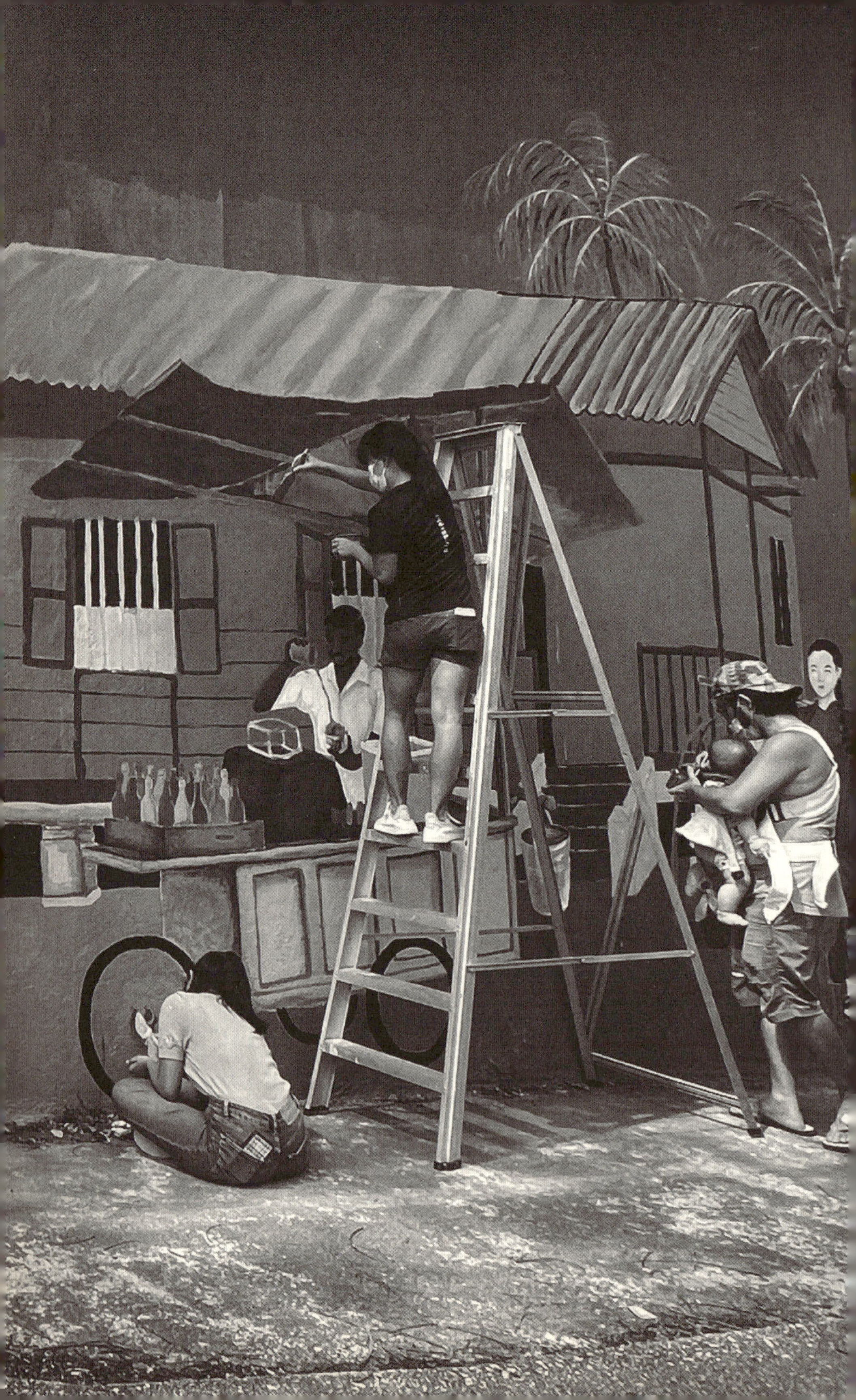

CHAPTER 8

Lifting the Human Spirit

There is no judgement, just individual expression and creativity.

When the Spirit is Caged

At first, everything seems slightly off. We are still in the middle of a pandemic, but the restaurant is packed to the brim. A baby screams in the corner; the young mother tries to pacify her with little success; the grandparents look apologetically around. An older waiter clears the table as the family stands up to go. As he turns, right hand lifting a teapot, a bluish-green tiger tattoo greets me. My eyes quickly scan the other wait-staff. Jeans, loose T-shirts, weathered but attentive faces. I look down at the menu; the name of the restaurant is *Breakthrough*. It all starts to make sense.

Yew Chong's eyes look at mine; he smiles. Of course. This must be a restaurant that employs reformed ex-convicts and those at the margins of society. John Soh, who had joined us to see an art exhibition earlier, does not miss a beat.

"Let's have dim sum," he says with a lift in his voice.

We started with the congee because that's what goes best with the quintessential Hong Kong dim sum. The porridge is smooth while the rice grains are soft and tasty. Next up, the bamboo baskets of bite-sized dim sum. I pick the *feng zhao*, or chicken feet. I loved chicken feet growing up, and age has only intensified this enduring love; today I literally worship the chicken at its feet. John also orders steamed pork ribs, which have both the soft and firm portions. The meat is both tender and chewy; they melt in my mouth. The *siew mais* are good too but the char siew rice rolls do the trick of filling us up and making all of us happy.

Breakthrough is an admirable project; people who have done wrong are allowed a second chance to right that wrong, and together they have done so deliciously and meaningfully. In particular, I like the unpretentious vibe about the place.

"I like it here because the food is good and cheap." It is clear the casual restaurant environment suits the artist. "And it's in Chinatown, close to my studio and not far from where I live. And I like to support this project's meaningful cause."

Yip Yew Chong tells us that he mentors reformed ex-inmates who aspire to be artists. He says art provides a special outlet to someone who is confined in a space for prolonged period. Art helps them focus their mind and allows their hopes and dreams to be expressed. And because it is subjective, there is no judgement, just individual expression and creativity. "They can become very good artists when they devote time to the craft, but more importantly, it is a skill that they will have when they return to society." The artist believes in supporting the cause, so he agreed to an invitation to give a talk and to conduct an art project management course at Changi Prison for the inmates. He received the invitation from a prison officer through CANVAS, a volunteer group he joined to mentor ex-inmate artists.

"It was my first visit to a prison, and it was a long, long walk into this big complex to meet a group of inmates." Security was tight; he was even given a gadget to wear that would set off an alarm if he felt at any time unsafe or threatened. "All the officers carried one of those, so I was given one. But honestly, I felt safe, I was not nervous at all. And even though I was in the Changi Prison, everything I saw resembled the world outside."

"Did you have to go to a special place to see them?" My mind is influenced by what I see in the movies.

"Yes, I was at the visual arts hub," he says lightly. "It was like a gallery where they did their arts and crafts. I must say, prisoners or inmates, call them what you like, they look just like you and me. And I was impressed by the high quality of some of the artworks there, some of them are so much better than mine. Many of them are talented; they just need a good platform, and be given the right opportunities."

He clarifies that it was a male prison and most of the eight inmates who turned up were his age or younger. Being there got him thinking about solitude and art. "The Covid pandemic confined me, forced me to stay put, and for the most part of the two years, it forced me to focus, to think about what I want to achieve, what I want to create. It was a kind of confinement too. But it was very good, because I couldn't paint murals, it forced me to focus on canvas painting. So being in a confined space can also force the mind to focus and think about what a person wants to achieve. After visiting the visual arts hub, I saw what they could do, in multi-medium, from oil to ink to sculptures, even pencil drawing. It wasn't dabbling in art to pass time, it was learning a skill and then striving and excelling in that skill. I am sure other inmates focused and excelled in other skills as well. But for the visual arts, they will enter society with art as a skill honed in prison."

I want to know what meeting the inmates was like, the questions they asked, and if they knew who he was.

"In prison, they are not allowed to have access to the internet freely." Yew Chong smiles. "So, they didn't know about me, they only knew someone who paints murals would come to first talk to them, and then conduct an art project management course. So, for the talk, I did a slide show, gave them a taste of what my murals and paintings were like. A background of myself and how I became an artist. I had one and a half hours, so I had time to talk to them in some depth on what I do and answer their questions."

"Art questions or practical questions about being an artist?" Prison artists must be terrified of the prospect of being real artists.

Yew Chong looks at me knowingly. "After the first slide of a mural, one hand went up. 'How much did you charge?'" Yew Chong laughs. "Very practical question! That was the first question, but I expected it as the prison officer already told me, they want to know what to expect when they get out there, what they can do, what's viable for them. They are very practical. The next question asked was, 'Are you coming back to guide us?' Then, the next question, 'Will you hire an ex-inmate?', 'Do you need assistants?' They were all related to jobs when they get out, and the likely chances they might be given as ex-prisoners. They even asked the type of clients I have and what these clients want. They were assessing, is art worth a try as a skill, or should they try something else."

They look like you and I, Yew Chong reminds me, everyday people,

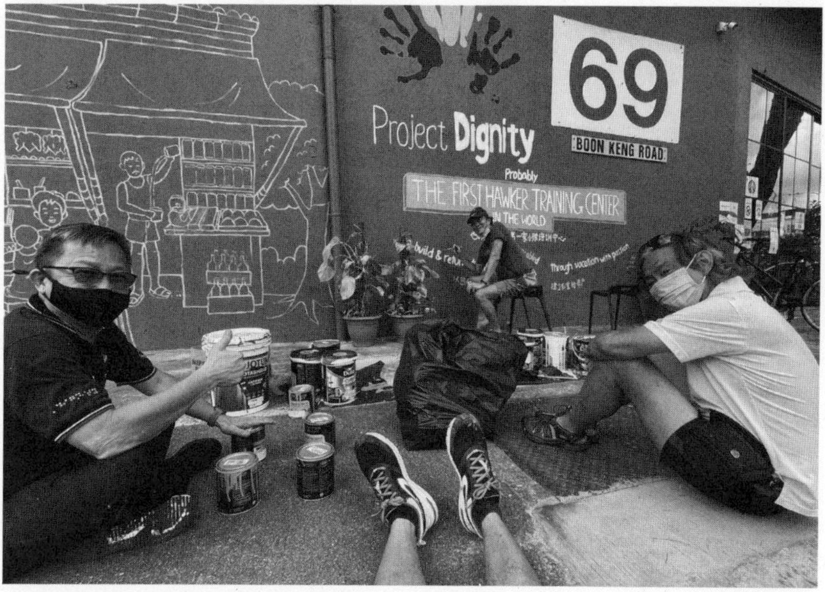

Dignity Kitchen provides training and work opportunities to the disadvantaged and disabled.

mild-mannered, no trace of anything untoward. Some look very young, like in their 20s. "Of course, I didn't know what they did to land them in prison, what I saw was an eagerness to learn something, and hope in their eyes. After the introductory talk, a month later, I went in again to conduct a three-day art project management course. The prison officer and I agreed that the inmates lack the skill to manage art project opportunities. They already have the skill or training to create art, but not enough skill to manage, such as how to present a concept to a potential client, how to price, what are an artist's rights. These are the exact same skills I mentor ex-inmates in as well. Not so much of doing the art. What they need help most isn't the technique, as many of them are already good artists. What they need are the administrative skills or the admin aspects of being an artist. How to talk to a client, how to

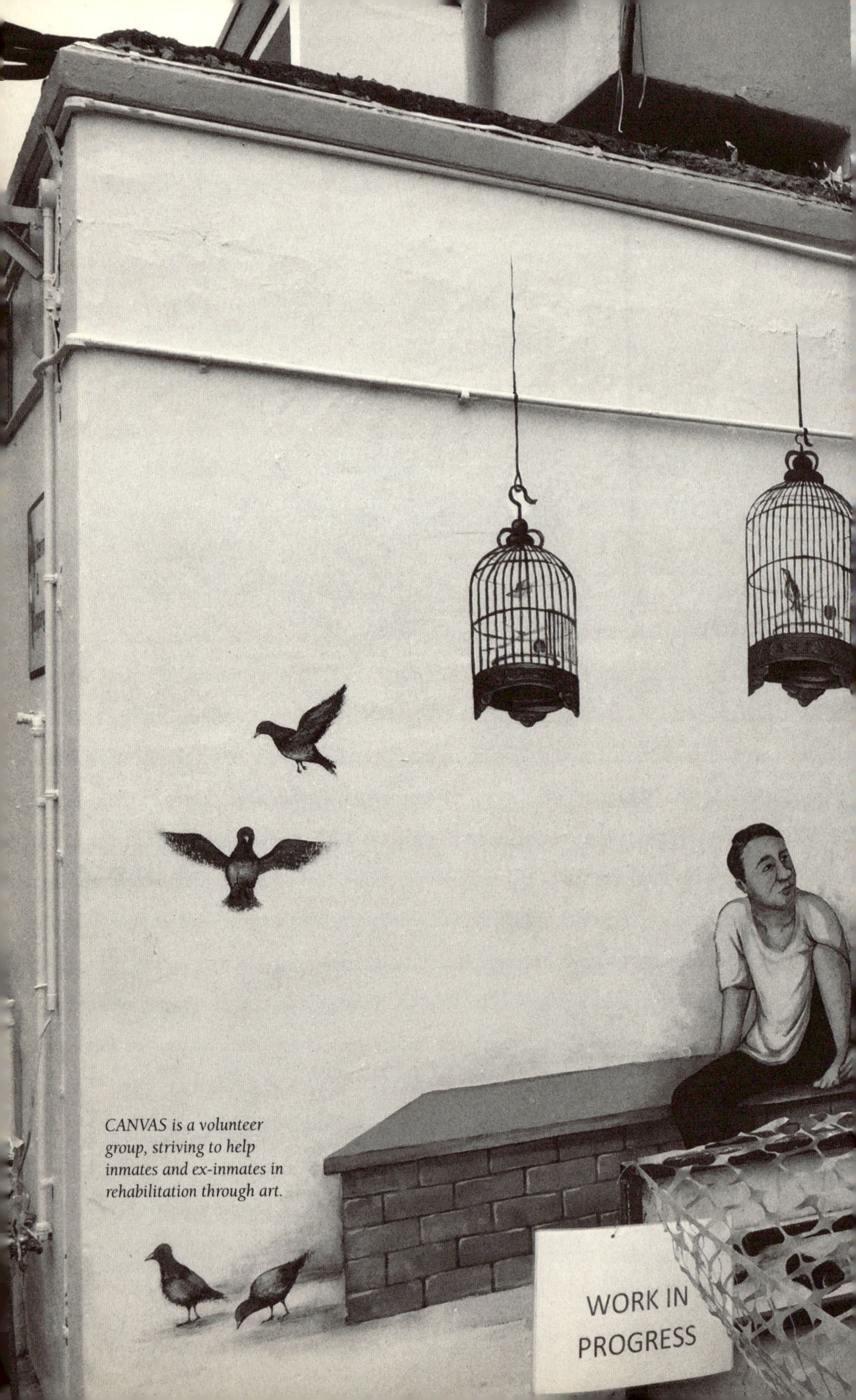

CANVAS is a volunteer group, striving to help inmates and ex-inmates in rehabilitation through art.

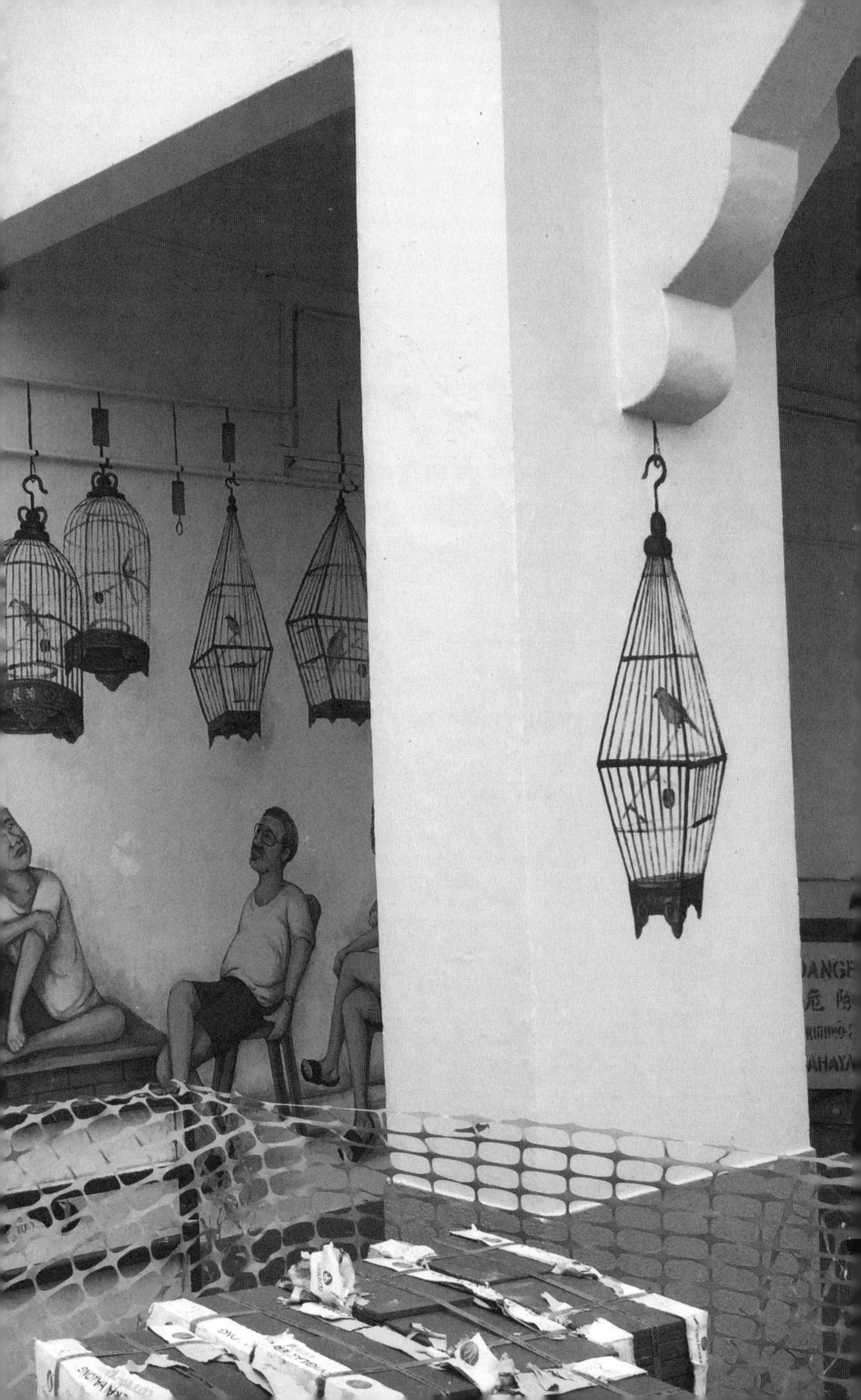

prepare a proposal, present a concept to a potential client. The business part of art is what they need to learn most. For example, one of them asked me how he would market himself; he was a good artist but he lacked the confidence and connections in the art market."

With CANVAS, Yew Chong is assigned to assist a few ex-inmates. They converse and text each other regularly. "I also invite them to see me paint my murals." This reminds me of another place Yew Chong brought me to Dignity Kitchen on Boon Keng Road. It was a hawker centre cum hawker training centre to provide vocation training and jobs for the disadvantaged and disabled. There, Yew Chong gave advice to Dignity Kitchen to create their murals.

I present Yew Chong with a metaphor: a white canvas, but it has been stained. The artist paints over the stain and it is now a new painting. Is the memory of the stain important?

"If the new paints are not good, you'd still see the stain." Yew Chong's face balances a smile and a frown. "Rehabilitation begins in the prison, and even when a person is released, rehabilitation continues. I am just one of many people in a large community helping in the rehabilitation process. It is important that the new painting is good. The memory of the stain serves to remind and instruct. Over time, it is good to just keep it as a faint memory."

Blue and Yellow

The last war in Europe, for most of us, was the Second World War. Even then, most of us had not been born to experience what a war was truly like. The world, for the most part, had gotten used to peace, even taken peace for granted. We would not believe that outright war could happen in broad daylight, right under our very noses. Few of us bothered with the details, or kept up with the current affairs of the world. If we did, we'd have known that Vladimir Putin meant it when he warned Ukraine not to join NATO. He acted in 2014 bringing Crimea into his fold; he would most definitely act again. But Ukraine continued to defy Putin with the encouragement of the West. So, when Russian tanks rolled into Eastern Ukraine on 24th February 2022, people were shocked, including many civilians from Ukraine and Russia.

Luda Zueva is a Russian marketeer living in Singapore for the past six years. She is familiar with China, Hong Kong, and other Asian cities, and she considers Russians to be Eurasians, not Europeans. But Singapore is her 'big love'. "Singapore has progressed beautifully," she says with a broad smile. "On the one hand, you have MBS, the Marina Bay Sands, so modern and so splendid. Yet, you know to keep Chinatown close by. So, while you march forward, you don't forget your heritage. I have a good feeling that things that are good would be kept while the country builds and explore the new. It is always good to keep a sense of nostalgia in a country."

It was her interest in Chinatown that introduced her to Yew Chong's murals. "There was something 'human' about the murals that I connected with straightaway. And the small details fascinated me. I was drawn in. Although it was art, it unfolded like a human documentary movie, so real, so true to life of Singapore years ago. I found them remarkable, this very personal style of his. I like how he brought his entire family into his art. The art was very powerful, very good." And so, she sought the artist out, and over the years, got to know more and more about him.

On 24th February, she felt helpless, but told herself she had to do something, although at that time she didn't know what she would do. Then, she remembered the situation in Belfast, Northern Ireland, in 1969, where people were killing each other, brothers and sisters, Protestants and Catholics. Her mind went back to the peace movement and the huge murals on the sides of a houses in Belfast. She knew if she was going to send a peace message to the world, it would have to be visual and huge. Yew Chong's murals came to mind, but where? Who would contribute a 'peace wall' for Yew Chong to paint on? Would the government allow a mural with a political message?

"How we would do it wasn't so important, we would find a creative way," her practical voice asserts. "With the big art and the talent of Yew Chong, we want to scream to the world, STOP IT! Let's live in peace."

Now divorced, her former husband is half-Ukrainian (his mother is Ukrainian). Her close personal friends are also from Ukraine; they worked together in big MNCs. Before the war, when asked if the war was imminent, she would dismiss it, "Putin cannot be so crazy, it won't happen. Now, I am suffering, and people are suffering from both sides. Ukrainians fleeing and Russians like myself who are against the war feel conflicted. I know some Russians are also fleeing because they fear they may be punished for their views, or they don't want to betray their friends in Ukraine. They flee to any country that allows them in without a visa. The situation is just so bad because most of us consider Ukrainians as our brothers and sisters."

"How are you suffering now?" I ask because she said she was suffering.

"Since the war started, I notice people have started to avoid me, some are openly hostile." Her voice continues to be firm. "Ukrainians, some of them close friends, distance themselves. It is as if just being Russian is bad. So, I know, I need to do something for peace, for Ukraine."

In discussing with Yew Chong, the mural idea was ditched, it would take too long for clearance, not to mention finding a wall big enough for this message. Clearance will also be unlikely as there is a political element. The creative way out is a three-metre by three-metre mural-like canvas to be painted by the Singapore artist and to be auctioned by Hotlotz for Red Cross Humanitarian Aid to Ukraine.

What does she want to say with this artwork?

"Through the talent of Yew Chong, what I want to say is, No War! And that's not negotiable," her voice tightens. "Not negotiable," she repeats. "And the more subtle message is personal; it is not fair to blame Russian civilians, we are not our government; we are not Putin. We should separate the Russian people from the Putin administration. We should not be cancelled as a country, as a people. It's not fair. I don't like cancel culture."

And why does she have faith using art as a medium?

"Art is much more powerful than words, especially when the artist has the ability to paint it big and bold." She allows a smile now. "And art is probably the only 'language' available now; Russians and Ukrainians do not talk to each other; Russians themselves cannot talk to others, even in English. No one wants to listen to us. So, we are completely lost in translation. Art is our only language; it needs to be understood at once glance, no explanation needed. And it is good it is from a Singaporean artist, his personal subjective and creative view, not from the West, not from Russia, not from Ukraine. From an artist, art, the universal language, like music."

"Okay, I am going to get a little political." I look her in the eye. "Singapore, to the surprise of many, has taken a position. Unlike China, India and the rest of Southeast Asia, Singapore has condemned the war and even decided to impose appropriate sanctions and restrictions against Russia. As a Russian, how do you feel?"

Her face brightens. "I understand Singapore's position," her voice assures. "If Malaysia one day decides Singapore should be part of Malaysia again, what would Singapore do? So, Singapore builds up its military, and the signal to the rest of the region is, don't even think you can violate our sovereignty. Don't even think about it. Singapore is a small country in a region of relatively big countries like Malaysia and Indonesia. Singapore's foreign policy decisions are usually carefully thought out and thought through. On Ukraine, I actually admire what Singapore did, what your Prime Minister did, he took it personally. It's Singapore's national interest."

Even though she has only been in Singapore for six years, she knows the Singapore psyche well. "Ukraine is a young country, became a nation only in 1991, barely 30 years old. Younger than Singapore, yet already such a nationalistic country. What will happen to Ukraine as a country now? Is this the beginning of Ukrainian nationalism?" I ask.

"I think the 'nation' of Ukraine has just been born," her voice quivers. "I just hope it doesn't get to be ultra-nationalistic. In the case of Singapore, Lee Kuan Yew was sharp enough to know Singapore wasn't a Chinese country, that it was also Malay, Tamil, and others. Similarly, I hope the Ukrainians wouldn't become ultra-nationalistic and proclaim

Ukraine just for the Ukrainians; there are also other nationalities there. It shares a lot of Russian culture too, and many people speak Russian there."

I decide to bring the focus back to the artwork. What does she want to do with this artwork?

"On top of the important message of peace," she stops, and composes herself. "I also want to be pragmatic; I wish the auction will be successful, and we will have some money, and some kids will have diapers; hungry people will have some extra food, and those injured will have some medicine. I can't go to Ukraine; I am not crazy, but I want to do something, so that those suffering will get some relief."

This project, what has been the single biggest source of inspiration? Has it been easy to put together?

"This was put together in very quick time. I then realised many people wanted to help, do something, except they didn't know what to do." She smiles. "I had problems getting the Ukrainians and Russians to come together, that I completely understand. But all the others, they genuinely wanted to contribute, they genuinely wanted to help. So, from this Singapore project, this Singapore 'initiative', from a Singaporean artist, was a breeze. Very quickly, I got a warehouse space for Yew Chong to paint this big canvas; someone offered to bring food and wine; others volunteered to help paint, it was literally organised in a week. There is something about art that brings people together. In Russian history, some of the most enduring survival of Russian humanity has been its art. So, in this war, this massive war, people need to be reminded of the humanity on both sides. And I think Yew Chong's art, his ability to bring out the humanity in each and every one of us, is what I count on. He is able to make very simple everyday things relevant to everyone, make us think about things that are simple but important. He told me the painting would go with the symbolism of the Ukrainian flag, blue and yellow, and would have a sunflower motif. I can't wait."

Can We Fly Kites?

Saturday, 19th March, 20 Depot Lane Industrial Estate. I was told Yew Chong would start to paint at noon; I decide to arrive a little early to get a feel of the space. I book my Grab at 11.15 am and arrive just past 11.30 am. The door to the warehouse is open.

The artist probably arrived early; when I step into the warehouse, he has already divided the massive canvas into two distinct shades, blue and yellow. The canvas, I find out, is actually denim, the fabric apparel designers use to make jeans and jackets. And this time, it is on the floor. The artist would need to navigate this piece differently from his murals and canvases.

"You are early." Yew Chong looks at me with a roller brush dipped in white paint. "When I arrived to set up, they were all already here, so I started early." He walks gingerly on the denim, applying white paint with the roller brush, simulating clouds, across the blue sky. The denim on the floor looks like a Ukrainian flag, the two colours many netizens on social media have started to add to their profiles as a war 'protest' and also to show solidarity with Ukraine.

The warehouse is rented by Pier Rizzardi, a bald, bearded, young Italian artist who is also an architect. Luda Zueva offers me water, and points to fruit, juices, and other tidbits she brought. There is no air-conditioning but the tall ceiling and fans keep the big warehouse relatively cool. The place is very bright, warm but not stuffy.

My focus is on the artist. His clouds across the blue are big, long waves that culminate in a circle that is the sun. The artist has decided to keep the sun stylistically white as well, adding any other colour to the sky would distract from the blue and yellow motif.

Then, Yew Chong suddenly kneels on the floor and starts using a brush to apply hot pink on the denim. I am curious. The painted pink portion is in the shape of an arrow. Below the pink, he applies a yellow strip of paint, and then green. Ah, this is a colourful kite in the sky.

Just at that moment, a Russian friend of Luda, Katya, arrives holding a bunch of sunflowers. Yew Chong looks up, smiling. "To encourage you, to cheer you on," Katya says with a Slavic accent. When she puts the sunflowers in a tall vase, the whole warehouse literally perks up. It is as if she has brought the morning sun inside.

The artist moves down to the yellow part of the denim and begin drawing a face, and then the limb to what seems like a child in a joyful stretch. Ah, this child is controlling the kite. Another child, and then another, all playful with their arms open to the blue sky. It is clear now; these children, painted in different colours, are manipulating many more kites in the sky.

"Wow, what a happy painting!" I cannot control myself; there is something liberating and free about kids and kites flown in the clear blue sky. My heart opens. The artist knows how to release joy, how to send a happy message without even a single iota of war in his art. Even at this stage, perhaps a third of the way to completion, I can see what

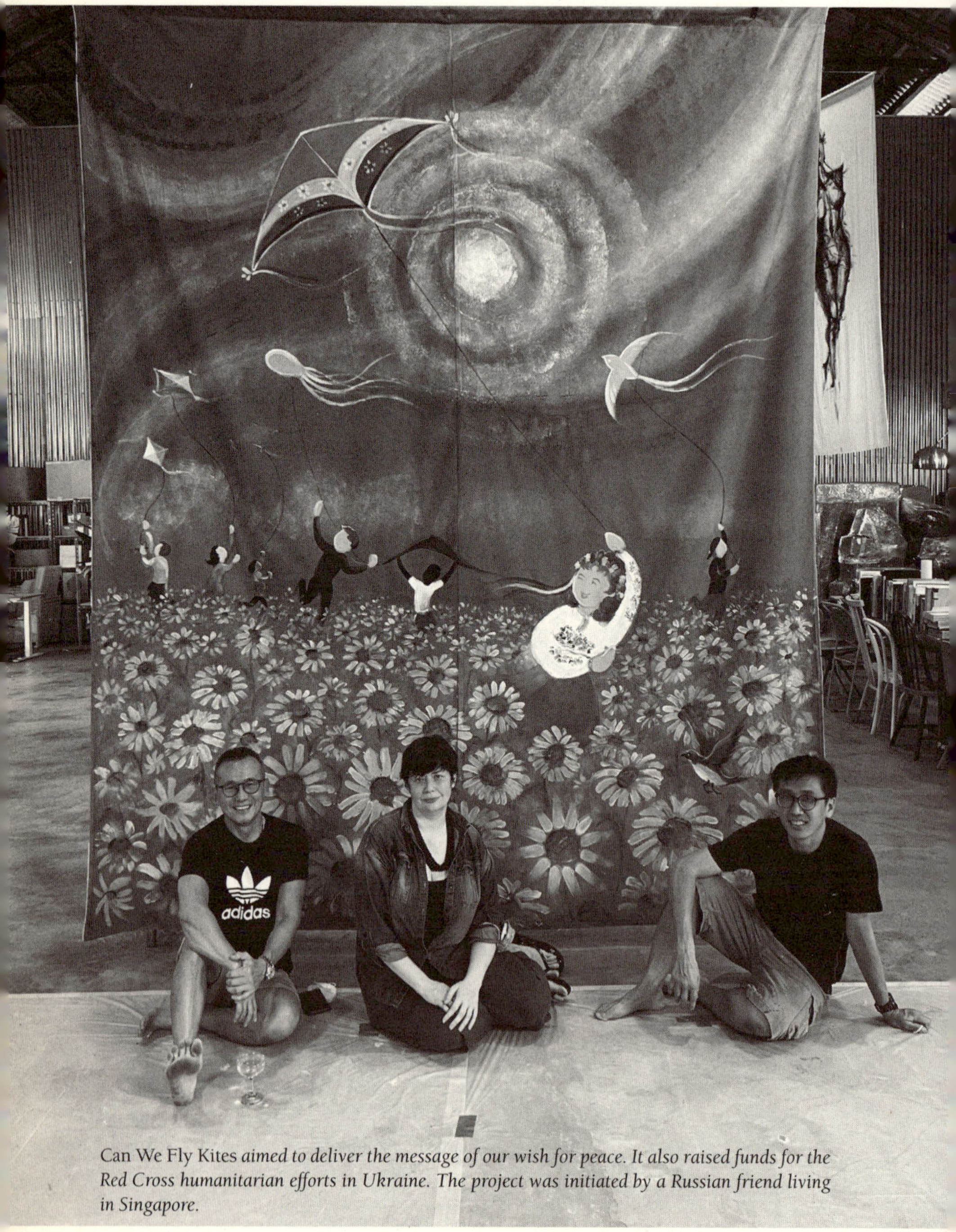

Can We Fly Kites *aimed to deliver the message of our wish for peace. It also raised funds for the Red Cross humanitarian efforts in Ukraine. The project was initiated by a Russian friend living in Singapore.*

he wants to say. Instead of fighter planes and bombs, he replaces them with free-flying kites; instead of rifle-wielding soldiers, he replaces them with kids, each controlling a thread to the kites, enjoying themselves on a sunny day.

"Why are the kids painted in different colours?" I ask.

He looks up with a grin, "Different nationalities."

The main child, a young girl, wears a Ukrainian wreath, her hair flowing to the waves of the clouds. Behind her, a boy with dark complexion holds up a kite about to be launched. The artist is now painting more kites and adding the tails to each. I begin to feel the draughts in the room, as the kite-flying moves in full gear on the denim.

A Dutch entrepreneur arrives wearing shorts and a loose t-shirt. He stares at the artwork intensely. "Ukrainian colours," he says to himself. Just then, a Chinese woman walks in.

Luda strolls over to the artist, "This is Yew Chong!" she exclaims. "And this is my Singaporean friend, Christina."

A younger woman carrying a bag walks in from the back entrance. She walks to Luda and says, "I am Nicole Cheah from the *The Straits Times*."

"Ah." Luda had alerted the national newspaper and is happy that they have actually sent a journalist. "I think the artist is halfway through."

Nicole walks over to the artwork and introduces herself to Yew Chong. The artist decides to take a break, gets himself a bottle of water, and joins the journalist and Luda by the sofa in the middle of the warehouse.

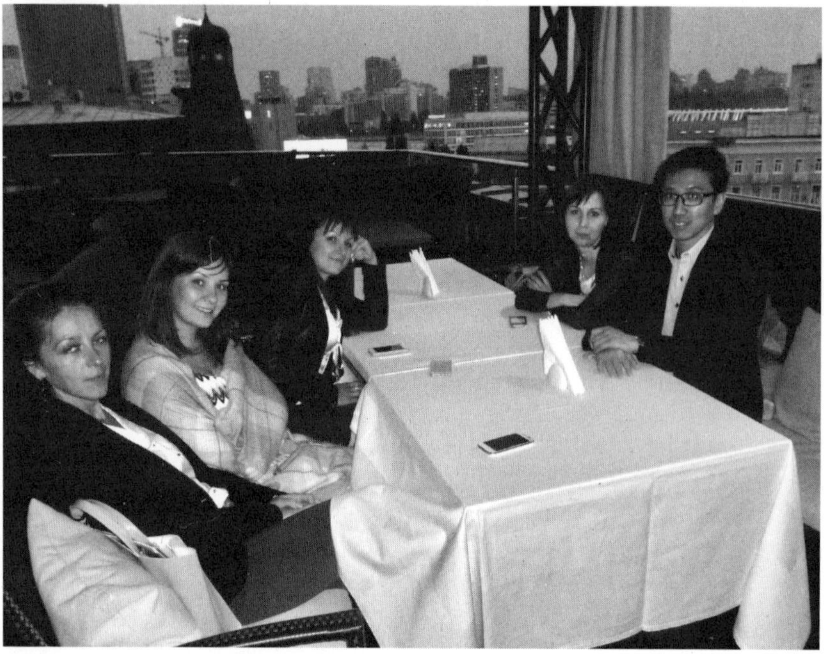

Kiev, 2013. Yew Chong with his Ukrainian and Russian colleagues at a rooftop restaurant in Kiev.

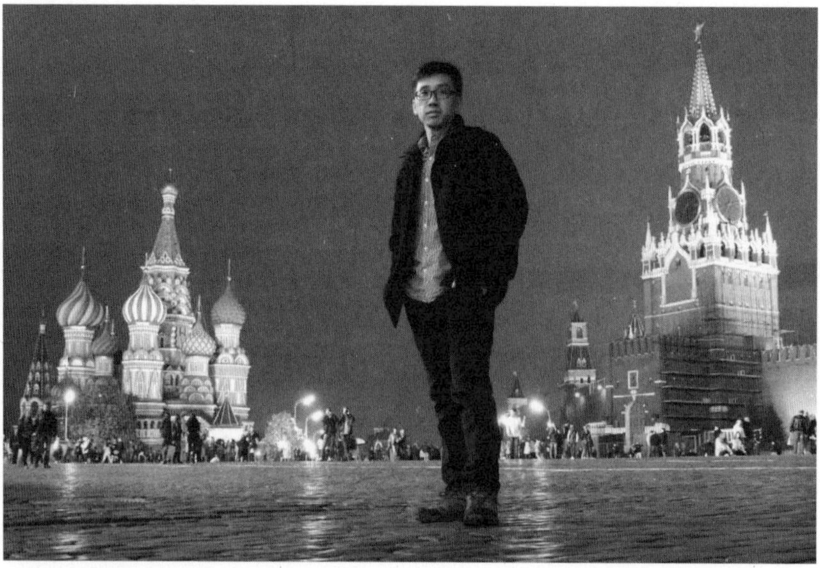

Moscow, 2013. Yew Chong's finance work brought him to various parts of the world.

"How did this all begin?" Nicole's fingers type on her iPad as her eyes stare at the artist.

"10 days after the war in Ukraine erupted, Luda contacted me," the artist nods at Luda. "She is Russian and wanted to express her wish for peace. As it is a meaningful message, I readily agreed."

Yew Chong has an audience now; those who dropped by to watch him paint have now gathered around to hear him. And the audience is international: Russian, Italian, Chinese, Singaporean, Dutch.

A woman, balancing many lunch packages and two bottles of wine, comes in from the back entrance. "Lunch is here." She catches her breath. "I am Angeles Herrero; I am Mexican." Lunch is beef tacos with fried tortilla chips, and they look mouth-wateringly good.

"So, this is an international gathering to support this peace message." Nicole's eyes scan the audience. "Impressive." She turns back to the artist. "Tell us, how did you decide on your message?"

"We explored various ideas and feasible ways to deliver the message," Yew Chong continues. "Things moved quickly. Other friends gave logistical support and arranged to auction the artwork for refugee relief efforts. I think the overall effort itself is symbolically meaningful, regardless of nationalities, races, and geo-political viewpoints, people can work together for a humanitarian cause…"

He walks to the denim on the floor. "*Can We Fly Kites* is the name of the artwork, it will depict children of different colours, from various places, flying kites in a sunflower field. I will invite everyone to help me paint the sunflowers, so every sunflower will have a different style. The sky is blue with wavy white clouds; the sun shines subtly. To make it Singaporean, I will include a mangrove blue and yellow flycatcher, a native bird in Singapore fluttering around the sunflowers."

"Lovely." Christiana beams.

Angeles puts her hands together in a mock clap. "Bravo."

Nicole continues to write on her iPad. "Tell us what you want to say with this artwork."

"The scene represents the wish for peace." The artist returns to the middle of the warehouse. "So that the children can fly kites again. Joyful scenes are my usual themes, as this painting is, but I changed the style to be kiddy, like a children's book cover. Children are naturally innocent, pure and they are our future. The joyful scene is what should be happening in the sunflower fields."

"I understand you have been to both countries." Nicole stops writing and looks at Yew Chong, eyes searching.

"Personally, I have several friends currently in Ukraine and Russia, and friends from these countries living in Singapore. I have been to both countries on business trips, about a decade ago." The artist grows slightly pensive. "Thinking back, I cherish the dinner I had in a rooftop restaurant in Kiev with Ukrainian and Russian colleagues in 2013. I cherish the weekends when I hiked in the outskirts of Kiev and Moscow. Some of the photos are on my website."

"My photographer will come at four." Nicole looks at the denim on the floor now. "Do you think it would be done then?"

"Let me continue painting." Yew Chong smiles as he gets up. "Yes, it will be done by 4pm."

With a thin brush dipped in deep red, the artist introduces the dress of a young girl, her left arm reaching out to the sky. Next, the blue shirt of a boy with his back to the girl. To the right of the girl, another boy running with arms open. He has now drawn seven kids, in various sizes, small ones in the distance, and the Ukrainian wreath girl biggest, with the most details.

More kites… some shaped like birds, others look like octopuses with their tentacles free in the sky.

"I am going to paint the sunflowers now." Yew Chong looks at his live audience and gives them a smile. "I will start off with a few small ones, then each one of you can contribute your own sunflower, just the yellow petals, I will fill in the seeds which are the centres."

Between bright and mustard yellow, he applied each petal of the flower deliberately. Soon, the line between blue and yellow is drawn over by bright sunflowers. I start to see the beginnings of the whole painting, kites and sunflowers. What an optimistic happy painting. The message of joy and hope shouts through.

He offers the brush to Christina, who sits next to him watching. "Here, paint your sunflower. Remember, the sunflowers get bigger as they get lower and lower from the horizon, because they are closer to the eye."

"I don't want to spoil the painting," Christina says, laughing. "I will paint a small one."

Yew Chong laughs, "You can't go wrong with yellow petals. We are not painting still life; don't worry, go for it."

Gradually, the sunflower field fills up, the small flowers near the horizon, and they get progressively bigger and bigger. The artist takes over the last row, where the biggest sunflowers greet the eye.

It is three-thirty, almost time for photographer to take his shot. "I have two more parts to paint, and it will be done." The artist is visibly more relaxed. "The local bird among the sunflowers and the threads linking the hands to the kites."

The audience in the warehouse has grown in the last hour, and most are sitting and standing around the three-metre by three-metre denim. The blue and yellow flycatcher is painted in flight among the bigger flowers. Its wings and upper body are blue and lower body yellow, almost like a Ukrainian flag flying.

Yew Chong now divides his body between the blue and yellow of the denim, and with a point thin brush, connects the kids' hands to the kites in wavy threads of dark brown and black. It is an emotional moment, like adding the black dot of the eyes to a human or animal, the last act that brings the subject to life. The threads pull the lower part of the denim to the upper, the human figures to their aspiration, freedom. When the denim is hoisted up and seen from some distance, the kites take prominence, soaring across the sky with easy grace. Freedom. The ultimate message. No war, but peace… so that we are free to be who were want to be.

"I need you to stand on a stool and go through the motion of painting with a brush," the photographer says to Yew Chong. "This will be a very good picture for the paper."

A very good picture indeed. It is on the front page of *The Straits Times* on Sunday morning.

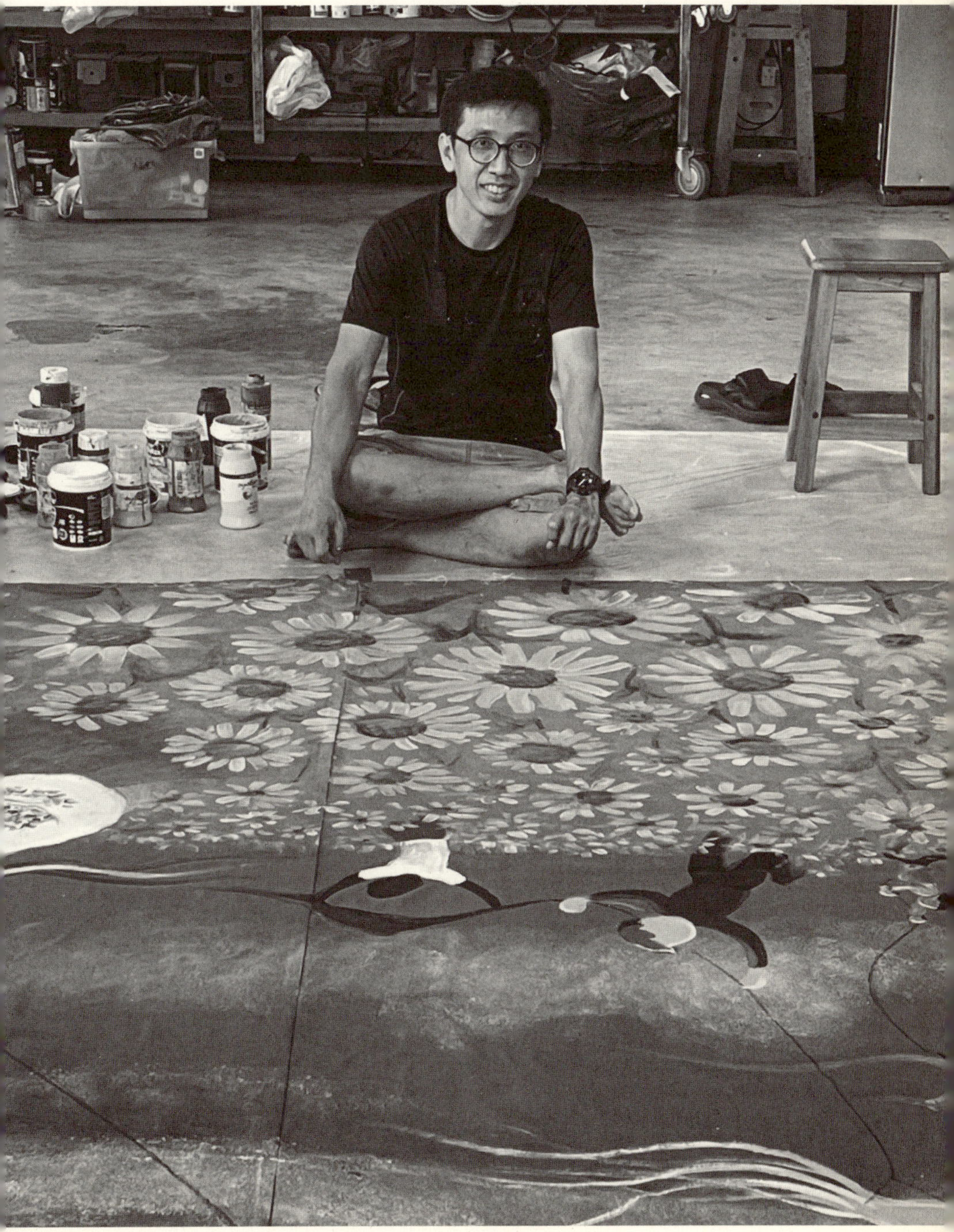

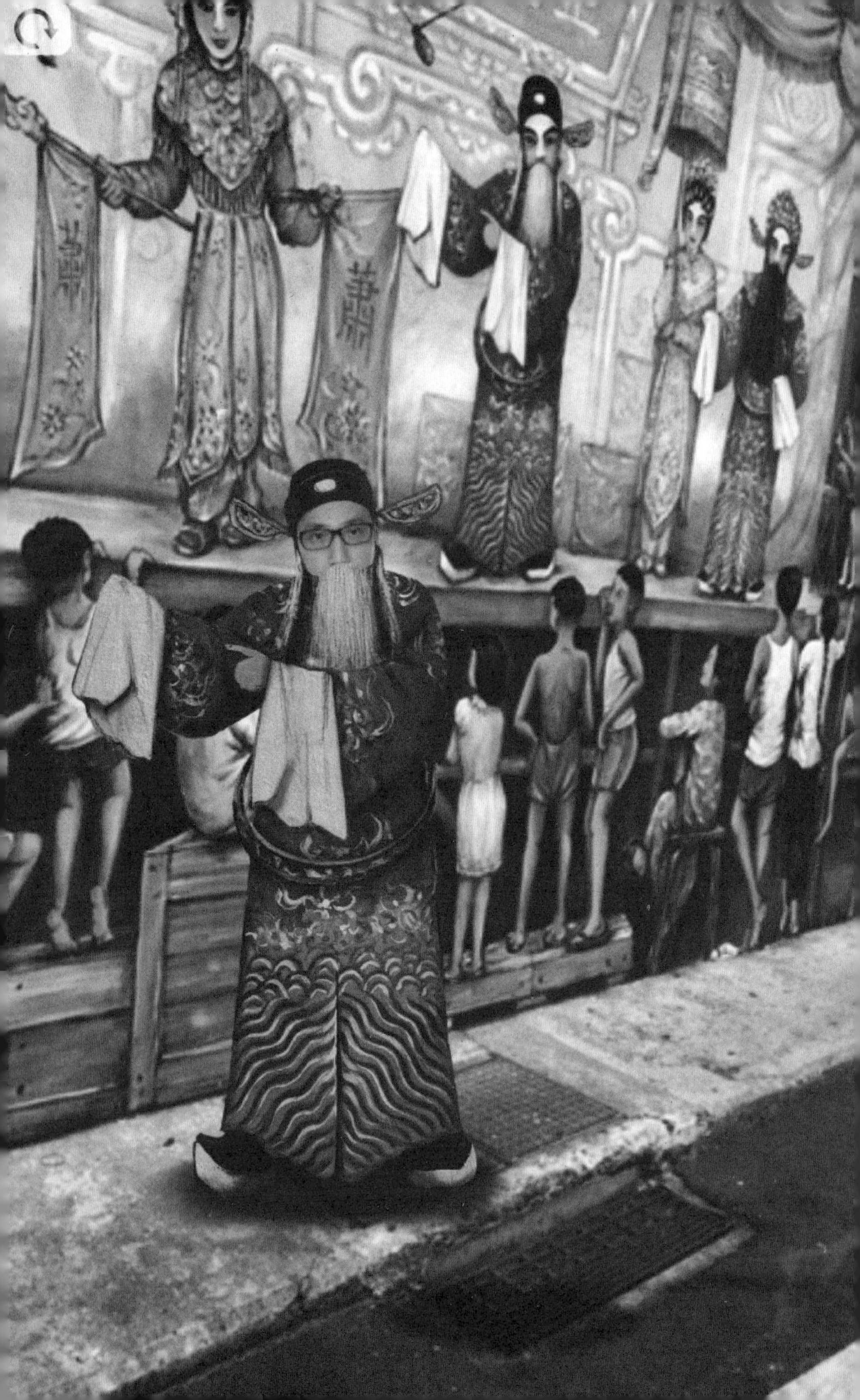

CHAPTER 9

Reinvention Story

Even after the switch, the accountant never leaves the artist.

Operating on Parallel Paths

Meeting Wong Su-Yen is a highly rewarding experience, albeit also an intimidating one. Her voice has the soothing quality of a broadcaster and her choice of words reminds me of an accomplished public speaker. I find out later that she is indeed a professional speaker, and has addressed audiences from the United States to Ukraine. Her audiences are typically CEOs and business leaders, ministers and government officials, unionists, entrepreneurs and educators. Looking at her LinkedIn profile is also humbling. Professor of global leadership, independent director serving on the Boards of several public, private, and not-for-profit organisations across the world, adventure traveller, musician…

I first met her in Yew Chong's art studio and knew her and her husband as art collectors. When I dug a bit deeper, I realised she is well- known in art circles and beyond, and as I had suspected, a chat with her would invariably go beyond art. Su-Yen is keen on focusing on 'the future of work' and what she calls an individual's reinvention story. To her, it is important to think of one's second or even third act because most of us will live to eighty, ninety, or even a hundred years old. Just being happy doing one thing, living out one career and then retiring may no longer be realistic, not to mention fulfilling. Yew Chong, to her, is an example of living one passion and keeping a second alive, and then going on to live the second passion, and in his case, making it better than the first.

The Yip Yew Chong story is an extraordinary one, a perfect example of how one envisions, plans, then executes a second act. Her interest in the artist began with his street art, something few were doing at that time. "We don't have a tradition of street art, he was one of the earliest." Her voice is confident without being authoritative. "Here is this guy, creating scenes that are past, and taking up wall space that wasn't used before and putting them to good use. Some other countries have a more involved street art history; for Singapore, it's pretty new. I was curious, who is this guy? In the early days, there wasn't that much written about him, and for me, I was really intrigued by what I call his reinvention story. This is what I do professionally; I help people navigate their reinvention."

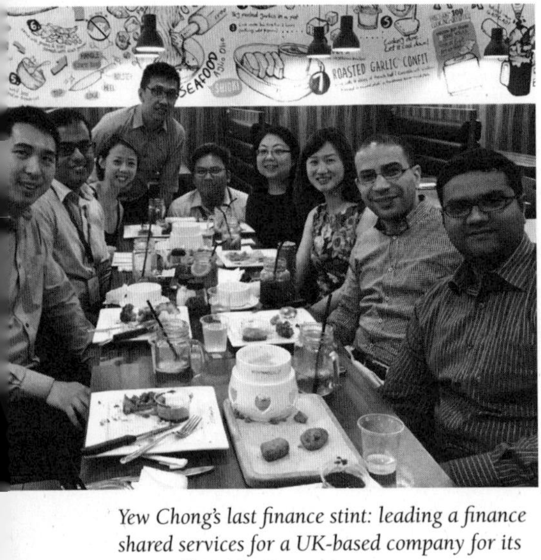

Yew Chong's last finance stint: leading a finance shared services for a UK-based company for its Asia and Middle East region.

Yew Chong's first and second acts cannot be more different from each other, and therefore, he is a rare and good role model. "It was probably difficult to fathom for most, here was a straight-laced guy, an

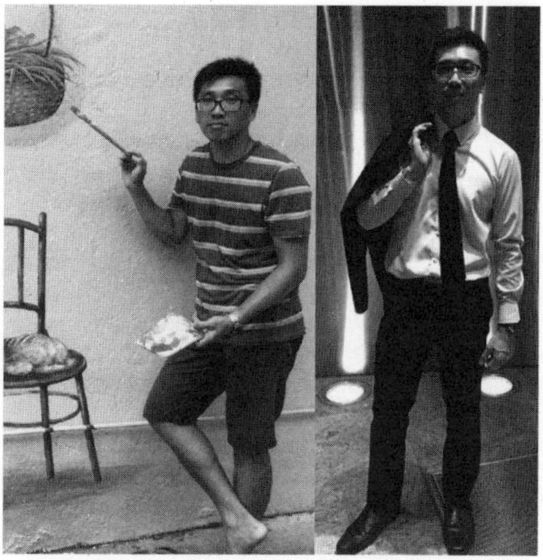

Between 2016 and mid-2018, Yew Chong painted murals on weekends while holding a full-time finance job.

accounting career with an MNC doing a regional job, a hired gun, yet he made the space to develop a parallel path, painting murals, while still doing his first job. At what point did he have confidence to make the switch? When he had enough saved, and when his so called 'hobby' was taking up more time than his real job."

It all boils down to planning, financial planning. Yew Chong knew that painting, or more specifically mural painting, would not be as financially secure as a job in Finance or Accounting. So, he saved. And even when he was doing well, got promoted, his lifestyle stayed the same. "He is financially savvy," Su-Yen asserts. "If you manage or maintain your lifestyle as your salary increases, then you have more flexibility to pursue different options later. He also built up a client base for his art to have the confidence to make that switch. That took time, and that to me was his path over the years that enabled him to do what he did."

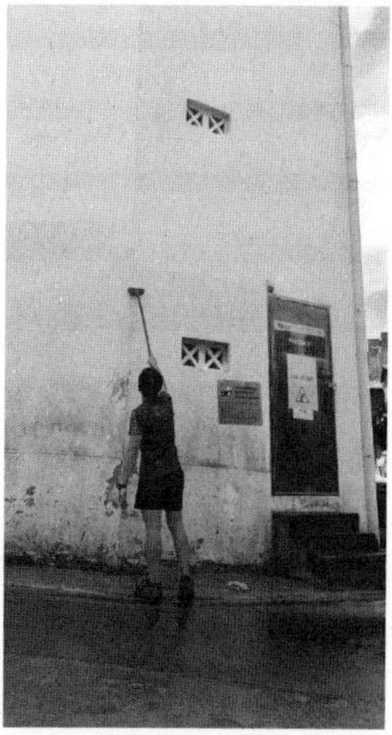

From working in the office to scrubbing walls on the street. (Photo by Echo)

Even after the switch, the accountant never leaves the artist. The accountant always

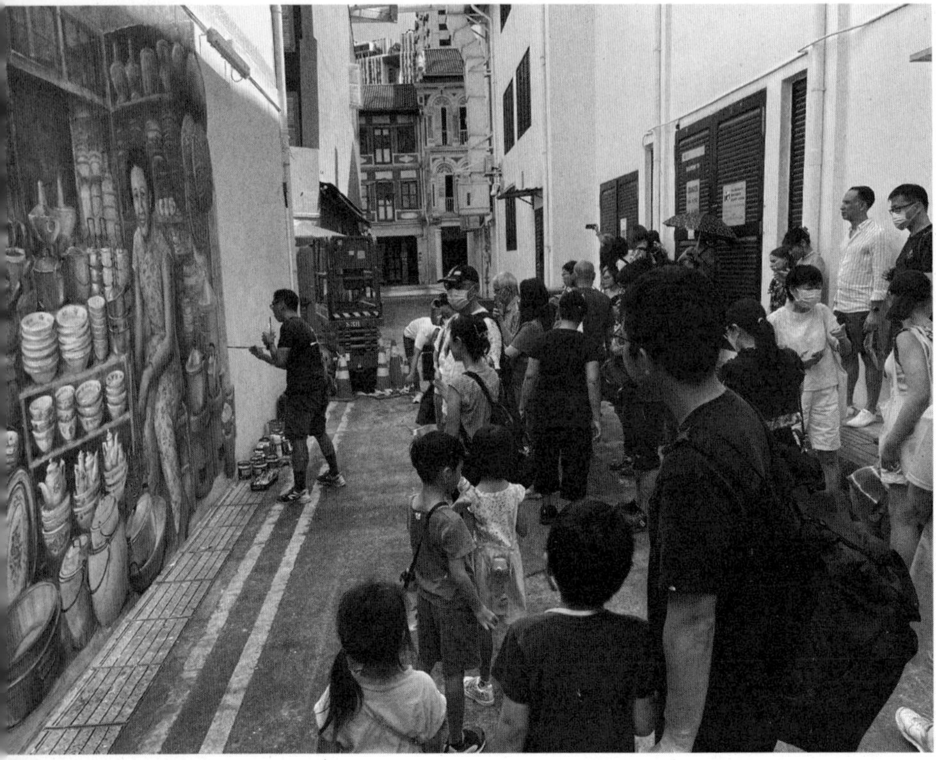

reminds the artist how he needs to stay viable, how to expand his client base, how to expand his fan base. While each mural is located in a back alley in an old part of Singapore, social media expands it beyond small Singapore to a global audience. "For some artists, the only thing that matters is the output. For Yew Chong, he thinks about the purpose of his art as well, that it must reach a global audience. It's part of being savvy. How can I ensure that what I do touches the maximum amount of people? By honing his skill with social media, his audience becomes global, not just Singapore. Being the accountant that he was, he is totally keyed into the business part of art as well. And the business of it involves how to create awareness, create fans, people who are loyal to you, so that they can follow your journey. He understands that in art, there are those who will buy your work and there are those who appreciate your work, both are important. Like Picasso. I am not going to buy a Picasso, but I appreciate Picasso. Nurturing a base is important and he is conscious of that. He has done it extremely well through social media and personal interaction. He lives in the 2020s, and is able to take full advantage of it."

Why has she decided to collect Yew Chong's work? How does it fit into her collection? "First, let me say his art speaks to every demographic. For people in their 60s and 70s, it is about reminiscence, nostalgia, reflecting on childhood experiences. To a child, the scenes are familiar, yet not quite. Like a street opera, familiar yet foreign. For tourists, it is culture that they don't see walking down Orchard Road. His art is universal and one takes away whatever one wants to take away. And that's why his art is powerful."

Su-Yen pauses. "For me, it is about how Singapore has evolved. He captures memories, Singapore's past; people in our generation can still remember those scenes even though how we live today is very different. Most artists today aren't doing that, so he is contrarian that way. He is doing what artists in the 1970s and 1980s were doing, trying to capture Singapore before it changes. He is able to put himself back to that time and capture the realities then, yet without being representational. The art in the 1970s and 1980s were representational, like the Singapore River while it was evolving, Chinatown while it was evolving. But his are memories based on extensive research, yet there is creative imagination. That's what attracts me to his art, imagination based on reality. Thematically, he fits into the second-generation artists who were documenting changes in the 1970s and 1980s, but his is done with a twist. He captures Singapore as it is transitioning."

But Su-Yen brings it back to why she thinks he is a wonderful role model for how people can think about structuring multi-chapters in their lives. "Remember, we are all going to be living till we are 100, 90, 80, whatever it is. Even if you spent 25 years pursuing one career, doctor, lawyer, teacher, that puts a person at 45 or 50. Then, we need to think about what's your next chapter, find something that is meaningful and fulfilling and that you are good at. Sometimes, people are not so open to these possibilities. They go into a particular path and their identities are so tied into it, tied to their chapter one, and they find it difficult to even think about chapter two. Yew Chong is a very good example of how one can think about chapter two, that draws on our chapter one. His business skills he puts to good use in terms of how he manages his art, the business part or the commercial side of his art, like how you price your art, and at the same time, it's all radically different. That is something that we need more role models of. Most of us, after our first chapter, would easily have another 20 years for something else. If you step away at 45 or 50 and not think about doing something else, I think that's quite sad. And he has been able to marry being an accountant and being an artist seamlessly together. He is an example of nurturing multi-interests. People focus on the one thing they are good at doing. But it is also important to have divergent interests in life because it gives you options and he is a perfect example of somebody who's done that, doing it along the way. He had an interest in drawing since he was a boy, doesn't mean he has to put it away; it also doesn't mean you need to get your first job as an artist either. He

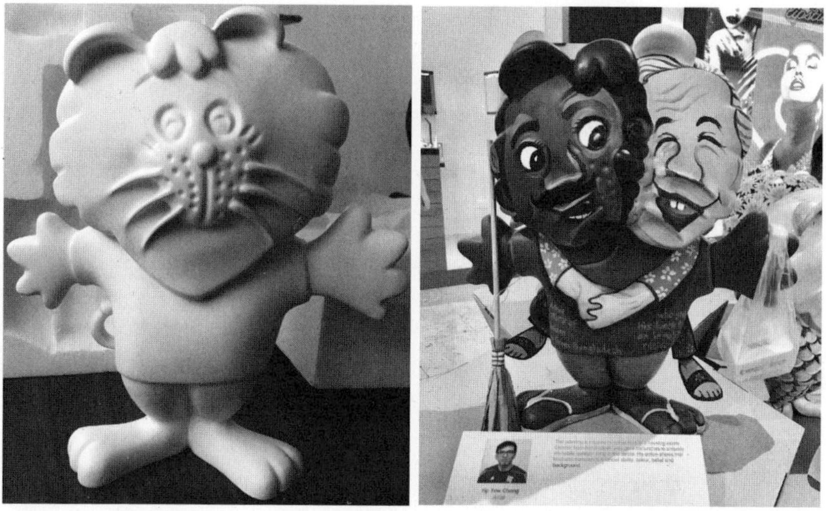

Reinventing something familiar to something surprising, yet still looking familiar, 2019.

didn't give up his passion, so he did it along the way. And the more he did, the better he became, until the day came when he knew he can switch with confidence."

All this talk about one's second act makes me think about my own reinvention. When I was in broadcasting, I nursed a secret. I wanted to be a writer. Occasionally, I allowed myself the luxury to dream, that I would casually walk into a bookstore, and there my book would be displayed, next to famous authors like J.K. Rowling and Stephen King. While it seemed far-fetched, it was a little fire I fed on the back of my mind. I paid special attention to the scripts I wrote for my current affairs stories and my documentaries. Perhaps one day. My heart would open when my stories were praised, and when my scripts were singled out, I was literally beside myself.

I reached the pinnacle of my broadcast career quite early. I was in my late 40s. While I was having the time of my life, I was also becoming restless and bored. The year was 2007; I was producing a documentary for Cultural Medallion artist Tan Swie Hian. When it was done, he looked at me and said simply, "This documentary should be adapted into a book; I have not seen the visuals for the documentary, but I enjoy reading the script."

Long story very short, I published my first book the following year. It was also the year I decided to leave MediaCorp. I explored many things after that, started my own company, joined a law firm, had a two-and-a-half-year stint in Myanmar running an entertainment channel. Throughout the decade-long search to find something else to sink my teeth into, I never stopped writing. I published a novel, then a self-help book on crisis management, then a book on another artist.

I terminated my stint in Myanmar in February 2019; COVID-19 had just started and there were murmurs of a military coup. I arrived at the Singapore Changi Airport in the late afternoon and decided to pick up a few magazines from the airport bookstore. On the way out, a familiar yellow book cover caught my eye, and when I walked closer, my heart skipped a beat.

It was not next to J.K. Rowling or Stephen King, but under the Singapore Literature section, next to Catherine Lim's short stories, was my first novel, *Riot Green*. It didn't seem real; even though I had continued writing, I never really saw myself as a writer. But there, in the Changi Airport bookstore, somehow, my thinking changed. Perhaps I should seriously consider writing as something I can do full time. Today, I am commissioned to write, and I also write for my own interests. Knowingly or unknowingly, I have gravitated towards fulfilling my secret dream, or what Su-Yen calls reinvention. I don't have Yew Chong's financial savvy; I am a poor writer. But boy I am glad I nursed a parallel interest to broadcasting, and throughout my first act, never let my second out of sight. Reinvention is something we need to embrace, all of us. Listening to Su-Yen, I find my own reinvention lacking the financial dimension that Yew Chong so meticulously planned and executed with forethought and precision. He is the role model.

Even in Art, a Parallel Run

25 years in the financial world, and now entering one decade as a full-time artist. Murals, big wall murals, have served Yew Chong well. Highly visible, each wall has captured the attention and imagination of the public in ways he had not dared to dream or imagine. 54 now, the question is, what's next?

"If I continue to do this, more and more of this..." The artist's eyes betray a fatigued mind. "Sooner or later, and I think sooner rather than later, the public, people who follow what I do, will get tired of me. So, in the last two years, and also because of COVID, I have become very selective when it comes to murals. One or two a year, and the site must be unusual and unique to allow me to try new approaches."

Reinvention from the financial to the art world was the first and crucial transition. Within art itself, Yew Chong is also planning for long-term sustainability. So, new approaches to murals alone would not be sufficient, he needs to reinvent his art too. "The last thing I want is to be known as a one-trick pony. I am keenly aware that to some critics, I am not even a proper artist. My art does not fit into a known genre, and I am sure I don't even fit into the traditional definition of a street artist. Yes, my art has connected with the layman and woman, and for that, I am grateful. I need to plan, as I get older, how I can get better, how I can continue to engage the public, not just through murals, but through another platform in art."

Along the River During the Qingming Festival (Qingming Shanghe Tu) is a handscroll painting by the Song Dynasty painter Zhang Zeduan (1085–1145). The scroll is 25.5 centimetres (10 inches) in height and 5.25 metres long. It captures the daily lives of people and landscape in the capital along Bian River (in present-day Kaifeng) during the Northern Song. The theme is celebrating the festive spirit and worldly commotion during the Qingming Festival. From right to left, as a viewer unrolls it, successive scenes reveal the lifestyle of all levels of the society from rich to poor, the business activities in rural areas and the city, and offer glimpses of period clothing and architecture. The painting is considered to be the most renowned work among all Chinese paintings, and it has even been called China's *Mona Lisa*.

As an artistic creation, the painting has been revered, and artists of subsequent dynasties made hundreds of replicas, copies of copies and even forgeries of well-regarded copies, each following the overall composition and the theme of the original but differing in detail and technique. Over the centuries, the Song original was kept by private collectors before it was eventually returned to public ownership. The painting was a particular favourite of Puyi, China's last emperor, who took it with him when he was forced to leave the Forbidden City in 1924. It was recovered in 1945 and kept at the Palace Museum in the Forbidden City. The Song original and later versions are regarded as national treasures and are exhibited only for brief periods every few years. Scholars believe that approximately a hundred versions exist today, in private hands and in major museums around the world, demonstrating just how much influence *Along the River During the Qingming Festival* has exerted in Chinese art over the years.

For a three-month period in the World Expo 2010 presented at the China Pavilion, the original painting was remade into a 3-D animated, viewer-interactive digital version, titled *River of Wisdom*. At 128 x 6.5 metres, it is roughly 30 times the size of the original scroll. The computer-animated mural, with moving characters and objects and portraying the scenes in four-minute day and night cycles, was one of the primary exhibitions in the Chinese Pavilion, drawing queues of up to two hours with a reservation. From 7th December 2011 to 6th February 2012, in an exhibition titled *A Moving Masterpiece: The Song Dynasty as Living Art*, the digital reproduction was exhibited at the Singapore Expo.

Yew Chong looks at me and smiles. "*Qingming Shanghe Tu* is an inspiration." His white teeth almost glisten. "It shows the impact art can create, not just over the years, but over centuries. I can do something even longer, something very manageable in terms of height, and the length could also be manageable if I painted a panel at a time. I want to transit from murals to something more sustainable. My reinvention, if you like to call it that, is really from emulsion to acrylic, from mural to canvas. I started to paint with acrylic on canvas even before I started painting murals, but stopped to focus on murals. The pandemic has brought me back to canvas. Now, I want to make this evolvement more permanent, more public by painting a long, long canvas. Acrylic on canvas would last much, much longer than wall murals, where the average lifespan is at most seven to eight years. Acrylic like oil on canvas can last for centuries if maintained well under a controlled indoor environment. So, this switch, if successful, would redefine me as an artist. I want to be known as an artist, not confined to just a mural artist."

On 31st July 2021, Yew Chong made his dream public in a post on Facebook:

> *I've dreamt of creating a long canvas painting. I was inspired by the famous Song Dynasty painting* Qingming Shanghe Tu. *I wanted to create a Singapore version showing her everyday life in the 1970s, 1980s. In my eyes, Singapore's physical cityscape transformed most dramatically during these two decades.*
>
> *While* 'Qingming Shanghe Tu' *is 5m long, I am aiming to paint it much longer, maybe 10 times longer. It's not a mural. It's canvas painting, so hopefully it is less transient. It will also take a very long time to complete.*
>
> *In the inaugural section, I've painted a cross-section interior of a three-storey shophouse in Chinatown....*

And so, the long, long canvas takes off. Over the next one and a half years, Yew Chong would update his social media base location by location, panel by panel, metre by metre.

4.4m completed! 45.6m to go! He declares on Facebook and Instagram. Panel by panel, location by location, the artist teases his vast social media base with dramatic and striking images of various parts of Singapore that most of them still recognise even though most

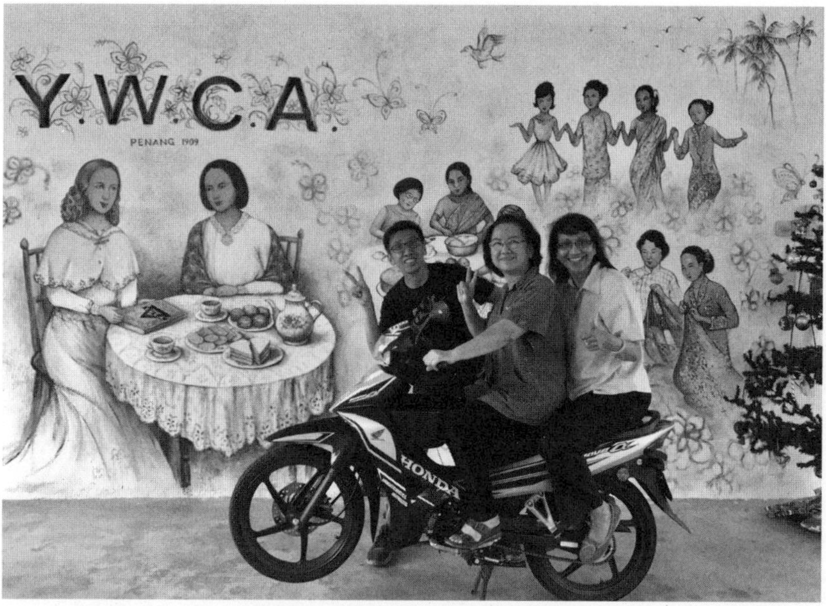

New territories and new connections can lead to new opportunities.

of these cityscapes have either changed drastically or are no more.

To many following him on social media, there is no transition, no change. The artist is still painting landscapes, cityscapes. The subject matter is still vanishing Singapore, and his style is unmistakably realistic and colourful.

"My switch to acrylic and canvas is subtle to the lay public." Yew Chong leans back, folding his arm. "The switch is important to me but it doesn't need to be apparent to them. For them, so long as my art stays relatable, it's all good. For me, I have opened up another medium, more manageable and it allows me to paint under a much more controlled environment. Sure, the art is not public, but I intend to put them in an exhibition. Where and how, I have not figured that out. Social media makes it public, and it will generate interest to see them in real life."

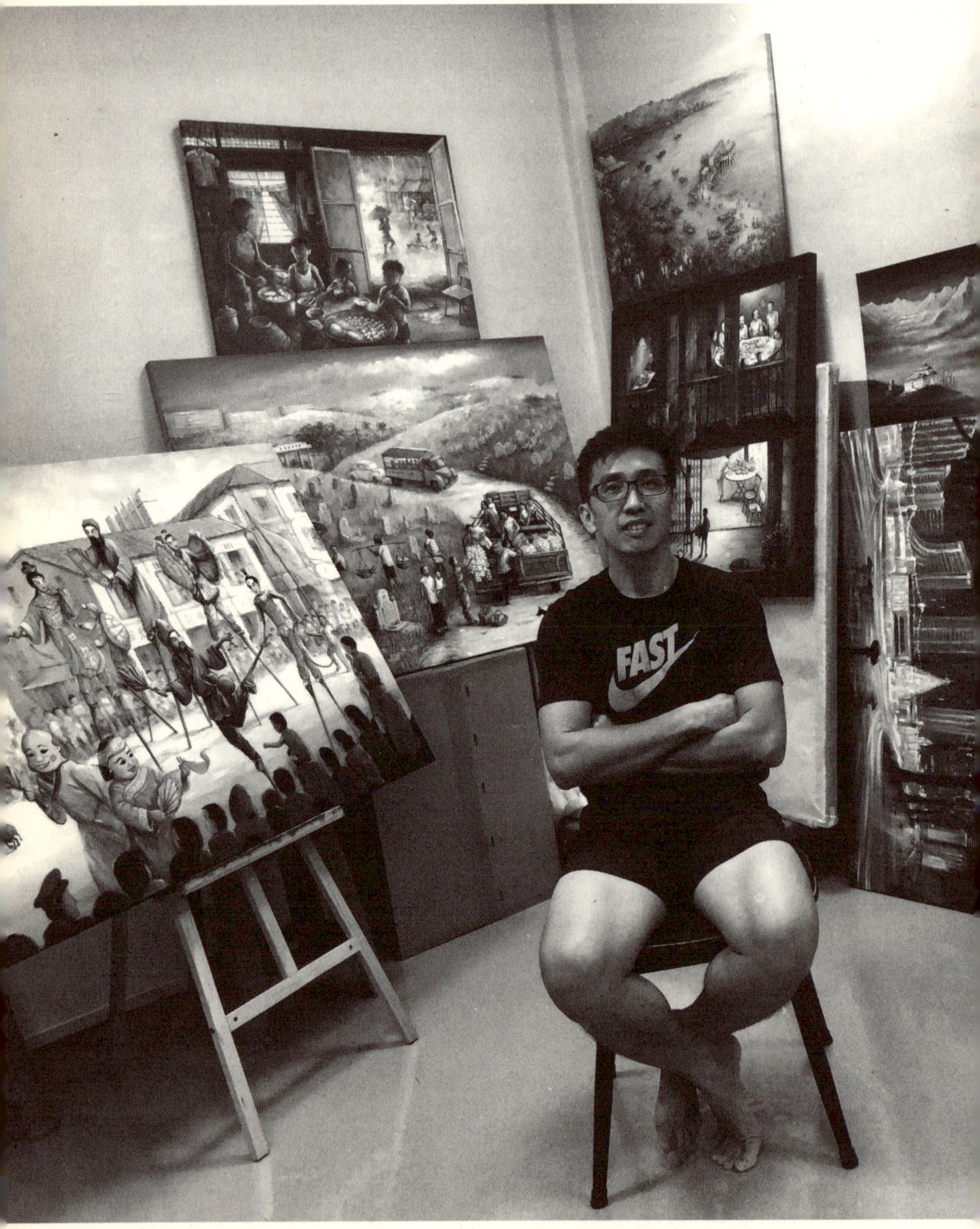

Painting Stories from Yesteryear *in his studio during the pandemic.*

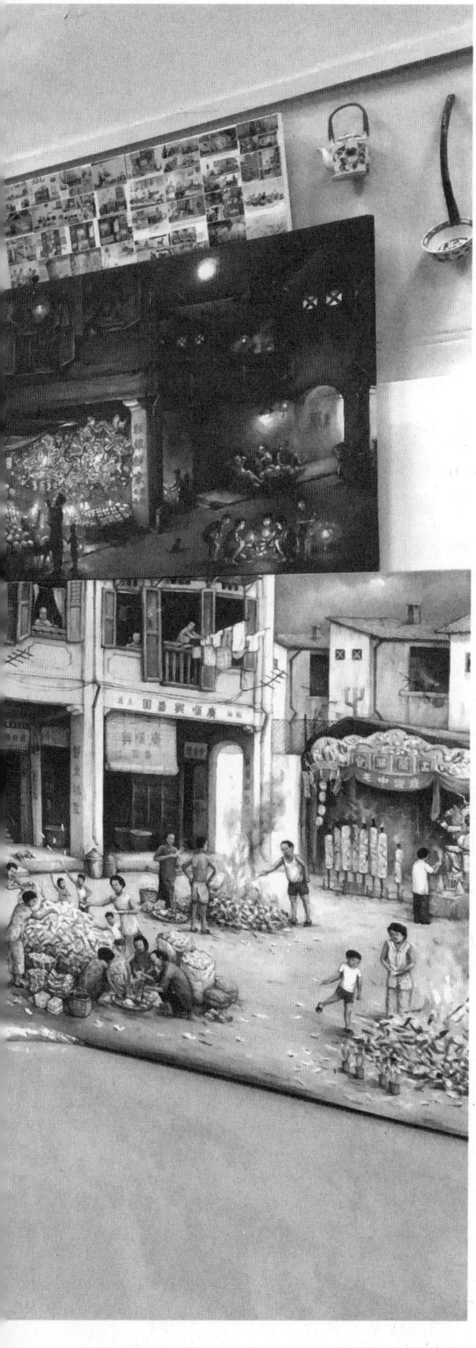

Using social media to update his public, allowing them to participate and interact, Yip Yew Chong's art looks set to continue its mass popularity as his art-making moves into the studio. Because each canvas is smaller than a wall, his style is now finer, crisper and the true talent of artist plainer to see. "I no longer use a wall-paint brush." Yew Chong laughs. "I use brushes other regular artists use. But I treat acrylic very much like watercolour, not oil. So even as I use different paints now, my style of painting stays the same."

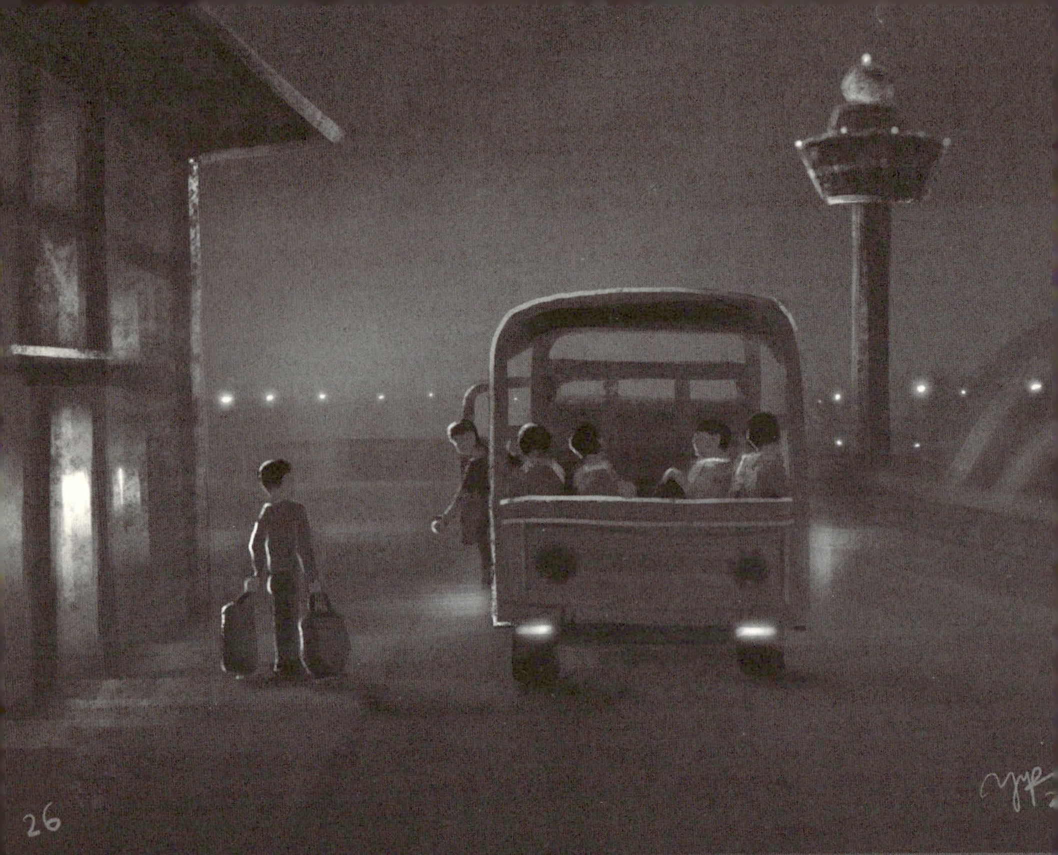

26

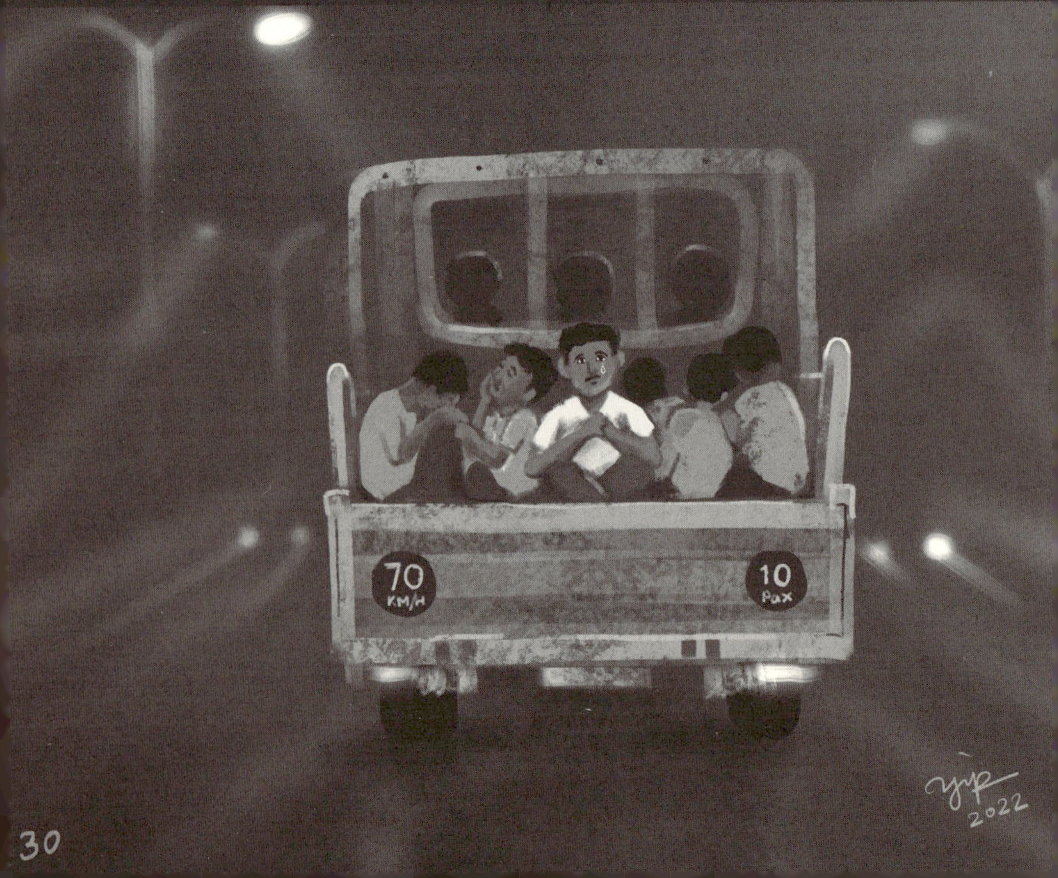

30

CHAPTER 10

Journeys

I count my blessings and consider myself so lucky to be born in my time and place.

A Journey by Lorry

I first stepped on Singapore soil on 28 October 2015. I arrived at the airport at 6am. The company sent a driver with a lorry to receive me. When I got into the lorry, I saw many other people sitting there. I was feeling very dizzy from sleep deprivation. After going for a while, I suddenly flipped upside down due to the car shaking. My forehead was badly bruised when the lorry driver pulled the brake very hard, and my head hit a metal bar in the car. The scar is still visible on my forehead. Later, this scar became a bad omen in my life.

When I went to see my bride for the first time for an arranged marriage, she liked everything but rejected the proposal because of my scar. I have not been able to get married till date.

The lorry journey was a dark chapter of my life which I can't forget even if I want to.

Mohammad Sharif Rana

Yew Chong texted me about an exhibition, *A Journey by Lorry*, at Projector X: Riverside Point. I was intrigued by the title of the exhibition and also the unusual venue. It was a busy week; I did not ask him about the exhibition or think too much about it. I just put it in my diary as something I needed to attend.

24th September 2022. Saturday 7pm. I am familiar with Riverside Point as it was the venue where I conducted my media training, but I have not heard of Projector X. I arrive at number 13 on the fourth floor, but the place is quiet; there is no hint of an exhibition anywhere. My heart sinks; I must be at the wrong address.

A young Indian man walks towards me. "Projector X?" he asks, looking equally perplexed.

Ah, I am at the right place! This man is also here for the exhibition. Just then, I receive a text from Yew Chong. *I am running a bit late; please go in first.*

An Indian woman walks out from a side doorway, "You are here for the exhibition? Come in. You follow this corridor, all the way down." She points to her right.

The Indian man steps in front of me and walks towards the corridor; I decide to follow him. Presently, I hear people talking, but not in English. The corridor opens up to a big auditorium-like hall, rows of chairs have been arranged, facing what looks like a makeshift stage. The room is filled with South Asians, most of them male. The man I followed waves at his friends and turns to me with a broad smile. "Welcome," he says in English. *A Journey by Lorry* ...ah. The whole 'scene' is falling into place; the title of the exhibition starts to make sense now. I walk towards a poster on the left.

This exhibition features a collection of stories and poems by migrant workers reflecting on their experiences riding at the back of lorries to work. They collaborated with local photographers and artists, who provided them images and illustrations in response to each poem or story.

Yew Chong's involvement becomes clear to me now; he is one of the artists who has used his art to illustrate and support the stories and poems written by the migrant workers. My heart opens; what a meaningful collaboration! Just then, I see Yew Chong walking through the corridor with his daughter. "My daughter has asked to come along; she wants to see the exhibition." Yew Chong is in a grey T-shirt and blue jeans; he fits right in with the crowd. As he walks further in, a few men stand and shake his hand.

Walking through the exhibition, I begin to realise Singapore may have become a first-world developed country, but how we treat those who have come here to work, especially in jobs Singaporeans do not want to do, leaves a lot to be desired. Each poem, each story, shows how little I know about them, especially how they feel. What they have to say is perhaps not what we want to hear, but as Singaporeans, we need to know. Suddenly, the exhibition takes on a socio-political dimension I did not see earlier. "I am glad you are involved in this exhibition." I look into Yew Chong's eyes. "More Singaporeans should know about this exhibition."

But the exhibition is not easy to get to. The Projector X: Riverside Point is a pop-up cinema hall which was previously an abandoned disco. Tucked or almost hidden on the fourth floor, if no one tells you

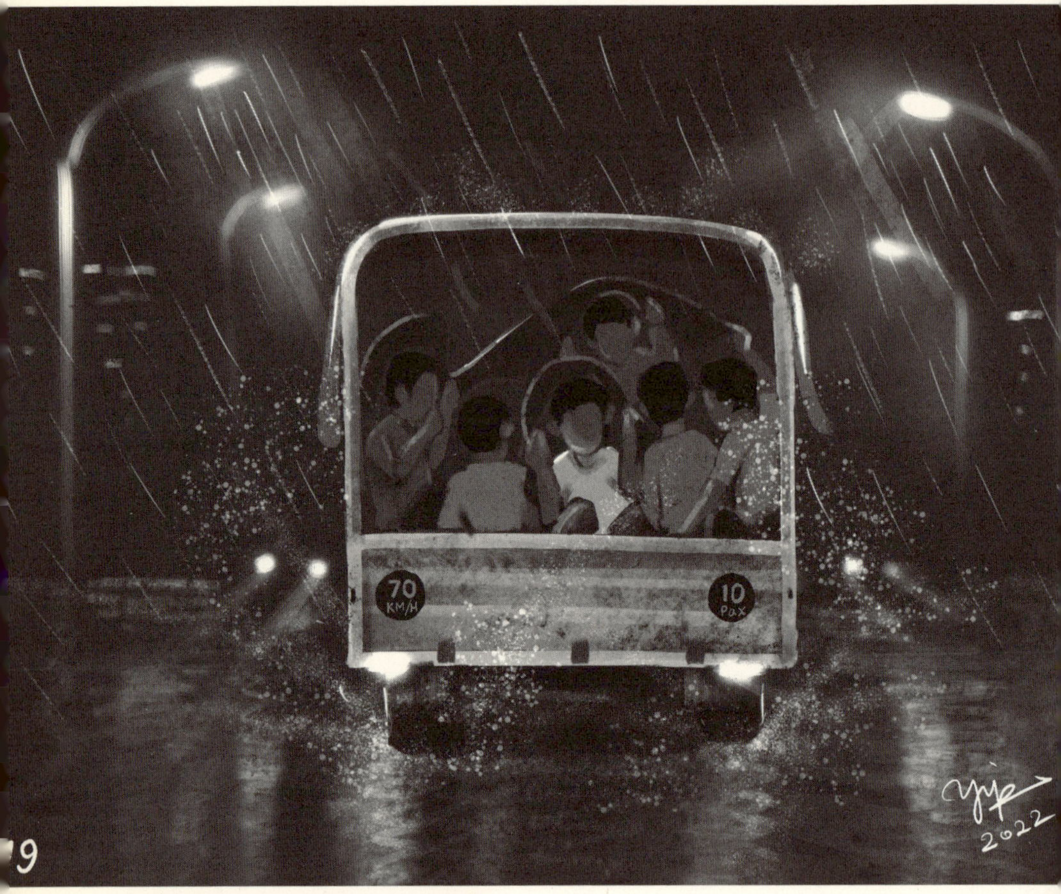

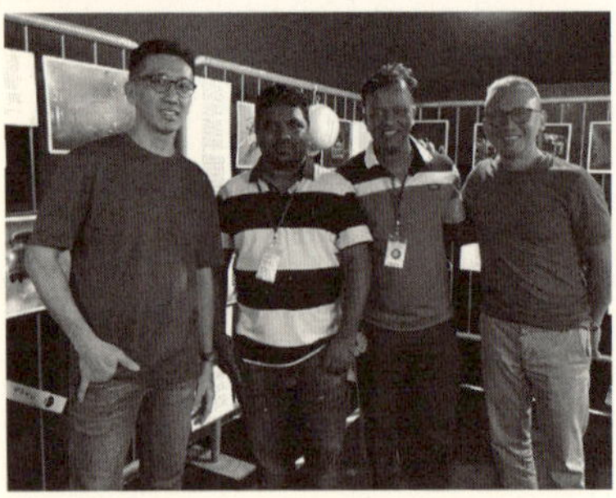

When Bhai Sharif and Ripon approached Yew Chong to contribute some artworks for the A Journey by Lorry *exhibition, Yew Chong readily agreed. Yew Chong believes the unsafe practice is not right.*

about the exhibition, you won't chance upon it walking around the riverside. So, even though each story, each poem underlines the danger of the decades-long practice of ferrying migrant workers on the back of lorries in Singapore, the chances of the message getting to the average Singaporean is low.

A quick Google search: in May 2021, there were three accidents involving lorries that were carrying migrant workers. The accidents sent dozens of migrant workers to the hospital and resulted in the death of two. In Parliament, members of parliament (MPs) asked if the government would review the safety regulations to introduce more measures to protect the safety of migrant workers, specifically asking for buses instead of lorries to ferry migrant workers. Yet, for a host of practical and cost considerations, construction workers would continue to be ferried in lorries.

Yew Chong has contributed eight digital illustrations to accompany eight poems and stories. There are 120 on show. The poems and stories were originally written in Bengali, Tamil, Tagalog, even Chinese, and have been translated into English. As I pace from one story to the next, I am ashamed to admit how little I know about the plight of these migrant workers. The stories are raw, wading in self-pity and anger, written in the first person, talking to themselves, talking to us.

> *Every morning and afternoon, when I see this car, I feel like we are some uncivilised folks living in a civilisation. It feels like we are some kind of inferior animals, who have to get drenched whenever it rains, work in a drenched body, come home with a fever of 100 degrees in the afternoon, and there is no such thing as home. We just spend the night in a shelter and ride that weird car to reach work in the morning.*
>
> *It is very sad that all the developmental work we do in Singapore for such a small salary is only to risk our lives, but in this civilised society we are hardly seen as civilised! It is such a*

civilisation where civilised folks go to work in the morning in comfortable buses, on the contrary, we savages take lorries to build a civilisation!

Naxmol Hasan

The exhibition is an experience, a rare chance to get into the hearts and minds of migrant workers through the English language and the universal language of art. I am glad the exhibition will go on till 9th of October; on some nights, there will even be live music and panel discussions. We can do our part and urge our friends to come and see that the migrant workers in our midst as not just manual labourers; they are fathers, husbands, and sons; some are poets, storytellers, and musicians.

Yew Chong takes out his mobile phone and scrolls through his photographs. He stops and shows me an image of a migrant worker assisting him in painting a mural. "Whenever I did murals which required heavy machineries, or worksites under construction, I had the opportunity to interact with migrant workers." He turns and hands me a paper plate. A simple dinner has been laid out, rice, curry and vegetables; the spread, I gather, is a treat, much better than what they get to eat in their dormitories. "One of the most memorable was when I was painting a tall mural using a scissor lift. My benchman was from Bangladesh. He was in his early 20s. He was chatty. We chitchatted a lot. It was funny that he kept comparing me with his dad, who was the same age as me. He said his dad would never speak with him like that. I said I don't speak with my own children like that too! I soon realised he was actually well-educated, knowledgeable, and aspiring. When our work ended, he asked if I can hire him for more days."

I cast my mind back to the years I stayed with my sister; her maid was from the Philippines. She was a university graduate but could not find work there, so she left her husband and kids behind to be a domestic helper in Singapore. I walk towards two chairs at the corner of the hall with bottled water on the table. "Let's eat here."

"With my limited interactions, I can't say at all that I understand the migrant worker community here." Yew Chong takes a sip of water. "But I learn empathy. Many of them have worked in Singapore for many years, away from their families left behind in their own countries. I count my blessings and consider myself so lucky to be born in my time and place. I wonder how I will feel if I were in their shoes."

The following day, 25th September, Yew Chong posts his thoughts about the exhibition on Facebook. Accompanying the posts are the digital illustrations he did for the exhibition as well as photographs of migrant workers assisting him painting murals. I have seen these illustrations at the exhibition, but seeing them again on my mobile phone makes me feel so much better. I feel sure many more people will get to see the images now that it is on social media. A somewhat obscure art exhibition is now given the Yew Chong touch, reaching not just a national but international audience.

On my mobile phone, I can enlarge the images with the tips of my fingers, and suddenly, the details of each illustration are clearer to me than when I saw them at the exhibition. On the back of a blue lorry, a worker balances himself next to several others. He has been highlighted; his shirt whiter than the rest. Both his arms are folded with his hands placed closed to his heart as if in prayer. An exaggerated white tear rolls down his left cheek. While the lorry looks real, the figures are treated naively. The beams from the road lamps duct like the limbs of a huge spider. The overall effect of the illustration is surreal, like a Dali painting.

The same lorry in another illustration shows it in the midst of a heavy downpour. Here, the figures are seen trying to cover their heads as the rain splashes from all directions, top, sides, and from the wet road. Unlike the previous illustration, the beams hitting down from the road lamps are orange; they accentuate the rain pouring down and their reflections on the road make the lorry look like it is floating in a riot of water.

The post is shared 136 times. The images draw many comments.

Lee Hwee Chin: Such unexpected artworks! Poetic, poignant, and they tell the needed true story. Thank you, Yip Yew Chong; you are truly touching hearts with your work.

Hena Roy: Well narrated, Mr Yip. Yes, we are blessed to be born in our time and place.

Yip Yew Chong: We should indeed appreciate and be thankful to all who helped build our blessed existence here!

Kim Ang: Makes one realise that underneath our skin, we're all the same.

Janlyn Seow: Totally can relate to this. While taking my uncle's vegetable lorry in the rain back in the 1990s while sitting at the back. Offered to give me a ride home but the front seats were packed with vegetables stuff and my grandma. By the time my uncle reached my estate, I was soaked from head to toe by the rain at the back. He never noticed until my joyride ended.

Yew Chong ends the post with this plea:

If you are keen to learn more about their thoughts, come read the many stories and poems they wrote. The exhibition is a unique platform that allows them to express their feelings through art. It changes our stereotypical visions of them working at construction sites, cleaning our estates, pruning our trees. They are also authors, poets, storytellers, photographers, curators, and musicians. Join them for a few minutes, sitting at the back of the lorries, at 'A Journey by Lorry' *Arts Exhibition.*

Journeys to Italy and France

In 2017, the Singapore Hokkien Huay Kuan commissioned Yew Chong to paint a mural on the 44-metre long rear wall of the Thian Hock Keng temple, one of the oldest temples in Singapore. The mural was unveiled on 13th April that year, during the Singapore Hokkien Festival. The Thian Hock Keng mural is the longest mural Yew Chong has done. From right to left, it tells the story of young men leaving their families behind for a better life, the dangerous sea journey from China to

Singapore, and how the Hokkien Clan Association helped early immigrants in 19th century Singapore.

"It is the epic story of immigrants, of how the brawn and muscles of these men help build modern Singapore." Yew Chong remembers the long mural with warmth in his voice. "Unlike most of my other murals which are more heritage, this is historical. A fair amount of research and discussion went into it." The mural was done more than five years ago; Yew Chong's focus is now on acrylic on canvas done in studio, less on big murals on walls.

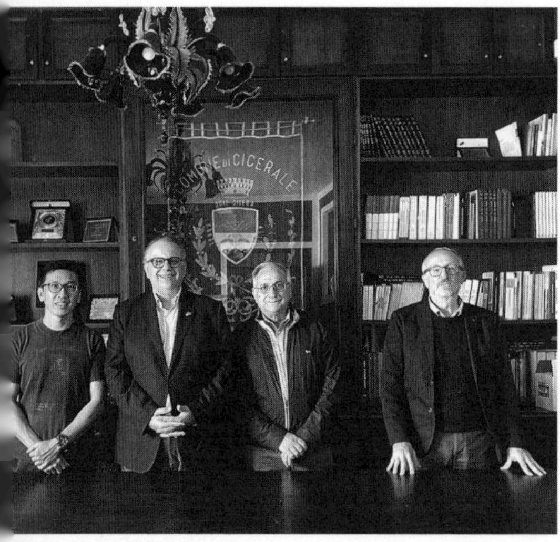

The curator, Gerardo, brought Yew Chong to the town hall to meet the mayor. Gerardo came across Yew Chong's works in Singapore and invited him to create three artworks in Italy.

Gerardo is an Italian curator. Working under the Edgar Degas Foundation, he is looking for both veteran and new artists for two jobs, to paint at an open-air museum in a small town in southern Italy, and a house which was once the Pope's residence. The search is for artists from all over the world, preferably artists who have had experience painting murals. Singapore is one of the countries in Asia he is keen to visit and speak to potential artists to travel to Italy. During his preliminary research on Singapore, he came across the Thian Hock Keng temple mural. When he arrived at Changi on a recce trip, he told the taxi driver to bring him to the temple. At the site, he was impressed. He thought the style, storytelling, and size achieved at the temple would fit what he wanted to do for the open-air museum.

"I was in Jordan in May last year." The artist recalls, still a little surprised by what happened. "I got a message from an Italian who wanted to meet me. He said he was coming to Singapore. I told him I would be coming back to Singapore just in time; we could meet. And so, we met up. He bought me dinner at a fancy Italian restaurant at the National Gallery Singapore." He looks at me with his brows raised. "It was kind of him, but I was not quite used to the food from such a high-end restaurant. It was probably a Michelin star restaurant. My first time." He laughs out, hands raised to his mouth. "The man is a curator, and he explained that he was setting up this open-air museum; he wanted to feature new and veteran artists from all over the world. He was touring from Dubai and now Singapore. After Singapore he would go to Ho Chi Minh, then to Australia, to look for artists to join him. He said he had invited Banksy, and Banksy accepted his invitation. It was all quite unreal."

Yew Chong was told he would be painting in Cicerale, a small town in the countryside in southern Italy. What was he supposed to paint? "It was clear to me during dinner that he was open and suggested I did some research." The artist smiles again. "We talked of painting philosophers, famous philosophers of Italy. Then, we went back to the mural of Thian Hock Keng temple, which was what caught his eye in the first place. How people came to Singapore, the Nanyang story. The painting should be like the mural, and it needs to be story-based. So, all these requirements are really up my alley. It is what I do. It sounds like a big project, a real opportunity to break from what I am doing in

Singapore. Of course, I don't know if it would really happen; it all sounds a bit too good to be true. So, I don't want to place too much hope in it; I don't want to be disappointed. At first, I was also apprehensive that it may be a scam. But I had done an online search on the curator before the meeting. I believe it is not a scam, but I am still cautious. If it is real, I am willing to put my 60-metre project on hold for a few months. I don't want to miss this opportunity."

Being an international artist has always been his ultimate aim. He has done several artworks overseas since 2016. Just before the pandemic, in February 2020, he was painting in Cambodia. He was set to paint in Pakistan in April 2020, and in Japan in May 2020. But the pandemic struck, and everything came to a complete standstill. "Everything was cancelled or put on hold indefinitely. Now, when the world has resumed to normal, I get the chance to paint in Italy! I don't know if it is officially an artist-in-residence stint and so I don't know if I can invite my wife. He told me it is like an artist-in-residence. The open-air museum is not opened yet. So, I get to be part of a museum opening. No matter how small or big, it is good to paint for a museum in Italy. Italians appreciate art. Even if it is a road-side mural, I would go. Murals are what I do anyway. At the dinner meeting, I was worried that it could be a scam. So, I did not reveal too much. I was wondering, are they real people? In Europe, there are many vanity galleries who invite artists, but you have to pay for entrance fees, registration fees, participation fees. And the worst scenario is I get kidnapped! I am still not sure if this is real. I hope it is."

Four months later in September, Yew Chong leaves for Europe, not just for Italy, but also Lyon in the south of France. At the eleventh hour, a French Expo company contacted him and asked if he could paint a mural at an Expo, immediately after his stay in Italy. Things have fallen into place like a dream. The anxiety of what to paint in Europe is also mercifully taken away; it turned out, both Italy and France want the subject matter to be Singapore, so scenes of Singapore would need to be painted there. They want the murals in the streets of Singapore to be brought to Europe!

The month of October sees Yew Chong blissfully lost in Cicerale, southern Italy. In a family-run country house, within a goat dairy farm and a vineyard at the back, it is the extreme visual opposite of urban Singapore, the needed break the artist longed for. "It fronts the beautiful

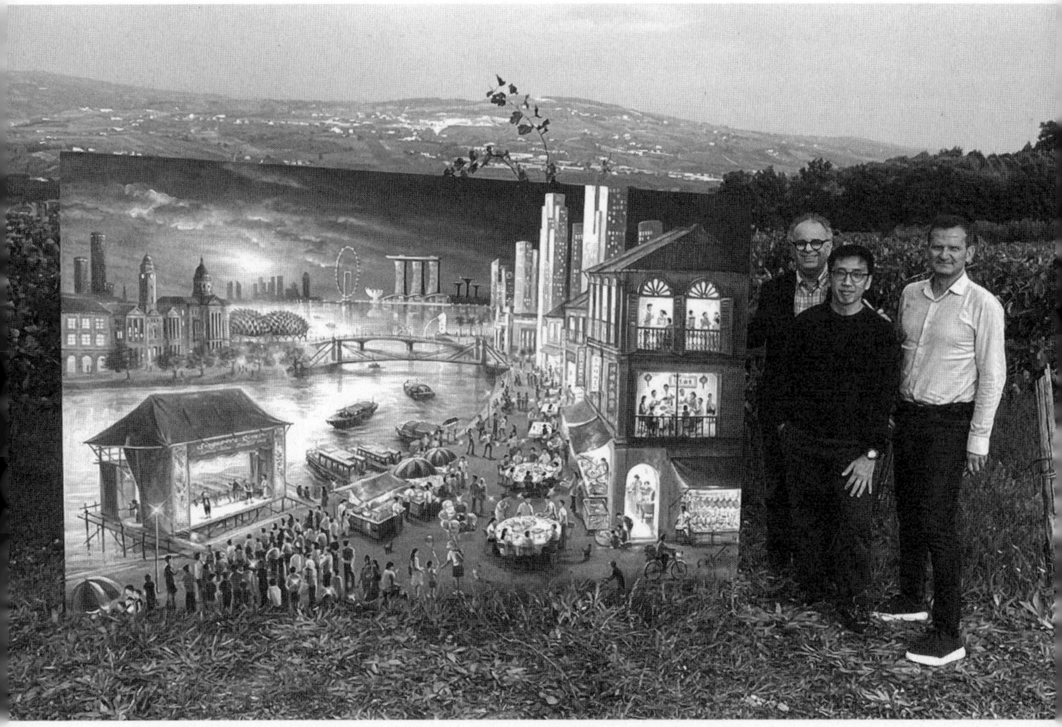

The painting will be displayed at the Benevento Wine and Art Museum.

Lake Alento; all around are rolling hills and ancient villages sitting high up on the ridges. The scenery is especially magical at sunrises, sunsets, and after showers, when rainbows arch over the lake." The artist's eyes are dreamy; this is a place he will remember forever. And he couldn't have asked for a better host; Marco and his wife Gemme, his father Claudio and their son, also named Claudio. "Marco is a superman, he does so many things in a day — cooking my meals, milking the goats, making cheese, and arranging my painting logistics. His dad Claudio takes turns to cook too, makes wine, and brings me out to the town for shopping and sightseeing. And Marco's son helps keep the dogs from barking at me all the time!"

Yew Chong was supposed to create two works in Italy, but he ended up painting four, all on wood canvases. In one painting, done partly in a goat and horse stable, and partly in a vineyard in Benevento, the artist depicts an imaginary dream scene of the Sannio Wine Festival happening along the Singapore River. He lines the riverbank with restaurants, people enjoying food paired with wine. The festival features mobile snack stalls and a traditional stilt tentage where an Italian opera is performing. The charming Sannio wine region surrounds the city of Benevento, which produces the ancient Falanghina white grape wine. While painting at Sannio, the Italian national TV channel TG Regione (Rai) was there filming the event; they interviewed Yew Chong in a segment featuring wine pairing with art. "It was quite surreal watching myself appearing on Italian TV!" The artist laughs.

The art piece that is most meaningful to him is his second one, the imaginary impression of the Cicerale Alento lake area where he stays. "At the bottom, I paint I Filadelfi 1828, the goat dairy farm where

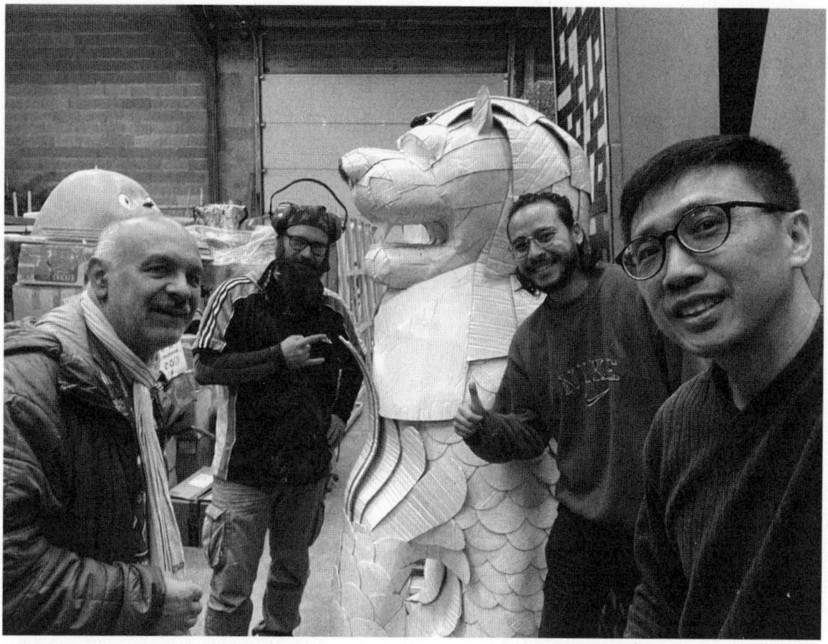

Preparing for the Salon De l'Asie in Lyon, France. Jean-Pierre, the CEO of the Expo, had visited Singapore earlier and invited Yew Chong to paint a mural for the Expo.

I am being hosted. When you look at the painting, you'd think I have imagined it, but it's real. I paint what I see every day there — the family's daily life. The farm owner Marco is milking his goats. His wife is picking lemons, olives, and berries. The children are playing. The owner's dad, Claudio, is harvesting grapes at the family vineyard. I paint myself too, painting this very painting, surrounded by cats. I also paint the farm worker Giuseppe, herding the goats on horseback, although in reality, he uses a motorbike!"

The top of the painting shows the Cicerale ancient town, sitting atop a ridge line overlooking the lake and looking up at the Cilento mountains. The ancient building with the tall wall is the Cicerale Degas Museum after its restoration. The painting, when completed, will be kept there. Edgar Degas was a French impressionist artist (1834–1917).

"Claudio told me I transformed theirs and my dreams into something we can see every moment." Yew Chong's voice is laced with emotion. "I told him I just painted what they built — the dreamland."

On the last day of his stay in Cicerale, the artist creates a small painting for the family. "This has been an opportunity of a lifetime, and while living and painting there, sometimes I have to pinch myself, is this real and not a dream? But what made it personal and unforgettable are my host and his family." The artist pauses; he tries not to let his emotion get the better of him. "In the painting, I painted myself playing with Marco's son, flying paper aeroplanes. May all our dreams come true!"

Unlike Italy where he painted mostly in a countryside stable, in Lyon, France, he paints in a warehouse in the suburb of Lyon city. "I am painting a portable mural about Singapore street food that will be displayed at 'Salon De l'Asie', Asia Expo, at the Lyon EuroExpo exhibition hall. Like most of my murals in Singapore, I will finish the mural live at the Expo. I will also be doing roundtable talks about street art and about Singapore culture in general. There are many things about Lyon I will not forget, not least painting at four degrees Celcius in the middle of the night. This is unforgettable."

3rd December 2022. Yew Chong is back from Europe and includes me in an event by the Islamic Religious Council (MUIS) where President Halimah Yacob is Guest of Honour. There are Malay celebrities like Rahimah Rahim and Aziza Ali in attendance. Both Yew Chong and I join them for lunch at Marina Square. After that, we have drinks at Orange & Teal, a café owned by former opposition member Chee Soon Juan.

Yew Chong is keen to talk about his experience in Europe. "You hear about legendary artists in Europe, like Van Gogh painting in Arles. We are also familiar with Asian artists going to Europe, particularly Paris, to be exposed to its tradition, to soak in the art vibes and lifestyle. It is almost a rite of passage for artists. This stint of mine was a gift; I did not believe it at first; then, it sunk in, and I told myself, I need to make the most of it." It is good seeing him bathed in a quiet kind of joy, still surprised that he was chosen, not quite believing what had happened.

"I told myself, I must feel different in Europe, so that I know I am not in Singapore; that way I will remember it better." His face relaxes into his signature calm, a knowing look and a slight smile. "The weather helped. It felt sharp, crisp, and different. In Italy, I was surrounded by goats when I painted. The horse stared at me, literally looking at me all day long. And the cats, just laying around, moving around me. So, instead of the solitude of my studio or being surrounded by an audience of Singaporean kids and families, I had these most unusual painting companions, animals. The experience was totally different, and really fun." He sits back and I feel he is searching for the right words. "I feel privileged to be there, just immediately after the world opened up. Privilege is the word I will use. I know many of my artist friends would have loved to have this opportunity. Some asked, how did you get this? They want it too."

He hasn't spoken much about Lyon, France. How did that come about? "The CEO of the Expo came to Singapore and asked if he could see me. And we met up. For that Expo, they were featuring Singapore, and they were interested in our culture. The timing was just nice, consecutive, one project after another. I did not need to fly back to Singapore; I just went on from Italy to France. I had no expectation of what the Expo would be like. France was plucked in almost at the last moment. At the Expo, I thought it was more of a cosplay festival, very young and hip. Everyone was dressed up in all sorts of attire, especially as Marvel characters. I quickly put on a wig just to fit in. For both France and Italy, they wanted to bring in international works. Singapore was well positioned for them to visit, we were opened. And I was lucky to be able to meet them."

Did he feel like an ambassador from Singapore? How would this Europe trip affect his work? "When I was there, I felt I was representing Singapore. Which also meant I had to be careful in my narrative and the presentation of images. I was presenting a version of the Singapore brand. An ambassador of sorts. It's an opportunity I have to be grateful for. I would keep this experience on the back of my mind, and there will be times when I will reflect on them more profoundly. After this trip, I feel more confident about my own style of painting. I have always thought my works were amateurish. When I made my way from Italy to France, I visited some iconic artworks of Michelangelo, Leonardo Da Vinci, Keith Haring etc. I looked at those artworks up close and learnt about their back stories. I learnt that at some points in their times, they were 'amateurish', experimenting their techniques, their styles. They grabbed the opportunities given anyway, just did it, developed it and let people talk about their works. Not all masterpieces were masterpieces from the beginning. And lastly, I should do more collaborations. If I want to do larger projects, I need to bring more

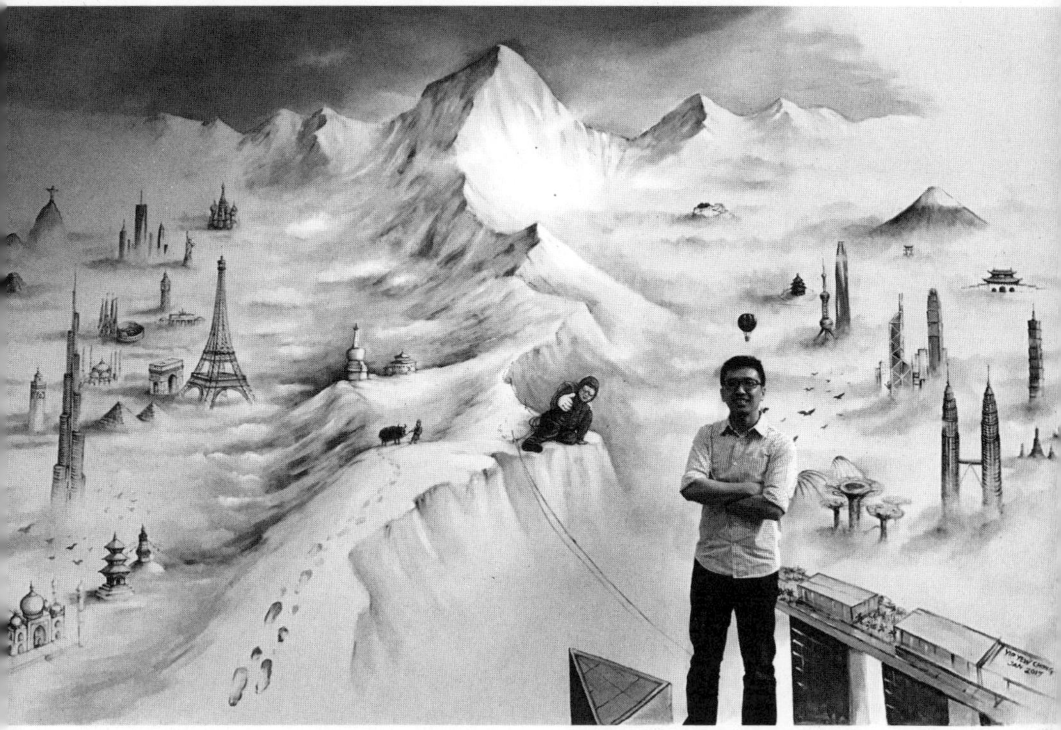

Yew Chong still dreams of travelling and creating art around the world.
World below Everest, *2017.*

people into the fold and work with more people. It would mean being flexible and seeing how to accommodate my style with theirs."

Two months away, in cultures very different from his own. Journeys, they bring us to various places, and they bring us back. In life, we place too much importance on destinations and goals, when sometimes, the journeys to these destinations are goals in themselves.

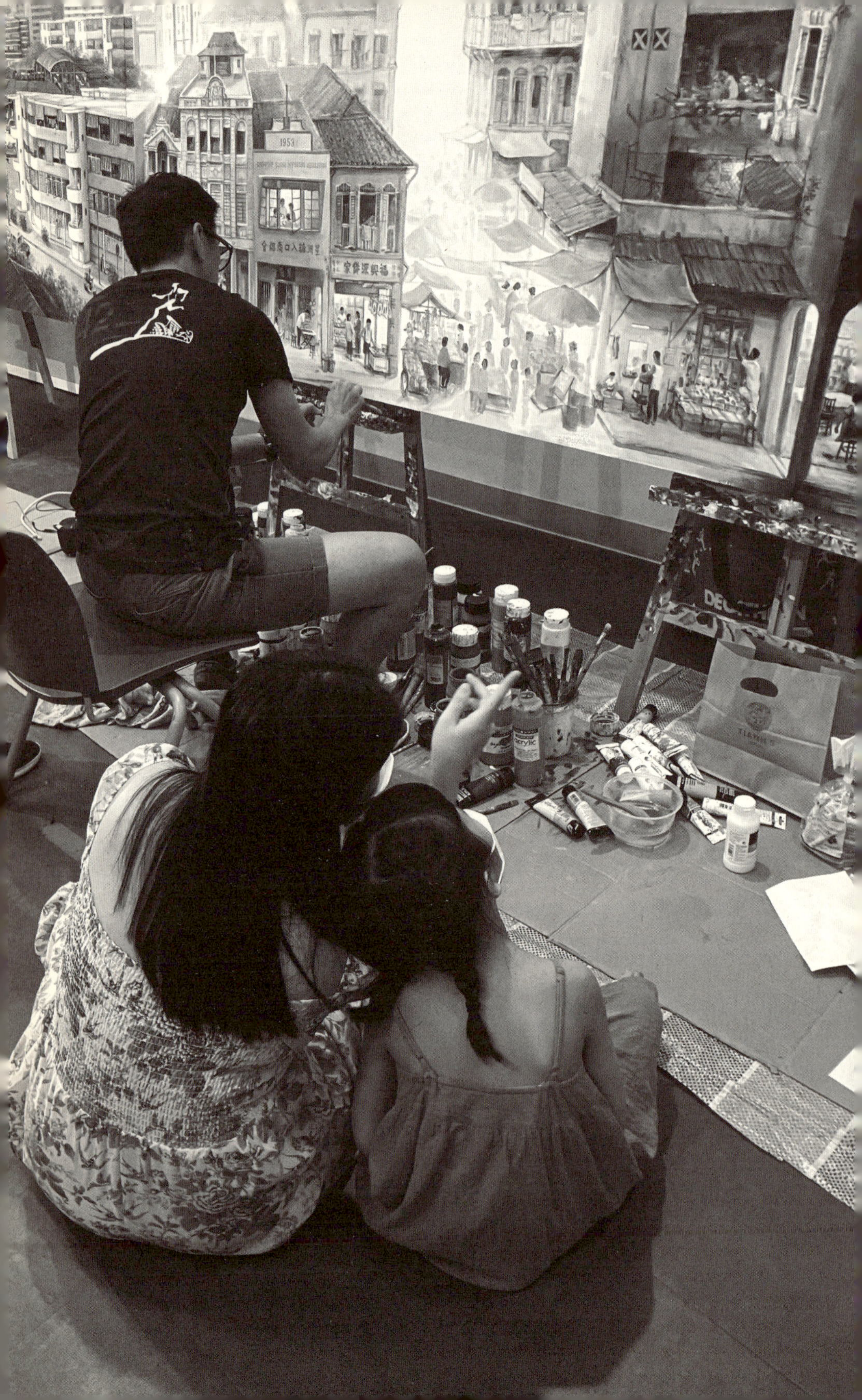
1953

CHAPTER 11

A Long, Long Canvas

I paint for ordinary men in the street — Singaporeans.

In August 2021, Yip Yew Chong began work on the first of what would end up being 27 canvas panels, his longest artwork. Over one and a half years, the artist painted the first 26 panels in his studio. When it came to his last panel, he decided to paint it with a live audience, like most of his murals. This took place at the Tiong Bahru Community Centre from 10th to 15th January 2023. This long, long canvas captures everyday Singapore in the 1970s and 1980s, the period when the artist "was growing up, as well as when Singapore was transforming rapidly. The old and new coexisted during these two decades." The artist has personal connections with all the scenes he painted. The first and last panels for example, show Chinatown in the day and at night, they capture his family's second-storey home where he lived for 14 years before it was demolished. On 15th January, Sunday, I was at the Tiong Bahru Community Centre; I joined other Singaporeans and foreigners together with media personnel to witness the completion of his long artwork. The mood was festive; students, family with kids, young professionals, retirees, expatriates, they all came to celebrate the end of this long journey with the artist. Spanning 60 metres when it was finally completed, *The Straits Times* likened the length to "five double-decker buses lined up head to tail".

When it was all done, I did a Q&A with the artist.

WTH: You are known for your murals. When did you start painting on canvas? We know your story with murals; tell us your story with canvas.

YC: Actually, I painted on canvases years before I started to paint public murals. I painted my first acrylic-on-canvas way back in 1992. My girlfriend (now my wife) bought me a set of acrylic paints because I told her I wanted to take part in the UOB Painting of the Year competition. Using the paints she bought, I painted a scene of my family having reunion dinner at my old family home at Sago Lane. I submitted it, but I didn't win. I collected the painting back and kept it till today. Subsequently, I did another painting using the same set of paints — a scene of the Himalayas, but didn't finish the painting till 2019. In 2006, I bought for myself a new set of acrylic paints and did five paintings to decorate my newly renovated home. You won't believe it if I tell you these are all the canvas paintings I did, until 2017 when I restarted. Just 7 paintings in 25 years.

In 2017, I picked up painting on canvases again. I painted my first 'serious' acrylic-on-canvas, "Mid-Autumn Night". From there on, I built up my momentum and painted more and more canvases such as "Pulau Kusu", "Winter Solstice", and "Hungry Ghost Festival". I considered these as my serious early canvas works. They were all painted between 2017–2018 while juggling my accounting day job and painting street murals on weekends. I chose these festive and nostalgic themes because I dreamt of holding a solo exhibition comprising of paintings of my childhood experiences. So, it wasn't really 'a switch from mural to canvas'. Rather, it's a parallel run, pretty much like the parallel run of my accounting career with art.

WTH: The pandemic must have kept you indoors, and that was when you focused more on canvas?

YC: The 2020 pandemic forced a reduction of painting murals on the streets and an increase in painting on canvases. In late 2019, I rented a small studio with the aim to paint more canvases. I dreamt of holding a solo show in 2021. I also aimed to do more overseas mural projects to move closer to my goal of going international. I knew I had already painted way too many murals in Singapore and I had to pace them out.

When the pandemic hit the world many of my planned mural projects were cancelled or postponed indefinitely. The pandemic kind of forced me to stop painting murals altogether and helped me to focus on canvas painting. It was timely! I locked myself in the studio and painted so much that I managed to hold two solo exhibitions in early 2021, *Something, Somewhere, Somewhen* at Art Porters Gallery, and *Stories from Yesteryear* at The Substation and Sofitel Singapore City Centre. Although the pandemic spoiled my plan of going international on murals, it boosted my canvas painting! I think in 2020 alone, I probably painted over 60 canvases. As I paint more, I can feel that I understand the medium better and better, and feel more confident of doing bigger canvases.

WTH: What inspired you to do a long, long canvas?

YC: During the pandemic lockdown, Professor Victor Choa forwarded me a viral post of a 200-metre long Chinese painting scroll by Tang Yaozhong titled: *Jiangnan Childhood Memories*. Prof Choa is the owner of the house where I painted my first public mural *Amah* in 2015. The Chinese scroll was painted between 1993 and 2013; it records the daily life of the Jiangnan people and customs in the 1950s and 1960s. What the artist achieved was grand, it showed me what could be done with a long canvas. It inspired me to do something similar for Singapore. It also reminded me of the famous ancient Song Dynasty scroll, *Along the River During the Qingming Festival*. Prof Choa said he hoped the scroll would inspire me, as he believed I had the ability to do it.

It was a simple text message, but it was a big push; his message inspired me to do the 60-metre long-painting. Earlier, after having successfully done the 44-metre long Thian Hock Keng temple mural, I had a similar idea of a long painting about broader Singapore, but the idea was that of an indoor mural. When I received Prof Choa's message, it gave me a new idea to do it on portable canvases instead.

When I finished the 60-metre long painting in January 2023, I had extensive media coverage, unexpectedly so. I shared one of the news articles with Prof Choa. He congratulated me for the achievement and said, "When I first saw the Chinese painting, I immediately thought of you. I never dreamt that you would take up the challenge!"

WTH: How did you decide what places to paint for the 27 canvases?

YC: Initially, the idea was to make it place-generic and representational, such as rural Kampong areas, HDB heartlands, forests, seasides, and so on, without identifiable real places. However, as I started to jot down the scenes, I thought that it was necessary to include real iconic buildings or events so that the viewer recognises and knows them to be in Singapore. I started to create a list that included a variety of landscapes and daily life activities. Then, I thought it would be nice if the viewer could follow a route, such as: from the Causeway, one moves anti-clockwise to Bukit Timah, Jurong, Sentosa, East Coast, and Changi. I estimated 50 metres would be roughly the length I would need to cover the key grounds. It is also a length I was confident to achieve without being too ambitious, or too draggy for a viewer. Having done the Thian Hock Keng temple mural at 44 metres, and the Changi Airport murals at 2 x 37 metres, 50 metres seemed right.

I drew up a list of the places I thought would be interesting, significant, or representative of the varied landscapes of Singapore. I tried to be as inclusive as possible, for example, both natural and cultural heritage; NSEW and interiors; land, sea, and air; all major ethnic quarters; night and day. Soon, my list became so long that I was in a dilemma. For example, if I had to choose between Bukit Timah Hill or the Singapore Botanic Gardens as our natural heritage, which should I choose? There were also aesthetic, historical importance, personal connections, and many other factors to assess. I know in the end, someone was going to ask, "How can you not include xxx place?" Ultimately, I knew they would all be my personal decision, but with inputs from many people.

WTH: How much of your scenes are reality-based and how much imagination? Do you follow the approach you do for you murals?

YC: All the scenes are imaginary; in other words, they are not real. However, they are all imagined based on real places, stories, and people. For example, the viewer will know the street depicted in Chinatown does not exist, there is no such street, in the past or present day. But the ambience is easily identifiable, one look and you know it is from the Chinatown area.

All the scenes are also viewed from a higher elevation than the street level. In reality, there are no such viewpoints (at least not at that time when drone photography was non-existent). I imagined these viewpoints based on a mixture of old street level photos, present day aerial views (Google Maps), and old maps.

Most scenes show condensed versions of real places, selectively showcasing the more iconic or representative infrastructures and leaving out the more repetitive buildings around them. It is like a composite drawing but painted in a more realistic than illustrative style. This way, the viewer can better focus on these featured icons without being distracted by overwhelming details had it been a real scene. For example, I reduced the number of blocks of a street, or columns of a building. The featured icons can then be more profound and viewed more closed-up. Stepping back, it also shows a better big picture of a place (for example, a condensed Little India scene shows how multicultural it really is, with multiple temples, mosques, and churches in the area).

I also reorientated some buildings to show their most iconic fronts, so that the viewer can identify them easily; for example, I turned the beautiful facade of the Al-Ahmadiah Press Building in the Kampong Glam scene to face the viewer, when in reality, only its back can be seen from the imagined viewpoint.

Lastly, I removed several walls or roofs of buildings to showcase the indoor activities, for example, the HDB flats, the school, library, army bunk, and even the Parliament House. This is of course not real but how else can I show daily life inside and behind the walls?

Most people accept these methods of condensing and distorting the reality of an area to give focus on selective stories and buildings. In fact, they found the imagined perspective refreshing. However, some cannot accept these discriminatory selections of focused areas and distortion of reality.

As you can see, I put a lot of thought into the panels before the actual act of painting. It is not a science. It is an art, a kind of trial and error. I enjoyed the thought process as much as the actual act of painting itself.

WTH: Why was research important since you are mixing reality with imagination?

YC: I must admit my research was superficial and my curation was inclined towards places and stories which I have a personal connection with. My research and curation were not all about how important or iconic a place is. For most of the scenes, I have personally been there, experienced the ambience at some point in time, or found the story compelling to retell. For example, I have wonderful memories growing up in Chinatown watching Cantonese operas on the streets, National Service (NS) training on Marsiling Hill and Pulau Tekong Camp 1, and enjoying school excursions to Haw Par Villa, Chinese and Japanese Gardens.

Having said that, I did try to make the painting generic by being as inclusive as I could in covering regions and cultures, so that they represent Singapore more collectively than just about myself. It was a fine balance.

Personal connections and past knowledge aside, research by referencing hundreds of old and present-day photos, aerial photos, real or hearsay stories, were important. They added a layer of connectedness to reality and collective memories, making the paintings look more relatable to more viewers. For me, that is more meaningful and important.

WTH: How did you manage the continuity from one canvas to the next? Scene to scene, day to day, and day to night.

YC: I normally don't paint long murals in sequence from right to left or vice versa. For example, when I painted the 44-metre Thian Hock Keng temple mural or the 37-metre long Singapore Rojak mural (at Changi T4), I started by painting a section somewhere in the middle and then jumped to sections on the left and right in a haphazard manner, and then join and blend the sections together.

This 60-metre canvas painting is no exception. Although I have a broad idea of the scenes and the areas I want to cover, I didn't paint them in sequence. The very first scene I painted was a night scene of Chinatown. Then, I jumped to the extreme left, Woodlands/Causeway, and then I jumped to the right, HDB heartland scenes. I continued to jump about, joining some scenes as I progressed, until all the gaps were filled. The last scene is a Chinatown day scene that

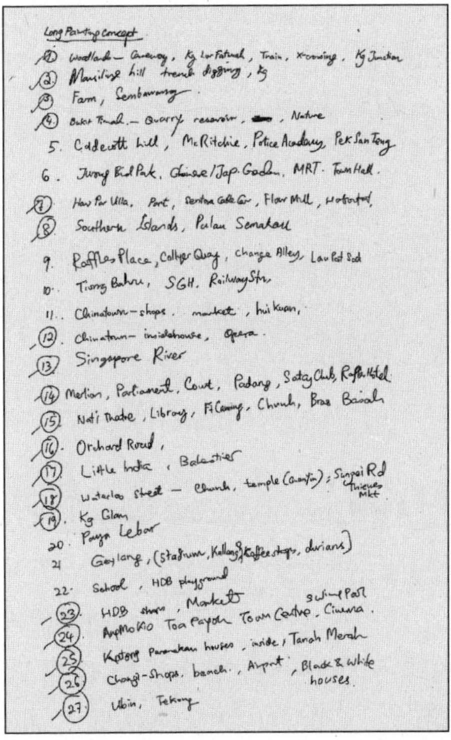

Yew Chong's broad plan for his 60m painting. The concept is in words and very fluid. The visuals are spontaneous.

joins to the very first scene which is the Chinatown night scene. I joined the back of the houses in the day scene (kitchens) to the front of the houses (the night scene).

There were two main reasons I did it this way: One, it gave me flexibility and options to change my mind as I progressed along. I could add new scenes that were not in the original plan, remove scenes that might look repetitive, or fine-tune the scene details. Because I posted my works on social media every time I finished a panel, I got a lot of feedback and received new ideas from the public. Some would suggest I include certain significant or representational icons. I might already have them in my broad plan, but if not, I could try to insert them. Here are three examples:

1. I added the Caldecott Hill/Police Academy scene because two friends happened to tell me in the same week that I need to add it. One said Caldecott Hill was significant to represent the TV/Radio broadcasting infrastructure. Another friend, who works for MediaCorp, also urged me to add it.

2. In the original broad plan, I had planned to paint the Balestier area so as to feature the intricate shophouses, cinemas, Tan Tock Seng Hospital, and so on. However, I decided to omit the Changi Airport in favour of an older looking Changi Village after I had to include the Paya Lebar Airport to represent civil aviation. Also, I felt the Balestier panel might look too similar to the Katong panel with the same intricate shophouses and cinemas, and I already had Toa Payoh Hospital and Singapore General

Hospital in the plan (no need to paint so many hospitals). There were also too many urban scenes but not enough rural scenes in the east. I had several rural scenes like Sembawang, Marsiling, and Bukit Timah in the west, so it may look lopsided. After considering the above, I thought it would be best to replace the Balestier scene with the Serangoon Corridor scene so as to showcase the Paya Lebar Airport and the eastern farmlands.

3. In the original plan, the West Coast/Haw Par Villa scene was to join the Collyer Quay/Raffles Place scene, because both scenes have the sea. The sea would be the common element that joined both panels. However, I soon realised the sea would look like a river because it would be too narrow. To make the sea look more like a sea, it needed to be more expansive. Inserting another panel with seas on both ends and joining these seas to the West Coast scene and Collyer Quay scene would broaden the sea. The southern islands would be an appropriate scene with lots of sea. The story of Pulau Seking being expunged and reclaimed to be part of Pulau Semakau would be an interesting story.

When I paint a long painting which straddles a long period, getting into the mood is important. It would be very boring to spend a lot of time painting several urban or rural scenes consecutively. Thus, I jump about when painting the scenes, so that there is variety to keep me motivated.

The method I used to join the different scenes together was to use a common pivot anchor and morph them, from one panel to the other. The anchor could be a building, a hill, or a water body. For example, Raffles Hotel in the Padang scene morphs into MPH bookstore in the Bras Basah scene. This way, each scene is appreciable on its own, yet the combined scenes form one continuous journey through different parts of Singapore. The transitions also become interesting viewpoints too.

As for the night to day, day to night, sunny to rainy to cloudy, these were easily morphed through gradual changes in the colours of the sky. This variety of weather and times of the day creates a rhythm of real life for a viewer. I intentionally put the rightmost and leftmost scenes to be sunny, and the second to be stormy. Most movies are like that too, and it works to swing the mood to keep the viewer interested.

WTH: This form of art, imagination from reality, you have your critics?

YC: I do have critics, especially for art that is supposed to depict Singaporean scenes. First, I am not formally trained in art or history. I paint from imagination. So the scenes are not geographically or historically accurate. My aim is creating ambience and story-telling. Nevertheless, the balance between aesthetics, self-expression, and historical accuracy was the main difficulty in painting this 60-metre canvas work.

People may expect canvas paintings to be more like fine art, compared to murals where precision is less important. For this type of painting, semi-realistic to realistic, people may expect it to be historically accurate, but I can't. Because I have to join Tiong Bahru to Chinatown,

Chinatown to Singapore River. How can I do it? I have to put in a lot of imagination. But to balance that is a big challenge because I can't meet everyone's expectations. I want to remind my audience that my art is not a historical document. My art is to evoke emotions and draw out their own memory.

WTH: Which panel or place proved to be the most difficult to execute?

YC: I don't think any particular panel or scene was more difficult than any other, to think about or to paint it. Each panel took about one to one and a half weeks to complete. The hardest part for each panel was to start it. The easiest and most enjoyable part was to fill in the details. For example, filling in the human activities after painting the buildings and streets. It thrilled me to see the paintings come to life when the human activities were added. Perhaps I would say the most boring things to paint were repetitive straight lines of buildings such as HDB flat windows and parapet walls. I did not have to be too precise when painting kampongs or shophouses. They could look crooked and still look right!

WTH: Did you, at any point during the painting, feel discouraged or thought it was all too much?

YC: I never felt discouraged for any moment. In fact, my motivation to do more (increasing from 50 metres to 55 metres, and then finally ending at 60 metres) was primarily due to strong encouragement from the public, as well as my own OCD to make it better — more inclusive, meaningful, and a stronger visual. But I do know that 50 to 60 metres for such a detailed painting is enough. The longer it gets, both mine and the public's interest will wane. I knew there was a limit to a viewer's interest in appreciating a work with so much detail. I like to compare it to a movie, no matter how good a movie is, two to two and a half hours is about the maximum an audience can be kept captivated before it becomes draggy.

I also need to move on to do bigger things. Having said that, I do enjoy the whole process. In fact, when the painting was coming to an end, I kind of cherish the last moments and know I will miss the entire experience. At times, I wish it can be 100 metres, so that I can include and cover all the places the public had wished me to include.

WTH: When it was completed, did this 'marathon' give you a different kind of satisfaction compared to the 'sprint' of a one- or two-week mural? Tell me about this feeling.

YC: Because this painting process is so much longer (about one and a half years) compared to a mural (two days to a month), the sense of relief is much stronger. However, since I haven't exhibited it yet, it also feels ironically incomplete, unlike a mural which stands proudly for all to see upon its completion. As long as I haven't exhibited it for public viewing, I will always feel the work is not yet complete.

WTH: Did you expect the public reaction to the completion of the 27 canvases?

YC: As expected, many supporters who followed this painting congratulated me. Many asked where and when they could view the painting in its entirety. What I didn't expect was the publicity from the media. I actually didn't call the media; I did not have a media release. I only informed Mothership who had interviewed me earlier; they reminded me to inform them when I plan to paint my last panel. When I announced my live-painting of the last panel and I had posted updates of the first few days' work, various media started to contact me, expressing their wish to cover the event. I did not expect mainstream media like *The Straits Times* or CNA to be interested. When the media came, and there were so many of them, I was really happy because I had always wanted as many people as possible to know and get interested in my work. The publicity was a good booster to the profile of this painting.

I paint for ordinary men in the street — Singaporeans. When more of them regard it as a uniquely Singaporean painting, that makes me feel good. A high general public interest is the best recognition of the painting's importance to the community. It becomes less important that the painting does not fit into any particular genre strongly. It is a bit of art, a bit of culture shaping, a bit of heritage. It's not too complex to understand. It touches varied interests and a wide spectrum of society. There is something in it for almost everyone to relate to. These are the reasons why I painted this long, long canvas, and when I see these objectives being fulfilled, it gives me a high degree of satisfaction.

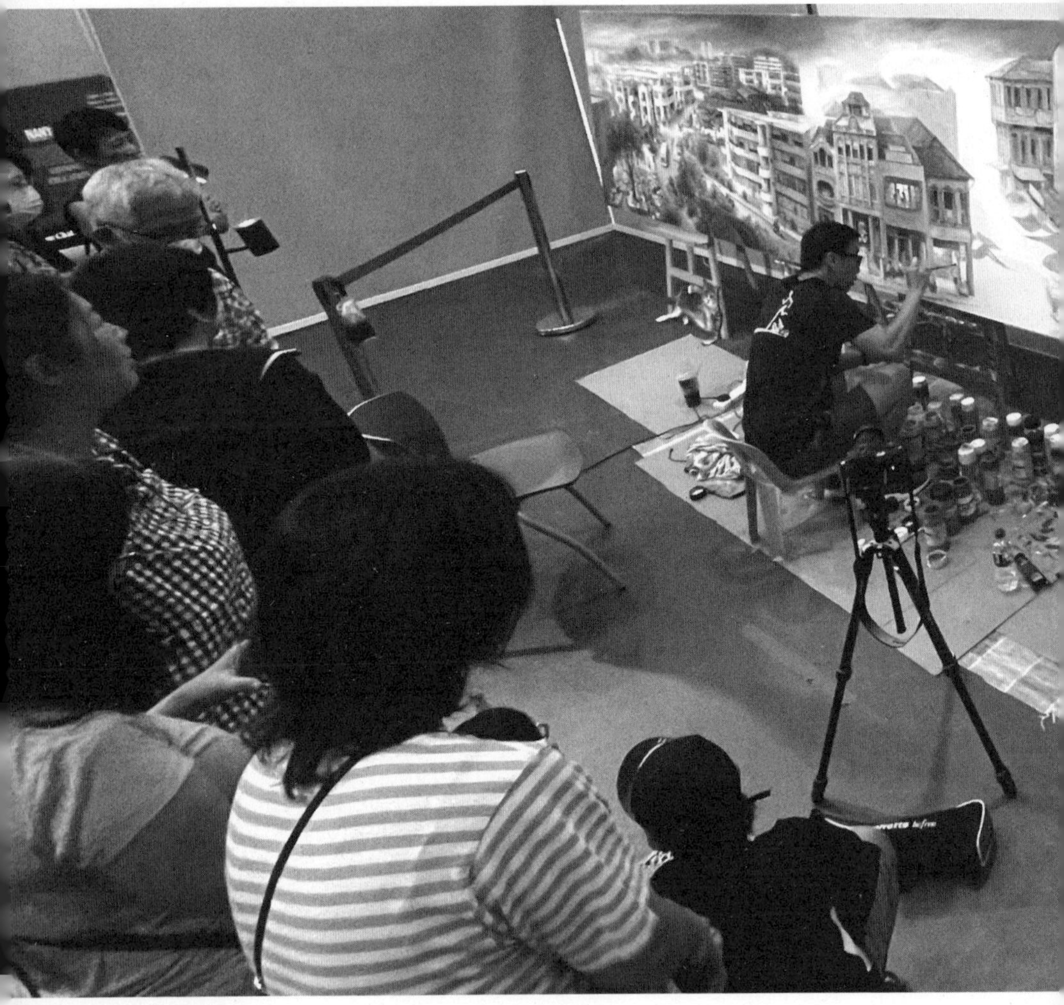

WTH: When it is all done, are you selling it or keeping it?

YC: Now that the painting is completed, I will send it for proper storage. The next foremost priority is to exhibit it for free public viewing. Of course, I wish to sell it since I had spent a lot of time and personal funds to create it, but I don't know how and when that can happen. I had thought of either selling it as one painting or as 27 separate pieces.

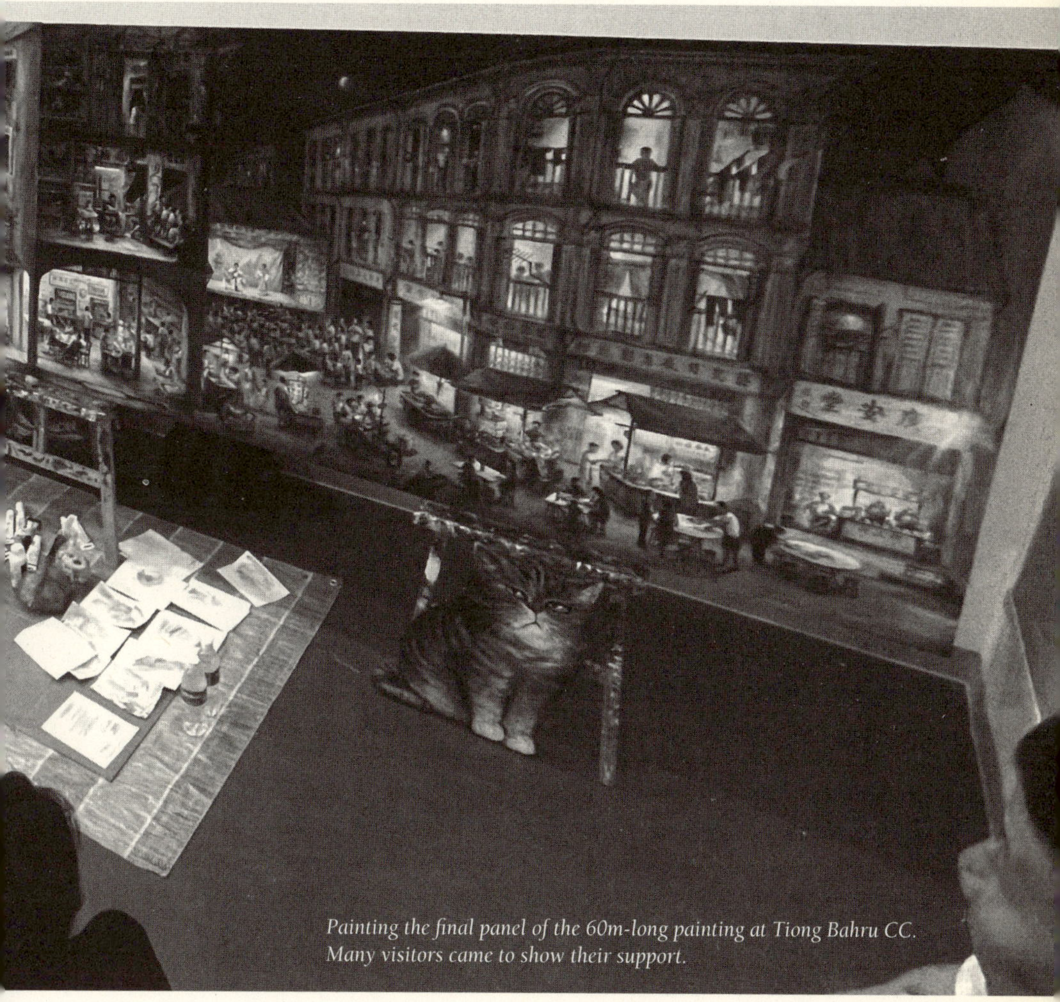

Painting the final panel of the 60m-long painting at Tiong Bahru CC. Many visitors came to show their support.

Selling them in pieces is more practical but my worry is, they will never be able to come together again as one painting. As the saying goes, "the sum of the whole is greater than its parts". Now that the painting is completed and there are some public interests, I will think about the options more carefully.

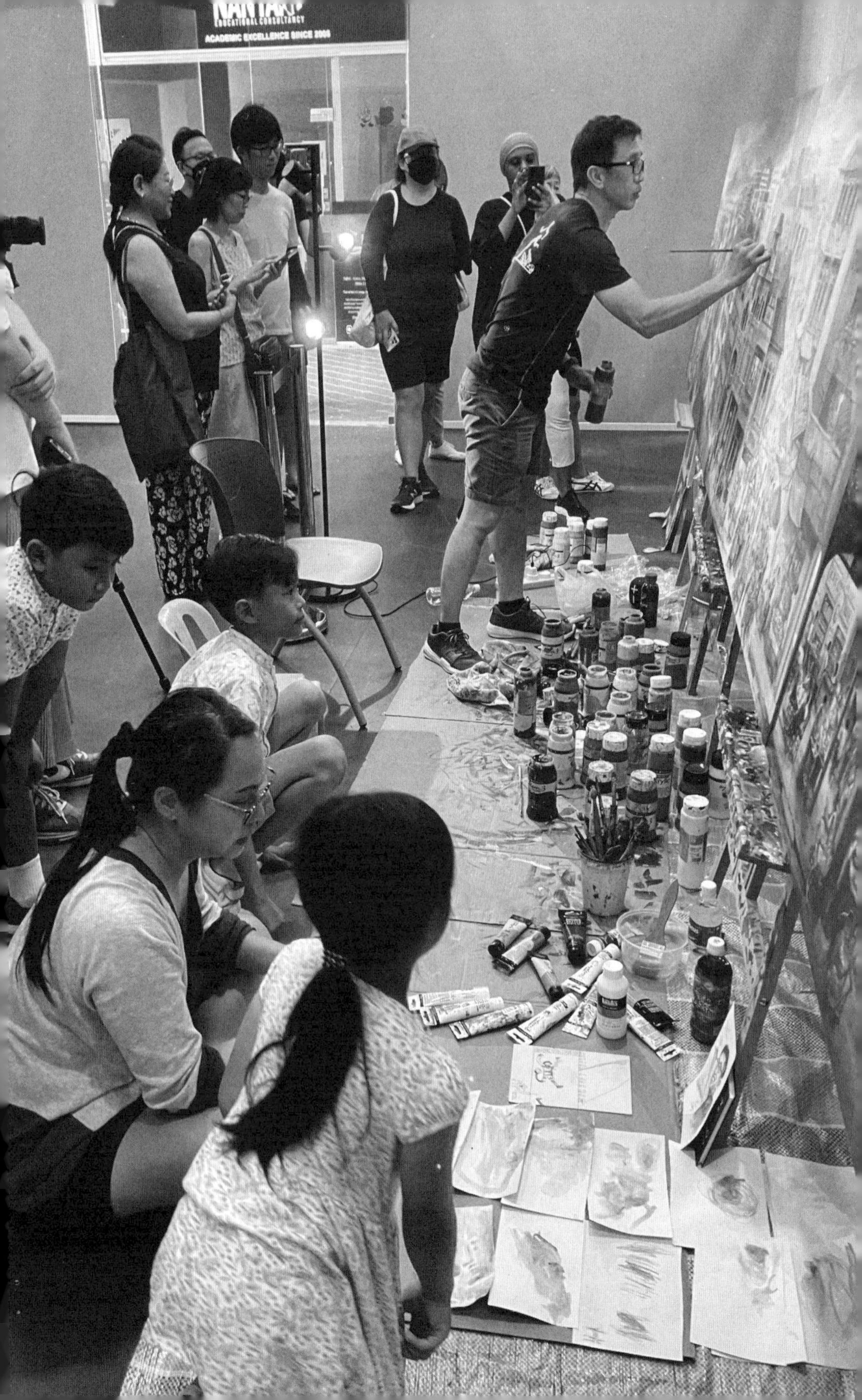
EDUCATIONAL CONSULTANCY
ACADEMIC EXCELLENCE SINCE 2008

CHAPTER 12

Postscript

"Don't praise me too much, tone it down."

I was an early Facebook friend of Yip Yew Chong. I made a special visit to Tiong Bahru when he was painting a mural of men relaxing with their bird cages on 28th February 2016. I remember being curious that he was painting on a wall without any reference to a picture or photograph. The artist was basically painting from what he saw in his mind. People would stop to stare at him and his wall; he smiled and was friendly. I took many photographs of him painting the birds and the bird cages, and recall a sense of joy watching him paint. The mural had a whimsical and liberating effect on me. Late that afternoon, I created a Facebook post, with three photographs and a line, "Watching a mural master at work".

From 2017 to 2020, I was running a TV station in Myanmar, but I monitored his posts on Facebook and Instagram. On weekends when I was back in Singapore, I would visit his murals in Chinatown and take photographs, posing with the murals. Again, I remember my sense of joy with his murals. My colleagues in Myanmar were also fascinated by the murals.

On 10th February 2020, I ended my two-and-a-half-year stint in Myanmar because of COVID and the unstable situation there. I came back and quite quickly got involved in writing *Soul of Ink: Lim Tze Peng at 100*. I was also writing *Transition: The Story of PN Balji*, and later, the three-part series, *George Yeo: Musings*. Even with all these commitments, Yip Yew Chong and his murals continued to interest me. In November 2021, I went down to Temple Street to watch Yew Chong paint his three-storey mural, and it was there that I decided I would write a book on him and how his murals brought so much joy to those who watch him paint. In December, through Facebook Messenger, I made an appointment to meet him and propose the book idea, the *Art of Joy*.

It has been more than a year of getting to know the artist and his family, seeing him in various situations and putting down what I saw and heard page after page, chapter after chapter. There were occasions when I would show him a chapter to verify the facts, and his feedback would invariably be, "Don't praise me too much, tone it down." He did not say this to sound humble; he genuinely did not want to come across as an artist who has 'arrived', or be seen as a 'star' artist. On one occasion, when someone suggested that he should be nominated for the Cultural Medallion, he was firm and quick to put a stop to it. "Please, I am not there yet. Perhaps after another decade."

This indeed has been the dilemma of this book. Almost everyone I talked to about Yew Chong sung his praises. It was difficult to get neutral comments, never mind negative ones. To prevent the book from being a 'whitewash', something the artist fears, I have included quite prominently at parts, what purists' view of his art had been, and how some would not even consider him a proper artist. That said, in most of my interviews with him, he was almost always self-deprecating. It is all about the tone, and I hope through my words and the photographs of the book, I have been accurate and fair to the artist, this fear of his notwithstanding.

In the final stages of editing this book, Yew Chong insisted I help him convey his thanks to everyone for encouraging and supporting him. I end this postscript with my own thank you list. First, I want to thank Yew Chong himself for this opportunity, sharing his art and his world with me, and for me to share it with my readers. On many instances, he made special arrangements to include me in his dealings with the art world, introducing friends to speak to me and, most importantly, availing his wife to talk to me. I know she is a private person; the frank interview she gave is a highlight of the book. I also want to thank Wong Su-Yen and Kelvin Ang for their keen insights into Yew Chong's world and art, as well as Faith, Charles and their children for being manifestations of the joy of his art. Finally, a special thank you to Hong Koon, Nicole, Claire, Lai Ann and Jimmy of World Scientific for believing in the *Art of Joy*.

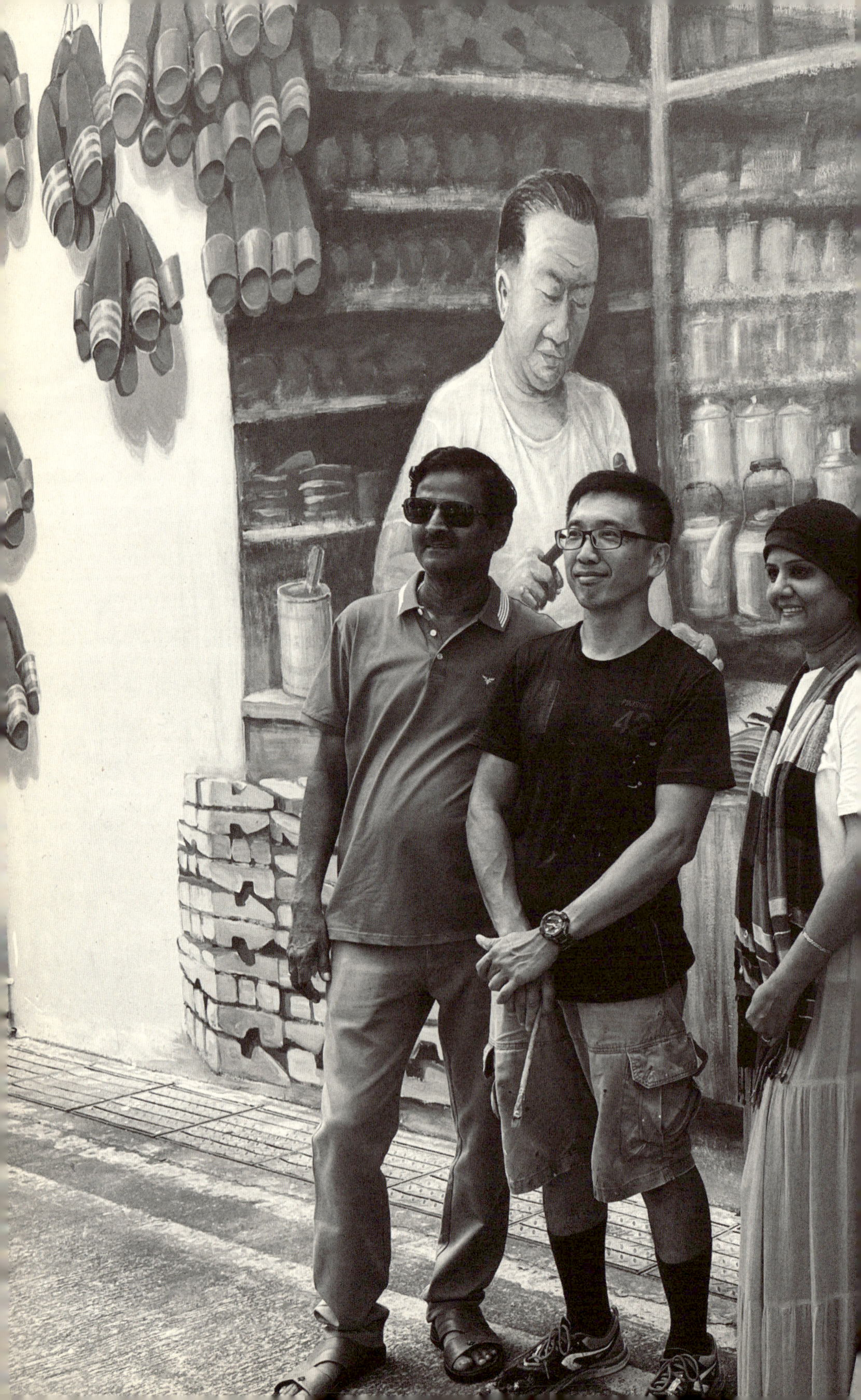

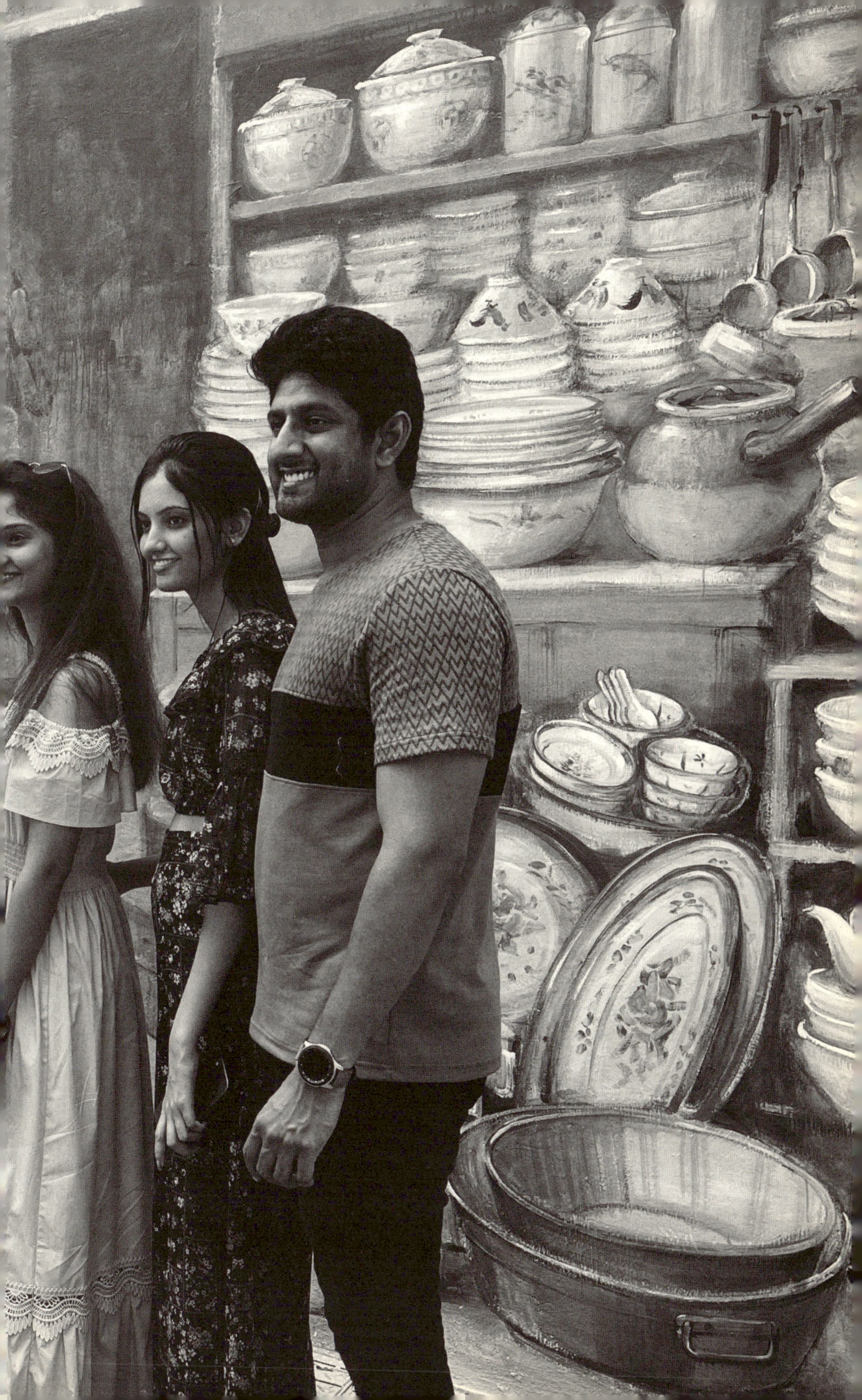

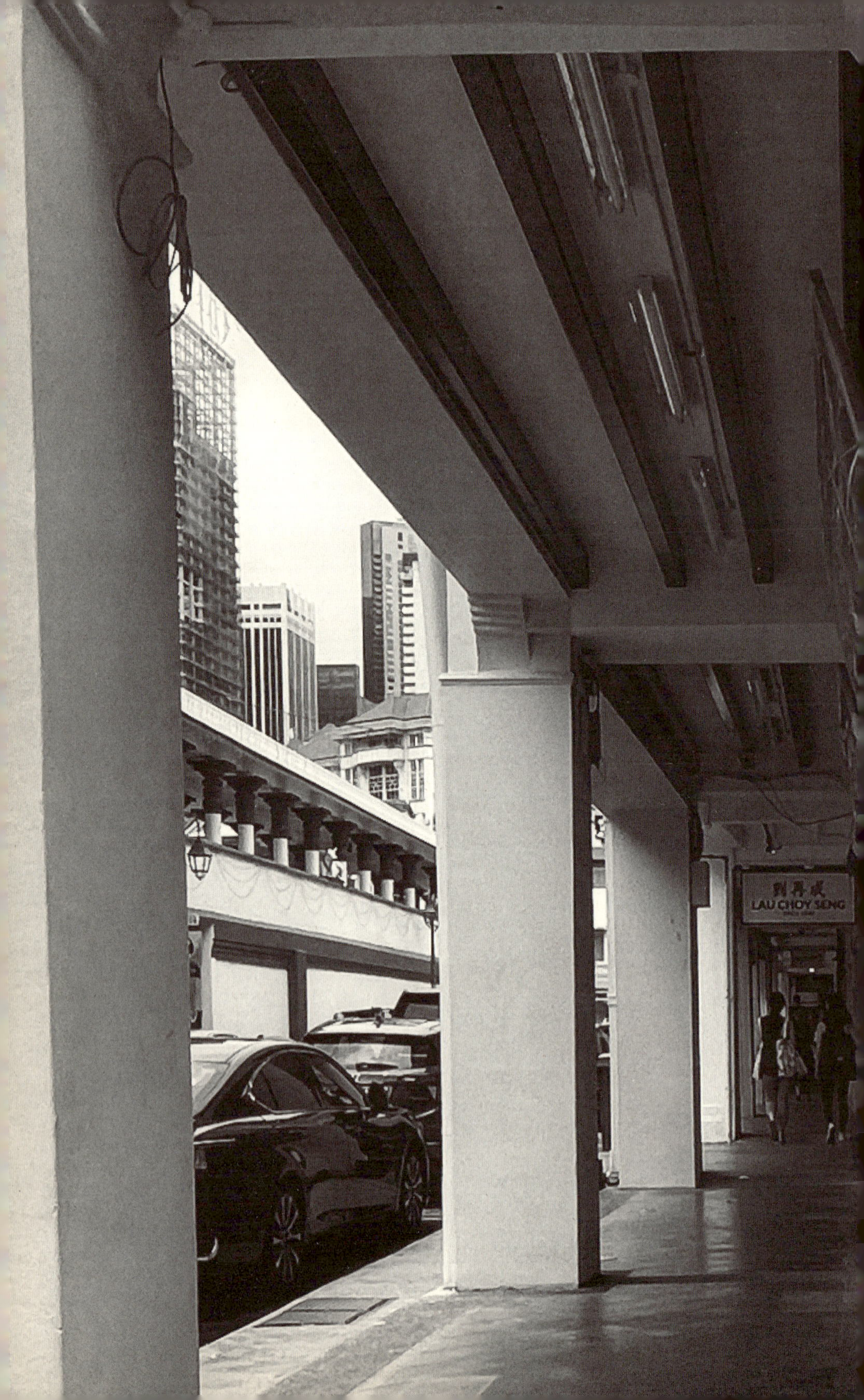
LAU CHOY SENG

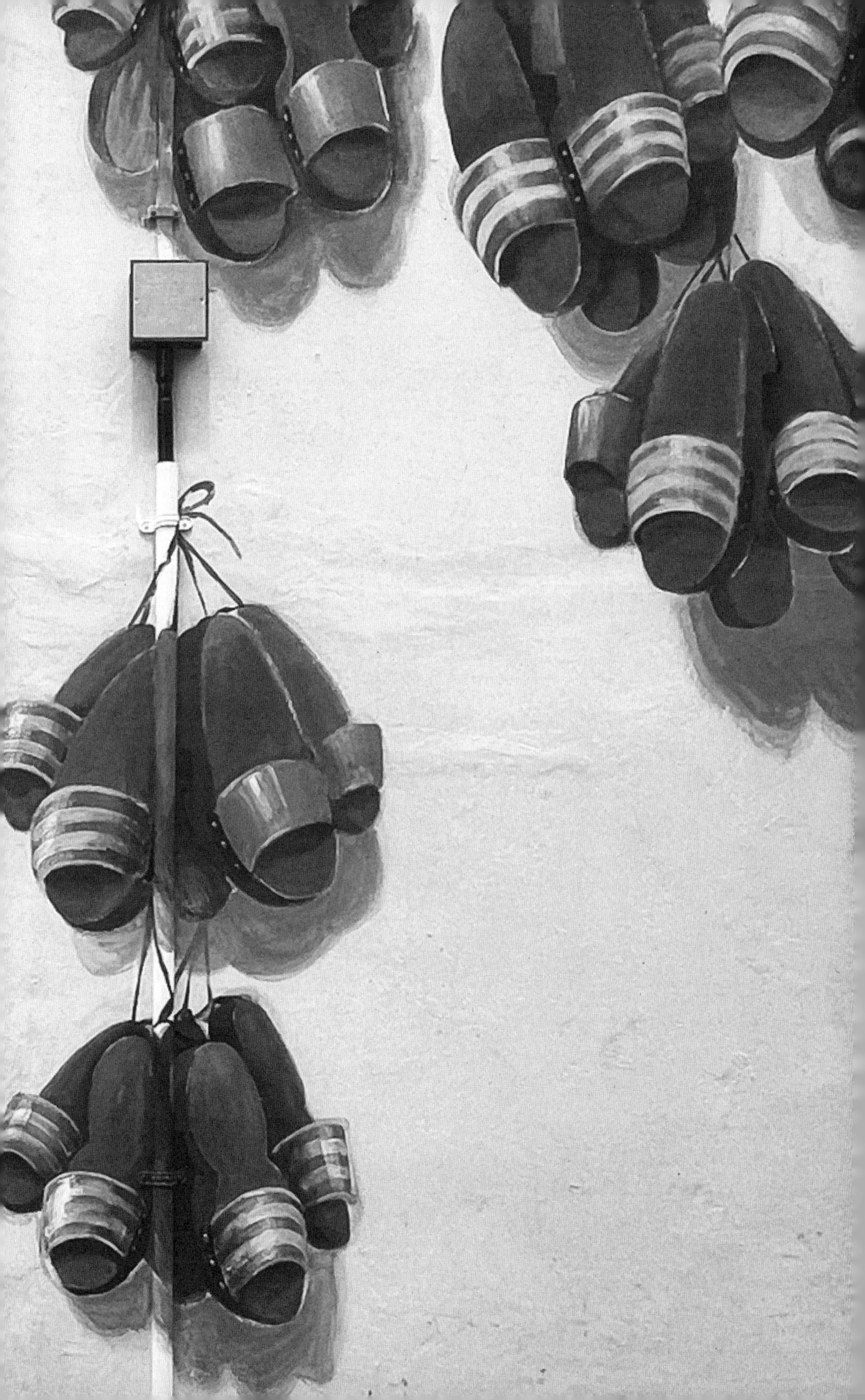

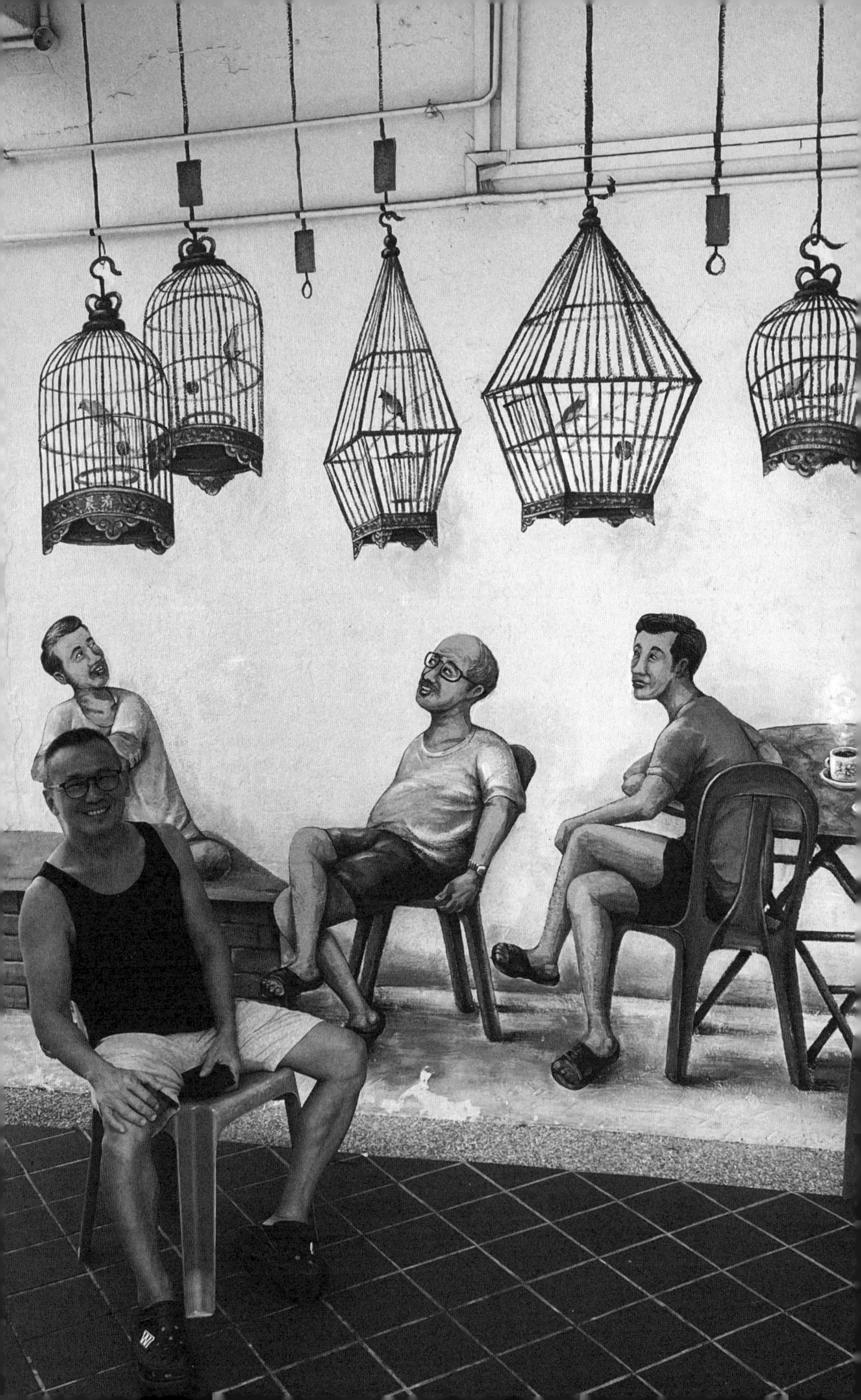

About the Author

Woon Tai Ho is a writer and media veteran. He wrote his first book, *To Paint a Smile*, in 2008. The genre-defying book weaved political, economic and social events into the art and philosophy of Singapore's renowned artist, Tan Swie Hian. Since then, he has been a prolific writer. Tai Ho wrote his first novel, *Riot Green*, in 2013. *Soul of Ink: Lim Tze Peng at 100*, written in 2021, was a finalist for Best Non-Fiction Title in the Singapore Book Awards in 2022. In the same year, *Transition: The Story of PN Balji* was also a finalist for the Popular Readers' Choice Awards. He is also part of the team working on *George Yeo: Musings*, a three-volume book launched over 2022 and 2023.

In media, he is best known for leading a team to start the Asia-wide news channel, Channel NewsAsia, in 1999. In the course of more than two decades, he launched news and entertainment channels across Asia, including MiTV and Channel K in Myanmar.